Children's
A to Z
Encyclopedia

Children's A to Z Encyclopedia

Miles Kelly

First published in 2004 by Miles Kelly Publishing Ltd
Harding's Barn, Bardfield End Green, Thaxted, Essex, CM6 3PX, UK

This edition printed in 2010

2 4 6 8 10 9 7 5 3

Editorial Director Belinda Gallagher

Art Director Jo Brewer

Project Manager Bethan Ellish

Editor Stuart Cooper

Editorial Assistant Chlöe Schroeter

Cover Designer Simon Lee

Designers Jo Brewer, Michelle Cannatella, David Gillingwater,
Simon Lee, Louisa Leitao, Debbie Meekcoms, Tom Slemmings,
Robert Walster, WhiteLight

Image Manager Liberty Newton

Indexer Gill Lee

Production Manager Elizabeth Collins

Reprographics Anthony Cambray, Stephan Davis, Ian Paulyn

British Library Cataloguing-in-Publication Data
A catalogue record of this book is available from the British Library

ISBN 978-1-84810-115-9

Printed in China

Made with paper from a sustainable forest

www.mileskelly.net
info@mileskelly.net

www.factsforprojects.com

Self-publish your
children's book

buddingpress.co.uk

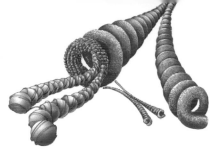

Contents

How to use this book

Your *First A to Z Encyclopedia* is bursting with information, colour, pictures and fun activities. The pages run from A to Z with a new subject on every page. This will help you find information quickly and easily. The index at the back of the book will help you look for more specific information.

Word box
New or difficult words are explained in the yellow panels

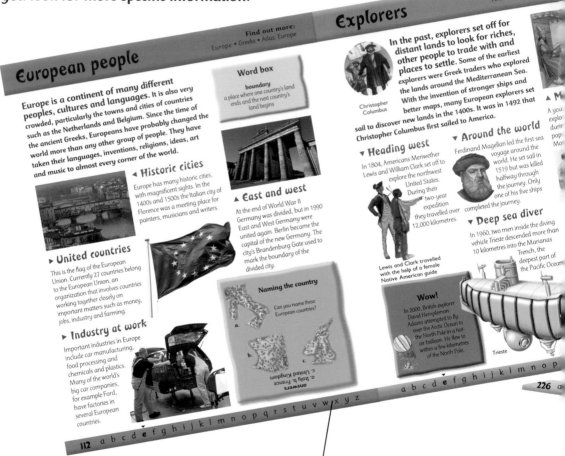

European people

Find out more:
Europe • Greeks • Atlas: Europe

Europe is a continent of many different peoples, cultures and languages. It is also very crowded, particularly the towns and cities of countries such as the Netherlands and Belgium. Since the time of the ancient Greeks, Europeans have probably changed the world more than any other group of people. They have taken their languages, inventions, religions, ideas, art and music to almost every corner of the world.

Word box
boundary
a place where one country's land ends and the next country's land begins

◀ **Historic cities**
Europe has many historic cities, with magnificent sights. In the 1400s and 1500s the Italian city of Florence was a meeting place for painters, musicians and writers.

▶ **United countries**
This is the flag of the European Union. Currently 27 countries belong to the European Union, an organization that involves countries working together closely on important matters such as money, jobs, industry and farming.

▲ **East and west**
At the end of World War II Germany was divided, but in 1990 East and West Germany were united again. Berlin became the capital of the new Germany. The city's Brandenburg Gate used to mark the boundary of the divided city.

▶ **Industry at work**
Important industries in Europe include car manufacturing, food processing and chemicals and plastics. Many of the world's big car companies, for example Ford, have factories in several European countries.

Naming the country
Can you name these European countries?
a.
b.
c.
answers
a. Italy b. France c. United Kingdom

Explorers

Antarctica • Explorers at sea

In the past, explorers set off for distant lands to look for riches, other people to trade with and places to settle. Some of the earliest explorers were Greek traders who explored the lands around the Mediterranean Sea. With the invention of stronger ships and better maps, many European explorers set sail to discover new lands in the 1400s. It was in 1492 that Christopher Columbus first sailed to America.

Christopher Columbus

▼ **Heading west**
In 1804, Americans Meriwether Lewis and William Clark set off to explore the northwest United States. During their two-year expedition they travelled over 12,000 kilometres.

Lewis and Clark travelled with the help of a female Native American guide

▶ **Around the world**
Ferdinand Magellan led the first sea voyage around the world. He set sail in 1519 but was killed halfway through the journey. Only one of his five ships completed the journey.

▼ **Deep sea diver**
In 1960, two men inside the diving vehicle Trieste descended more than 10 kilometres into the Marianas Trench, the deepest part of the Pacific Ocean.

Wow!
In 2000, British explorer David Hempleman-Adams attempted to fly over the Arctic Ocean to the North Pole in a hot-air balloon. He flew to within a few kilometres of the North Pole.

Trieste

112 a b c d e f g h i j k l m n o p q r s t u v w x y z

226 a

a b c d e f g h i j k l m n o p

Wow box
Look for the orange panels to read amazing true facts – the funny cartoons will make you laugh!

Alphabet strip
Your book is alphabetical. This means it runs from A to Z. Along the bottom of every page is an alphabet strip. The letter that starts the main heading is in bold. Above the letter there's a small arrow to highlight where you are in the alphabet.

Cross-references

Within the colour band are cross-references to other subjects. These tell you where you can find out more information about your chosen topic.

Colour bands

The coloured bands along the top of each page tell you which subject area you are in.
- The Natural World has green bands.
- People and Places has orange bands.
- Planet Earth has blue bands.
- Universe has yellow bands.
- Science and Technology has red bands.
- History has purple bands.

Find out more:
Earth features • Oceans and life • Water

...as cover more than two-thirds ...urface. Amazingly, they contain ...water in the world. The oceans are ...s deep on average, but in some places ...es down even deeper. The deepest ...the bottom of the Pacific Ocean – ...more than 11 kilometres below

Wow!
In December 2004, there was a tsunami in the Indian Ocean which caused waves to grow up to 24 metres in height.

ARCTIC OCEAN
ATLANTIC OCEAN
...CIFIC OCEAN
INDIAN OCEAN
SOUTHERN OCEAN

...arco Polo
...s of Asia
...as a
...ourt of the
...lai Khan.

...tic

...t Scott's second
...each the South Pole
...edy. When his team
...d the South Pole on
...8, 1912, they found
...at a Norwegian
...team had arrived
...there one month
...earlier. Scott and
his men died from
hunger and cold on
the way home.

v w x y z 113

wave movement

▼ Giant waves
Earthquakes under the sea-bed can produce giant waves that race towards land at speeds as fast as 970 kilometres an hour. These waves may be 30 metres high near the shore. They are called tsunamis.

...l harvest
...eaweed.
...eir own on plots on the
seabed. The harvested seaweed is a useful ingredient in products such as plant fertilizer and ice cream.

f g h i j k l m n o p q r s t u v w x y z

Ocean life

Find out more:
Oceans and seas • Sea animals • Water

The oceans are filled with living things. These range from the tiny shrimp-like creatures that float on the surface to strange-looking fish that crawl across the sea-bed. Most ocean creatures live in the warmer, sunlit waters near the surface, where most of their food supply is found.

▼ Ocean creatures
Sharks, dolphins and turtles live near the water's surface. Large mammals such as the sei whale dive to lower levels. The waters at the bottom of the ocean receive no sunlight. Only a few kinds of sea creatures such as deep-sea fish and starfish can survive in this cold, dark world.

▼ Floating life
Tiny plants and animals called plankton drift through the surface of the water in huge numbers. They become food for larger ocean creatures.

1 Dusky dolphin
2 Kittiwake
3 Northern right whale
4 Man 'o' war jellyfish
5 Great skuas
6 Pacific white-sided dolphin
7 Broad-billed prion
8 Ocean sunfish
9 Ridley's turtle
10 Cuttlefish
11 Tiger shark
12 Yellow-bellied sea snake
13 Tarpon
14 Banded sea snake
15 Yellowfin tuna
16 Common squid
17 Mako shark
18 Nautilus
19 Commerson's dolphin
20 Sei whale

a b c d e f g h i j k l m n o p q r s t u v w x y z **227**

Activity and puzzle boxes

Some pages will have activities, games or puzzles for you to do. Look for the green, blue or purple panels.

Africa

Find out more:
African people • Atlas: Africa • Deserts • Grasslands

Africa is the second largest continent in the world, after Asia. It is a land of great contrasts, with hot deserts, thick forests and grassy plains. Most places are either hot and wet, or hot and dry. The world's longest river, the Nile, flows through North Africa to the east of the biggest desert in the world, the Sahara.

▶ Amazing sights

Africa is a land of spectacular sights, including the Great Rift Valley and the towering Mount Kilimanjaro, shown here, which is the remains of an extinct volcano.

▼ Victoria Falls

The Victoria Falls are situated on the border between Zambia and Zimbabwe. Local people call them the 'smoke that thunders' because they make a deafening noise and produce a smokelike spray of mist.

▶ Hunters and hunted

Animals such as giraffes and antelopes roam across the African grasslands, followed by hunters such as lions. They share watering holes.

elephant

giraffe

buffalo

antelope

lion

warthog

hippopotamus

African kingdoms

Find out more:
African people • Explorers on land • Religion

Since around 3100BC, many kingdoms and and empires have been powerful in Africa. The first was in Egypt, where the pharoahs built great pyramid tombs. Later African kingdoms, all south of the Saharah desert, became rich through trade and conquest; their peoples lived by farming, hunting, trading and making fine craft goods.

▶ Circle of stone

From the 1000s onwards the Shona people of southern Africa mined gold and made bark cloth. They built a royal palace at Great Zimbabwe between AD1000–1500. Its huge stone walls still stand today.

▲ Fighting force

Few warriors could stand up to the armies of the Zulu people. They conquered large areas of South Africa in the 1820s. Their fighters carried spears, shields and wooden clubs.

▼ Statue of a hero

Legends from central Africa tell of Chibinda Ilunga, who lived in the 1500s. He was a prince of the Luba people but fell in love with Lweji, a Lunda princess. He came to rule over her nation and was wise and just.

▲ Mosque at Mali

In the 1300s, the West African empire of Mali was famous for its fabulous riches. Its merchants crossed the Sahara Desert by camel, travelling to North Africa. These merchants were part of an international Muslim community, and worshipped in religious buildings called mosques.

African people

Most of Africa's population lives south of the Sahara Desert. Many people of North Africa are Arabs, or have some Arab ancestors. Farther south, the people can be divided into more than 800 different groups, each with its own way of life and often its own language.

▲ Busy cities

Although more than half the population live in small villages, Africa has some large, bustling cities. Cairo, the capital of Egypt, is one of the busiest.

▲ Life in the desert

The Tuareg people live in the Sahara Desert. Traditionally they are nomads, people who move from place to place in search of fresh grazing for their camels, goats, sheep and cattle.

Word box

cassava
a thick root that is cooked and eaten like a potato

nomads
people who do not settle in one place, instead moving from area to area

▼ Which foods?

In the hot, wet parts of West Africa farmers grow bananas, coconuts, cassava, rice, cocoa and tea.

▼ Nelson Mandela

Nelson Mandela was the first black president of South Africa (1994–99). As a young man he fought for the rights of black South Africans. White leaders imprisoned him for his beliefs for 28 years (1962–90).

Air

Air is the mixture of gases that you breathe. You cannot see, smell or taste air but it is all around you. Layers of air surround our planet Earth, too, making up the Earth's 'atmosphere'. Oxygen is a gas found in the air. All animals, including humans, need it to stay alive.

▶ Oxygen-makers

Animals take in oxygen from the air and breathe out a waste gas called carbon dioxide. Plants do the opposite. They take carbon dioxide from the air and turn it into oxygen. The oxygen is given off through their leaves.

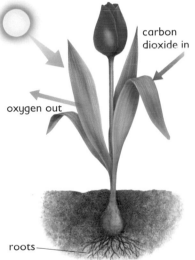

energy from the Sun

carbon dioxide in

oxygen out

roots

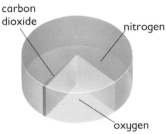

carbon dioxide

nitrogen

oxygen

▲ Gases in air

Nitrogen and oxygen are the two main gases found in the air. About one-fifth of the air you breathe is oxygen. Air also contains very small amounts of a gas called carbon dioxide.

▲ Moving air

When the wind blows it is really air on the move. If you stand outside on a windy day you can feel this flowing air as it rushes past you.

Wow!

On calm days a thick, yellow fog called smog hangs over the American city of Los Angeles. It is mainly caused by exhaust gases from traffic.

▶ Less air!

There are tiny particles in air called molecules, which are always bumping into each other. The more they do this, the greater the air pressure. Gravity pulls the molecules closer to Earth, so this is where there is greater air pressure. At higher altitudes there is less pull by gravity, giving lower air pressure and less oxygen. This is why mountaineers often wear breathing equipment.

How did the USA begin?

During the 1600s and 1700s, people from the British Isles, France and the Netherlands settled in North America. The places where they made their new homes were called colonies. These were ruled by Britain. In the 1770s, people living in the colonies rose up against the British. They wanted independance from British rule.

▲ What a tea party!

The people of Boston were fed up with paying taxes to the British government and getting nothing in return. They even had to pay a tax on tea. In 1773, in protest, some colonists crept on board three British ships and threw the cargoes of tea into the harbour!

▼ First president

The rebel army had been led by a soldier called George Washington. In 1789 he became the first president of the United States.

◄ A free country

In 1776, the American rebels declared the colonies independent from British rule. The war continued but by 1781 the British had lost. The rebels set up a new independant country – the United States of America.

▲ The war begins

In 1775, a man called Paul Revere discovered that British soldiers were marching to a village called Lexington to capture rebels there. He rode all night to warn them. When the British finally reached the village, the rebels were ready for them. The battle that followed sparked off the War of Independence.

Word box

independence
freedom from rule by another country

tax
money which people have to pay to a government, so that it can run the country

Amphibians

Frogs, toads, newts and salamanders are amphibians. Most amphibians are small animals with soft, smooth skins. They can live on land as well as in water and are found near ponds, streams and lakes. Amphibians usually breed in water.

▶ Lots of amphibians

There are more than 5,000 different kinds of amphibian. The largest is the Japanese giant salamander, which is more than 1.5 metres long. Newts are very like salamanders, but in general, they spend more of their lives in water.

Pacific giant salamander

◀ Poisonous frogs

Frogs and toads make up the biggest group of amphibians. This poison arrow frog lives in the rainforests of South America. Its poisonous skin helps to protect it from enemies.

▲ Confusing enemies

The fire-bellied toad has a bright red tummy that it uses to distract its enemies. When it is threatened it leaps away to safety, and the quick flash of bright red confuses the attacker, and gives the frog an extra fraction of a second to escape.

▼ From egg to frog

Tiny tadpoles hatch in water from the eggs of a female frog. As they grow, tadpoles develop four legs and a frog-like body. After a few months the tadpole has changed into a frog.

1. the female frog lays hundreds of soft eggs (spawn) in the water

2. the tadpoles hatch from the eggs

3. the tadpoles grow legs and change into froglets

4. the froglet loses its tail and changes into a frog. Frogs get bigger as they mature

Anglo-Saxons

Find out more:
Britain and Ireland

Who were the Anglo-Saxons? Their ancestors (relatives from long ago) were people called Angles and Saxons from northern Germany. Groups of them invaded southern Britain about 1,500 years ago and set up small kingdoms. Over time, the language they spoke developed into much of the English spoken today.

▼ Life in an Anglo-Saxon village

The Anglo-Saxons built villages of timber houses with thatched roofs. They farmed the land and raised cattle and sheep. During the AD600s and AD700s many of them became Christians and built stone churches.

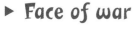

▶ Face of war

In about AD624, one Anglo-Saxon warrior was buried in his finest rowing ship, under a big mound of earth. It is thought the warrior may have been Redwald, king of East Anglia. He was buried with his gold coins, his finest jewellery, his prized weapons and this scary-looking helmet made from iron and bronze.

▲ King Alfred of Wessex

Around AD871–899, the most powerful of the Anglo-Saxon kingdoms was called Wessex. Its wisest king was called Alfred. He built new towns and a fleet of ships. His warriors fought against Vikings, who were invading the north and east of England.

Animals

Animals live in almost every corner of the world. They swim in the oceans, walk or run across the land, and fly through the air. The biggest animal on land, the African elephant, weighs as much as a farm tractor. You would need a microscope to see the smallest animals.

there are five main kinds of **vertebrates**:

birds

amphibians

mammals

reptiles

fish

▶ Animal groups

We divide animals into two main groups: vertebrates (animals with backbones) and invertebrates (animals without backbones). Within each group there are many kinds of animal. For example, roundworms and sponges are two different kinds of invertebrate, and lions and pelicans are two different kinds of vertebrate.

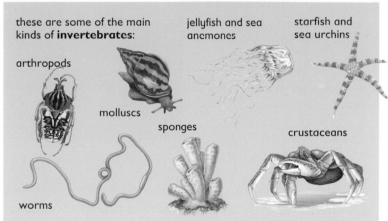

these are some of the main kinds of **invertebrates**:

jellyfish and sea anemones

starfish and sea urchins

arthropods

molluscs

sponges

crustaceans

worms

▼ Biggest of all

The blue whale is the biggest animal on Earth. An average female weighs as much as 120 tonnes and is around 26 metres in length.

◀ Lots of insects

Insects are the biggest group of animals. There are more than one million different kinds. All adult insects have six legs, and most can fly.

Wow!
Some large land tortoises can live to be around 200 years old.

Animals: behaviour

Find out more:
Animals: habitat • Birds • Mammals

Behaviour describes what an animal does –
its actions and movements. Some animals,
like worms and slugs, have very simple behaviour.
A worm does little except try to avoid light,
dryness and being touched, and will just eat
its way through soil. Other animals,
especially birds and mammals,
have complicated behaviour.

▶ Clever behaviour?

Some animals can use tools. The
Egyptian vulture picks up a stone
in its beak to use as a hammer. It
then smashes open an egg so it
can eat what is inside. But if the
real egg is replaced with a
painted wooden one, the vulture
still keeps trying to smash it. So
maybe this bird is not so clever
after all! The cleverest birds are
probably members of the parrot
and crow families.

Wow!
Some gorillas 'talk' to the human
guards who protect them from
poachers (thieves),
using the sign
language they have
invented themselves.

▼ Learned and not learned

An orb-web spider can make its
intricate web without watching or
learning from other spiders. Its
behaviour is 'built in' from the start,
rather than learned later. This is
called instinct. Many animals,
including spiders, insects and
frogs, have instinctive behaviour.

▼ Breeding behaviour

In the breeding season, male mammals like impalas, deer and goats
clash heads and fight each other. This behaviour is called rutting. The
strongest, healthiest male wins the contest and is able to mate with the
females. This means his offspring are likely to be strong and healthy too.

Shape puzzle

Can you put these shapes in an
order that makes sense?
Some chimps can!

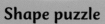

answer
The shapes in order are triangle,
square, hexagon (six sides) and
decagon (ten sides). Their number
of sides increases in this order.

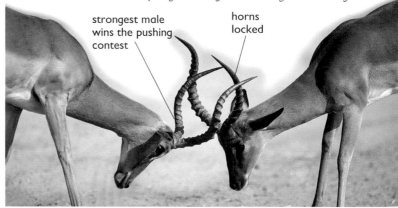

strongest male
wins the pushing
contest

horns
locked

Animals live in hot deserts and on snowy mountain-tops, in thick jungles and on wide, open grasslands. Where an animal or group of animals lives is called a habitat. For example, the hot, steamy rainforest of South America is the habitat of jaguars, monkeys and parrots. The frozen landscape of Antarctica is the habitat of penguins.

▶▼ Working animals

Across the world, people and animals work together to do different jobs.

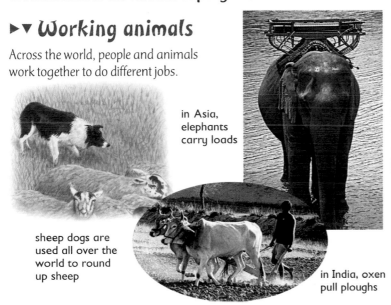

in Asia, elephants carry loads

sheep dogs are used all over the world to round up sheep

in India, oxen pull ploughs

▼ Animal travellers

Some animals travel huge distances to look for warmer weather or food supplies each year, usually to the same place and back again. This journey is called a migration. In North America, caribou travel thousands of kilometres to find food in winter.

▼ Animals and sport

For thousands of years, people have trained horses to take part in races. Races between horse-drawn chariots were held in ancient Rome. Horse races have been held in Europe since the early 1600s.

▼ In the cold

Polar bears can survive on the frozen land and in the icy cold waters of the Arctic. Their thick coat of fur protects them from the cold. A thick layer of fat below the skin also helps to keep them warm.

a large surface area from which body heat is lost

▲ Hot and dry

Animals that live in very hot places, such as the fennec fox, often have long ears and tails to help their bodies lose heat.

Antarctica

Antarctica is the world's coldest continent. This bare, icy land lies around the South Pole, the most southerly place on the Earth. Most of Antarctica is covered with a huge sheet of ice which is up to 3 kilometres thick in places. During winter, the South Pole is completely dark because the Sun never rises there.

◄ Big chunks of ice

Huge chunks break off the ice around Antarctica to form icebergs, which float out to sea. Icebergs are a danger to ships.

• South Pole

Roald Amundsen

◄ The South Pole

Explorers tried to reach the South Pole after people first sighted Antarctica in 1820. In 1911 two teams of explorers, one from Norway and one from Great Britain, began a race to the South Pole. The team led by Norwegian Roald Amundsen arrived first.

► Chilly research

These scientists are taking temperature readings in the freezing conditions of the Antarctic. Antarctica has more than 30 research stations, which are manned all year round by scientists from all over the world. Different types of scientists collect rock samples, observe animal behaviour, record weather data and study earthquakes and solar radiation.

Antarctica: animals

Antarctica is a huge frozen region at the South Pole. The cold Southern Ocean is rich in nutrients and plankton that are eaten by small fish, squid and krill. These then become food for larger fish, penguins, seabirds, seals and great whales.

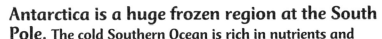

◄ Cold fish

The cold Antarctic water is full of cod, sea perch, ice fish and tooth fish. They are prey for the Southern elephant seal, which can dive down to 400 metres.

▼ Antarctic predator

One of the biggest predators (hunters) in the Antarctic seas is the fierce, sharp-toothed leopard seal. It is more than 3 metres long and hunts penguins, seabirds, fish, squid and even small seals.

▼ A chilly wait

Most penguins live in Antarctica. The female emperor penguin lays her egg and then goes off to feed at sea. The male stands with the egg on his feet all winter. He feeds the chick when it hatches with food stored in his stomach, until the female returns to take over.

► Summer visitors

Some animals only journey to Antarctica for the brief, warm summer. The Arctic tern migrates all the way from the Arctic, near the North Pole, to feed on small creatures at the water's surface. Whales migrate from warm, tropical regions to eat vast shoals of krill.

Wow!

The male Southern elephant seal is as big as a real elephant — almost 6 metres long and 5 tonnes in weight!

Apes

Our closest animal cousins are apes. Their body shape is similar to ours. They are clever and use tools, and most live in groups called troops. The smaller apes are gibbons of Southeast Asian rainforests. The larger apes are chimpanzees and gorillas, from Africa, and orang-utans, from Southeast Asia. All apes are rare and need our protection.

◄ Grooming friends

Chimps form large troops, of 100 members or more. Friends in a troop groom each other's fur and sleep in tree-nests at night. They eat plants, small animals and birds. Males can form a 'gang' to hunt monkeys or attack wandering chimps from other troops.

▲ The biggest ape

A full-grown male gorilla, or silverback, stands almost 2 metres tall and weighs over 200 kilograms. He defends his small troop of 5 to 15 against other gorillas and predators, such as leopards. But most of the time, gorillas just munch plants, sleep, groom or play.

Word box

territory
an area where an animal lives, feeds and defends itself or its group against other animals or danger

► The lonely ape

There are two kinds of orang-utans: Bornean and Sumatran. Unlike other apes, they live mainly alone, except for a mother and her baby. Like most apes, orang-utans are mostly vegetarian, eating fruits, shoots, buds, flowers and leaves. They rarely leave their trees.

▲ Noisy gibbons

Gibbons, such as the white-handed or lar gibbon, live in small family groups. They whoop and holler at dawn and dusk to defend their territory. They can make 10-metre swings through the treetops.

Arabs

The Arabs came from the deserts of Arabia, in southwest Asia. They lived in tents and herded camels. They also built towns and cities with the wealth they made from trade. Between the AD600s and AD900s, Muslim Arabs conquered areas of the Middle East, Africa and Spain. They built beautiful palaces and mosques.

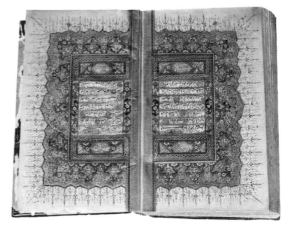

▲ Holy words

Arab design and Arab script, (way of writing), were often very beautiful, this is because Muslims believe it is the literal word of God. This is a copy of the *Qur'an* (the Koran), the Muslim holy scriptures.

▼ Dome of the Rock

Muslims captured Jerusalem in AD638 and built this mosque in AD691. It is one of Islam's holiest sites and is said to contain the stone from which the prophet Muhammad rose to heaven.

▲ Sailing the seas

The Arabs built big wooden sailing ships called dhows. These carried bales of silk and cotton, spices and coffee beans. The Arab merchants traded with East Africa, India, Southeast Asia and China.

Word box

mosque
a place of worship for Muslims

Muslim
a follower of Islam, the religion of the Prophet Muhammad

Arctic: animals

The Arctic Ocean, in the far north of the world, is almost totally covered in winter by a huge floating ice sheet. The land around is frozen, yet animals still thrive. Fish, seals and whales swim in open water. Polar bears, musk ox, Arctic foxes and hares roam the land. Snowy owls swoop around above the icy ground.

Word box

blubber
a fatty substance under the skin of mammals and birds, which keeps in warmth

tundra
treeless, boggy land around the Arctic Ocean covered in snow in winter

bowhead whale

▼ Adaptable bear

Polar bears eat meat, such as caribou, seals, birds, whales and fish. The female digs a snow den in early winter. Without eating any food, she stays here and gives birth to two or three cubs, feeding them on her milk.

▲ Giants in the sea

Some great whales, like the 20-metre-long, 60-tonne bowhead, stay in Arctic waters all year. Others, such as blue and minke whales, arrive only for summer. Like seals, they have a thick layer of blubber to keep them warm.

▲ Musk ox

Large herds of musk oxen roam the tundra. Their long fur keeps out the cold. They scrape away snow with their large hooves to find plants to eat. If a predator appears, oxen stand in a circle, facing outwards, to protect their young in the middle.

Wow!

The bowhead whale has the largest mouth of any animal, almost 10 metres around the lips!

◄ Winter white

Many Arctic animals, like snowy owls, are white in winter, to blend in with snow and ice. This camouflage makes them less noticeable to predators and prey.

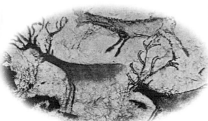

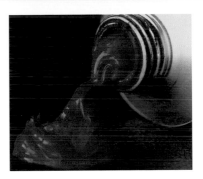

Early humans first painted pictures of animals on cave walls over 15,000 years ago. It is thought that early art was created for ritual practices connected with hunting or worship. Since that time, people everywhere have produced all kinds of painting, sculpture, carving and pottery – we call them works of art.

▼ Decorative art

Peter Curl Fabergé was a Russian jeweller, whose decorative art skills became popular with the Russian tsars in the 1880s. He is most famous for his beautifully decorated Easter eggs. Fabergé also made picture frames, clocks and other traditional items.

▲ Kinds of paint

Different kinds of paint produce different effects. Oil paints are thick and textured. Watercolours are much thinner and softer.

Wow!
Some paintbrushes are so fine that they are made from just one or two hairs. The artists work with a magnifying glass to see what they are doing!

Fabergé egg

▲ Pablo Picasso

Pablo Picasso was born in Spain in 1881, but he mostly lived in France. In many of his paintings, people and objects are turned into shapes and patterns.

▶ Looking at art

You can visit an art gallery to look at paintings and sculptures. This is the Guggenheim Gallery, in New York, USA.

Asia

Asia is the biggest continent in the world. It stretches from the Mediterranean coast of the Near East, to the islands of Japan, off Asia's eastern coast. A range of mountains called the Himalayas separates the warmer, wetter countries of southern Asia from the rest of the continent.

▶ Highest place on Earth

The world's highest mountain is in Asia – Mount Everest. It is 8,848 metres high. Mount Everest is part of the Himalayas, a mountain range on the border between Nepal and Tibet.

◀ Heavy rain

In southern Asia, winds called monsoons blow at regular times of the year. These winds bring very heavy rains.

▼ Sandy desert

Deserts cover most of southwest Asia. Little rain falls there and water is scarce in most of the region. The dry lands are no good for farming.

▼ Rare wildlife

The orang-utan lives in rainforest areas of Borneo and Sumatra. It is the only great ape to live in Asia, and is now a protected species.

Word box

monsoon
seasonal strong winds and heavy rains

rainforest
forests in tropical regions

range
a line of mountains

Asian people

Find out more:
Asia • Atlas: Asia

Around two-thirds of all the people in the world live in Asia. **Most live near rivers or by the coast, and make a living from farming and fishing. Many people are moving to the cities, where living conditions are often very crowded. Asia is the fastest developing region in the world, with many advanced industries.**

▼ Rice-growing

Nearly two-thirds of the rice in the world is grown in just two Asian countries — China and India. Rice is grown in flooded fields called paddies.

▶ By bike

The streets of Chinese cities are filled with people riding bicycles. The bicycle is the most popular way of getting around in China.

▲ River life

The river Ganges is India's busiest waterway. People come to trade goods, and many bathe in the water, which is believed to be holy.

◀ Following religion

This Buddhist statue is in Thailand. Asian people follow many different religions, including Hinduism, Islam and Buddhism.

▲ Tea trade

Tea is an important crop in Asia. The leaves are taken to nearby factories to be sorted and dried.

Word scramble

Unscramble these words to find the names of five Asian countries:

a. DLINHATA
b. ACNIH
c. TWIKAU
d. LEPAN
e. GLOAMOIN

answers
a. Thailand b. China c. Kuwait d. Nepal e. Mongolia

Assyrian Empire

Find out more:
Cities of ancient times • Empires and colonies

The Assyrians were a tough bunch. Their soldiers were famous for skinning enemies alive! But they were clever scholars, too. They were carvers of stone and builders of roads and cities. Between about 1700BC and 612BC, the Assyrians built up a mighty Middle Eastern empire over an area that is now Iran and Iraq.

▲ The last king

Ashurbanipal came to the throne in 668BC and set up a great library in the city of Nineveh. He was the last great Assyrian king. After his death there were revolts all over the empire. Nineveh was destroyed in 612BC.

▲ Chariots and bows

Big chariots pulled by two or three horses were used in war. Some had sharp, whirling knives fixed to the wheels. Assyrian soldiers carried deadly bows and arrows and iron spears and swords.

Wow!

Assyrian soldiers used inflated animal skins to cross deep rivers.

▲ Winged gods

The Assyrians worshipped gods of earth, fire, wind and water, and winged spirits or genies. The chief god of the Assyrians, shown in this stone engraving, was called Ashur.

CYPRUS
SYRIA
Mediterranean Sea
EGYPT
Euphrates River
•Nineveh
Tigris River
Babylon •
Gulf

◄ Many peoples

The great empire stretched from Egypt and Cyprus in the west to the Persian Gulf in the east. Many different peoples came within its borders.

Astronomy

Do you like looking at the stars in the night sky? Astronomy is the study of these stars. It is also the study of our Moon, the planets in our Solar System and all kinds of objects found in the Universe. In ancient times, people studied the Moon, planets, sun and stars to make the first calendars. Now astronomers use amazing technology to see farther into space than ever before.

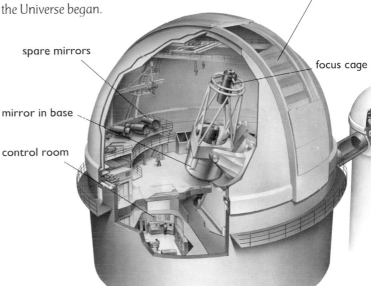

Make a star mural

Have stars twinkling on your own bedroom wall!
1. Cut out star shapes from shiny sweet wrappers. Glue the stars onto a large sheet of black paper.
2. Brush some PVA glue onto the paper and sprinkle glitter over it. Shake off any loose glitter.
3. Stick your star mural up on the wall with multi-purpose tac.

▶ Seeing by radio

The light you can see from some stars has taken hundreds of years to reach us. Some stars are so far away that we can't even see them. Astronomers also look at the skies using radio waves. Huge metal dishes called radio telescopes collect these radio waves. Some scientists think they have found radio waves left over from when the Universe began.

sliding roof

spare mirrors

focus cage

mirror in base

control room

▶ Watching the sky

Modern astronomers use huge telescopes with giant mirrors and lenses. These help them to see objects millions of kilometres away. The telescopes are kept in buildings called observatories. Parts of the roof slide back so that the telescope can be pointed at the sky. The telescope slowly moves around as the Earth turns, to watch the same patch of sky.

Atoms and molecules

Atoms are some of the smallest objects that exist – so small that they are invisible. Everything around us is built from billions of them. Atoms do not usually exist on their own, but join together to make molecules. Two or more atoms joined are a molecule.

▼ Inside an atom

An atom is made up of different types of tiny particles. It looks like a small version of our Solar System. The central part – called the nucleus – is like our Sun. The electrons are arranged like the planets that fly around the Sun.

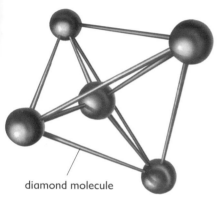

diamond molecule

▲ Coal or diamond?

It seems odd to compare a precious diamond with a lump of common coal, but they are, in fact, very similar! Both contain carbon atoms. In coal, the atoms of carbon are joined up in one particular way. In a diamond, they are joined up in a different way, to form the hardest substance known.

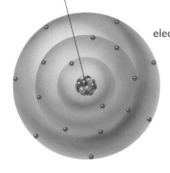

nucleus made up of protons and neutrons

electrons

chlorine atom

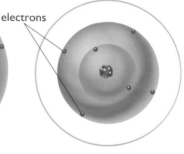

carbon atom

◄ Water-works

One drop of water is made up of millions of molecules. Each of these molecules consists of one atom of oxygen and two atoms of hydrogen. Hydrogen and oxygen are themselves gases, but when they combine, they form water.

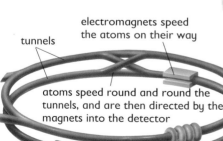

electromagnets speed the atoms on their way

tunnels

atoms speed round and round the tunnels, and are then directed by the magnets into the detector

particles collide here in the detector

◄ Atom-smasher

The only way to study atoms is to smash them open. To do this, scientists use a huge machine called a particle accelerator. The accelerator shoots particles towards atoms very rapidly so that they collide.

Word box

collide
crash into each other

particle
tiny object that the eye cannot usually see

The first Australians are called Aborigines. They came to Australia from Southeast Asia over 50,000 years ago. They fished and hunted animals, such as kangaroos. Dutch explorers sailed along the coasts of Australia in the 1600s. Then, in 1788, British people arrived at Botany Bay and began to settle the land.

◀ Ned Kelly

The 1870s were wild and lawless times in Australia. Ned Kelly and his gang of bushrangers stole cattle and robbed banks. When Ned was captured, he was wearing a home-made suit of armour.

◀ Ancient sounds

This Aborigine is playing an ancient instrument called a didgeridoo. Music, dance and storytelling recall the ancient history, beliefs and traditions of the Australian Aborigines.

▶ A new nation

The British used Australia as a place to send prisoners and to settle free people. They divided the land into separate colonies. Australia became a united country in 1901. This flag, which dates back to 1909, became the official flag of Australia in 1954.

Australia's flag

stars of the Southern Cross, the brightest constellation visible in the Southern hemisphere

Word box

bushranger
an escaped convict or gangster who lived in Australia in the 1800s

colony
an overseas settlement controlled by a stronger foreign nation

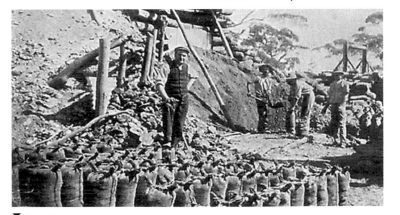

◀ Gold and sheep

In the 1800s, more and more Europeans arrived in Australia. They often attacked the Aborigines and forced them off their land. Many of the newcomers were sheep farmers. Others were miners – shown here at a gold mine in Western Australia in 1910.

Babies

A human baby spends about nine months inside its mother's body before being born. It takes about 40 weeks for a baby to grow from a tiny egg to a small human being – with eyes, ears, a nose, fingers and toes.

egg

sperm

◀ Life begins

A baby starts out as a tiny egg inside its mother's body. This egg has joined with a tiny cell called a sperm, which comes from the father.

▶ From egg to baby

The egg begins to grow inside its mother's body and it divides quickly into lots of other cells. These cells group together to form different body parts.

at 6 weeks the egg develops quickly and is called an embryo

at 8 weeks the growing embryo is called a foetus

at 12 weeks the foetus looks like a very tiny baby

▲ A newborn baby

Newborn babies cannot walk, talk or feed themselves. At first the baby feeds only on milk, either from the mother or from a bottle.

▼ Getting around

In Africa, many mothers carry their babies on their back. The mother has both hands free while the baby is held safely against her body.

at 6 months the baby is well developed but not yet ready to live outside its mother's body

at 9 months the baby is ready to be born. A newborn baby is about 50 centimetres long

▶ Learning to move

Babies can crawl by eight months. They take their first steps and usually say their first word at about one year old.

Wow!

By the age of eighteen months a child can say about 20 different words.

Bats

Find out more:
Mammals • Sound

Bats are the only mammals that can fly.
There are almost 1,000 kinds of bat (nearly one-fifth of all mammals) and most live in tropical forests. They are small, and flit about at night after flying insects. Bigger, more powerful bats hunt fish, small birds and owls. Most bats rest by day in dark, sheltered places like caves, hollow trees and the roofs of buildings.

flying foxes

high-pitched sounds echo off the moth

common pipistrelle

▲ Squeaks in the night

Most bats find their way in the dark helped by both eyes and ears. Bats make high-pitched sounds that bounce off nearby objects as echoes. The bat hears the echoes and can work out the position of objects as small as a gnat.

▶ Fruit bats

About 190 kinds of bats are fruit bats, called 'flying foxes' due to their long-snouted faces. They eat fruits, seeds, shoots and plant juices but can be pests and ruin farm crops.

Wow!

Bats have strong muscles to power their wings. Some can fly at more than 50 kilometres an hour!

▲ Bat roosts

Bats usually rest or roost by day in groups. They hang upside down by their clawed feet, wrapped up in their wings. The wings are the bat's 'arms', designed for flight. They are made of a thin, light, tough membrane, which is held out by extremely long finger bones.

Word box

echo
sound that has bounced, or been reflected, off an object

membrane
a thin layer of skinlike substance, on or inside the body of an animal or plant

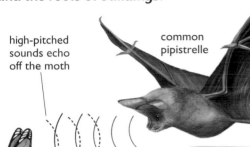

Bears

Bears are big, powerful mammals. They have a large head, wide body, massive legs, huge paws and claws and a tiny tail. Most live in forests and eat mainly plant foods. The biggest is the polar bear, which is white and eats meat, and the brown bear or grizzly.

▼ Sun bear

The sun bear lives in the trees of Southeast Asia. It stands about 1.4 metres tall and weighs around 50 kilograms, making it the smallest bear. Its tongue can stick out 25 centimetres to lick honey from bees' nests, grubs from wood holes and termites from their nests.

▲ Spectacled bear

The only bear of South America, the spectacled bear has pale eye rings and rarely leaves the trees of upland forests. It bends branches over to make a rough nest, to rest and sleep.

Bear senses

Do bears find their food and their way around using mainly their eyes, ears or nose? Put these bear senses in order, from the strongest to the weakest:

**ears and hearing
eyes and sight
nose and smell**

answers
1. nose and smell. 2. ears and hearing. 3. eyes and sight.

Wow!

The grizzly bear is the largest land-based carnivore (meat-eater), standing 3 metres tall and weighing up to 1 tonne.

▼ Fishing for salmon

Like most bears, grizzlies eat many foods – roots, nuts, berries, grubs, birds' eggs, honey and occasionally meat. In autumn, grizzlies gather along rivers to catch salmon. A grizzly then sleeps for much of the winter in a cave or den.

A–Z of bears

American black bear – north and central North America
Asiatic black bear – south and east Asia (mainland)
Brown bear (grizzly) – northern Europe, Asia and North America
Giant panda – west and south China
Polar bear – all around the Arctic
Sloth bear – southern Asia
Spectacled bear – uplands of western South America
Sun bear – Southeast Asia

Beavers

Find out more:
Mice and rats • Rodents

Beavers are big, stocky members of the rat-and-mouse group – rodents. They gnaw strongly with their incisor teeth and eat bark, soft wood, sap, fruits and leaves. Most common of the three types is the American beaver. It has a wide, flat, scaly-looking tail and lives in family groups across North America, and also in parts of northern Europe and Asia.

▼ Beavers at work

The beaver family is busy all day. The beavers build a dam from branches, stones and mud, across a stream. This holds back the water to make a lake where the beavers live in their lodge. Beavers keep busy repairing their lodge and gathering food — mainly soft bark, shoots, buds and twigs.

the lodge's living platform is dry and safe

▲ Mountain beaver

This secretive beaver has almost no tail and rarely swims. It looks like a big, fat rat and lives in a burrow in the woods along North America's west coast.

beavers gnaw around trunks to fell trees, using the branches to build a dam and lodge

Word box

incisor
a tooth with a straight, sharp edge, like a chisel or spade, at the front of the mouth

lodge
the den or 'house' of a beaver family

the lodge's underwater entrance and thick walls keep out enemies such as wolves

underwater, a beaver sees well and feels with long whiskers

Wow!
When well-fed in autumn, the European beaver is the second-heaviest rodent weighing over 35 kilograms (the capybara is the heaviest at 60 kilograms).

Beetles

Beetles are the largest single animal group on Earth. There are more than 350,000 kinds. These insects live in every habitat, from icy mountains to deserts and deep lakes (but not the sea). A beetle has two hard, curved wing-cases over its body, which are really its toughened front pair of wings. Underneath, folded up, are the second pair of large flying wings.

▲ Lady beetle

A ladybird's colourful spots warn other animals: 'I taste horrible, don't touch me!'. They are a gardener's best friend. Ladybirds protect garden plants by eating huge numbers of caterpillars and aphids (greenfly and blackfly).

▼ Ferocious beetle

The male rhinoceros beetle is one of the longest in the world, at 18 centimetres. The male uses his huge head horn to fight off other males and attract the smaller-horned female for breeding.

▲ Beetle lookalike

Cockroaches have a tough body covering and look similar to beetles. But they belong to a different insect group (*Blattodea*). Most kinds live in tropical forests. A few invade buildings, coming out at night to eat scraps of food.

▶ Great diving beetle

Most beetles eat plants or scraps, but the great diving beetle hunts tadpoles, pond snails, small fish and even baby frogs. It does this as a larva, too. It has to come to the surface for air, which it traps as tiny bubbles under its wing-cases.

Pest beetle quiz – who eats what?

A few beetles cause great damage, usually in their fast-eating grub or larval stage, often called a 'worm'. Can you match these beetle pests with what they eat?

1. Colorado beetles	**a.** potato crops
2. woodworms	**b.** oak beams
3. larder beetles	**c.** wooden items such as furniture
4. mealworms	**d.** meat or animal products
5. death-watch beetles	**e.** stored grains (wheat, flour)

answers
1a 2c 3d 4e 5b

Bicycles

Riding a bicycle is one of the world's most popular ways of travelling from place to place. We use bicycles, or bikes for short, to travel to school or work, to deliver things, to race as a sport and to take exercise. Each bike is specially designed for the job it has to do.

Wow!

There is a kind of cycling sport where cyclists race round a special wooden track. The bikes have no gears and no brakes!

▲ Fast bikes

A racing bike is light to help it travel quickly. It is made of a strong material, such as aluminium, plastic or carbon fibre. The rider changes gear to suit his speed. Thin tyres are also designed for speed.

▼ Mountain bikes

Mountain bikes are strong and chunky so they can move over rough ground. The wide tyres grip well on slippery, uneven surfaces.

▼ Bicycle taxis

In India and other Asian countries, bicycles are used as taxis. They pull two-wheeled carriages where the passengers can sit. These taxis are called rickshaws, and they are also used for moving heavy goods about.

Word box

carbon fibre
a strong, light material made from plastic and threads of carbon

gears
toothed wheels that help the cyclist to pedal more easily

▶ Early bikes

The penny farthing was one of the earliest bicycles. The first ones appeared in 1870. Its giant front wheel was about 1.5 metres high. Each time the rider made one complete turn of the pedals, the big wheel turned all the way round.

Birds

There are more than 9,000 different kinds of bird. The largest is the African ostrich, which can grow to be taller than a man. The smallest is the bee hummingbird, which could easily fit in the palm of your hand. Birds live in every corner of the world, from hot deserts to the icy lands of Antarctica.

bee hummingbird

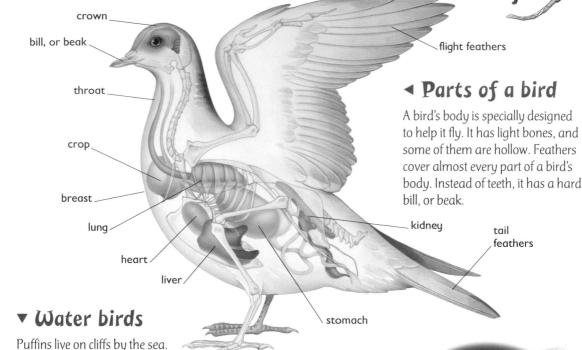

crown

bill, or beak

throat

crop

breast

lung

heart

liver

flight feathers

kidney

tail feathers

stomach

toes

◄ Parts of a bird

A bird's body is specially designed to help it fly. It has light bones, and some of them are hollow. Feathers cover almost every part of a bird's body. Instead of teeth, it has a hard bill, or beak.

▼ Water birds

Puffins live on cliffs by the sea. They dive into the water to catch fish. Their large beaks enable them to hold many fish at once.

► Birds of prey

Birds that are fierce hunters of other animals are called birds of prey. They include eagles, vultures, hawks and owls. They have sharp claws and strong, sharp bills. This owl is hunting a mouse.

Birds: habitat

Find out more:
Birds • Seashore life

Birds are the only animals with feathers.
All birds have wings too, but not all birds can fly.
Penguins cannot fly but they are good swimmers.
The ostrich cannot fly but it can run at speeds
of more than 60 kilometres an hour,
faster than any other bird.

▼ Making nests

Most birds lay their eggs in nests
made in trees and bushes, on cliff
ledges, in riverbanks, or in holes in
the ground. The weaver bird makes
a complicated nest by knotting
strips of leaves together.

large, powerful
legs allow the
ostrich to
travel long
distances

1. the male weaver
twists strips of
leaves around
a branch or twig

2. he makes a
roof and an
entrance

3. the finished
nest has a long
entrance, and
provides safety
and shelter for
the eggs and
chicks

▼ Breaking out

Many baby birds are blind and
helpless when they break out of
their shells. They are cared for by
their parents for several weeks.

1. the chick
chips at the egg

2. the egg
begins to crack

3. the egg
splits open

4. the chick
wriggles out

◄ Fast and big

Ostriches are the only birds with two
toes. They live in Africa in groups
and eat almost any kind of food
from grass to grubs.

▼ Different bills

Birds use their bills, or beaks, to get
food and to protect themselves. The
bill of the grosbeak is short and fat
– ideal for eating berries and seeds.

▼ Long-distance traveller

Some birds leave their home during
winter to find food in warmer
places. This journey is called
migration. The Arctic tern flies more
than 17,000 kilometres from its
summer home in the Arctic to the
Antarctic in the south.

Blood

Blood is the life support system for our bodies.
It carries the vital oxygen and goodness from food that we
need for life and growth. It also helps to collect dangerous
waste products from around the body.

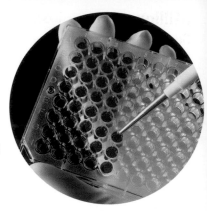

Word box

plasma
clear, yellowish liquid that
makes up most of blood

transfusion
putting blood from a healthy
person into someone who is
sick or injured

▼ Blood cells

Blood contains several types of living
cell, floating in a liquid called
plasma. Red blood cells are tiny,
flattish discs that take oxygen round
the body. White cells fight infection.
Tiny platelets help to stop bleeding.

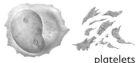

red blood cells   white blood cell

white
blood cell   white blood cell   platelets

▲ Which group?

People who have lost a lot of blood
through injury or disease may need
a blood transfusion. It is vital
that patients get blood from
someone who has blood of the
same group (type). To check this,
small drops of blood from the
person who is giving it are tested
carefully beforehand.

▼ Under pressure

Blood is pumped under
pressure round the body.
Doctors often check this
pressure, as it can cause
problems if it is too high or low.

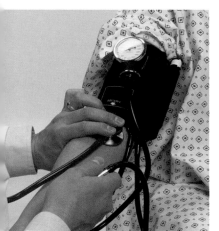

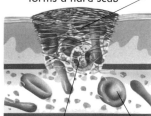

clot dries and
forms a hard scab   platelets

sticky clot blocks the cut

skin

white blood cell   red blood cell

▲ Stopping the flow

If you cut yourself, tiny structures called platelets release sticky substances.
These block the cut with a mass of fibres to form a clot. White cells swarm
into the cut to kill any germs, and repair begins. The mass of fibres and
trapped red cells dry to form a scab. Underneath this, fresh skin develops.

Books

Millions of new books are created every year. Some, like this encyclopedia, have words and illustrations in them. Some books have only words, some have mainly pictures and very few words. We read books to give us information as well as for enjoyment.

Wow!

A Chinese book called the Diamond Sutra is the oldest printed book – it was made over 1,100 years ago.

▼ Book beginnings

Authors are the starting point for most books. Some authors write out their work by hand, but many use a computer.

▼ Writing books

Charles Dickens (1812 to 1870) wrote some of the most famous books in world literature. His characters were brought to life in classics such as *Oliver Twist*, *A Christmas Carol* and *David Copperfield*.

▲ Religious writing

The main scripture of the Sikhs is called *Adi Granth*, or 'First Book'. It is a collection of the preachings of the first five gurus, and Muslim and Hindu hymns. They were written down between 1604 and 1704.

▼ Book characters

We all have favourite characters from the books we have read. How many of these famous book characters do you recognize?

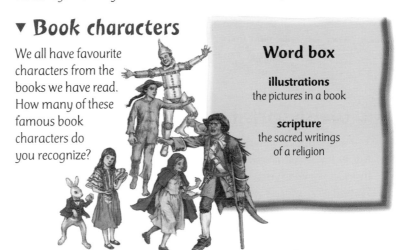

Word box

illustrations
the pictures in a book

scripture
the sacred writings of a religion

▲ Scotland's might

Parts of Edinburgh Castle are nearly 1,000 years old. Its high walls guarded the kingdom of Scotland from attacks by the English. From 1603 the Scottish king ruled England, too. Scotland and England were fully united in 1707.

The British Isles are a group of small islands lying in the shallow waters off the northwestern coast of Europe. The two largest islands are called Great Britain and Ireland. Today these lands are green, with a moist and mild climate. In 1801 Britian made Ireland part of the UK, although some Irish people did not want this. In 1921, after an uprising, Ireland was divided. The southern four fifths became an independant nation.

▲ For England!

England became very powerful in the Middle Ages. It fought many wars against its neighbours. This fierce battle took place at Agincourt, in France, in 1415. It was a victory for Henry V (Henry the Fifth) of England.

▲ Welsh uprising

The Welsh battled with the English, too, but were conquered in 1283. In 1400, the Welsh rose up against English rule, under a leader called Owain Glyndwr. The English were back in control by 1413 and the two countries were united in 1536.

◄ Irish freedom

England tried to rule Ireland for centuries, and it became part of the United Kingdom from 1801. In 1916, there was an uprising in Dublin against British rule. The southern part of the country won independence after December 1921 but the North remained within the United Kingdom.

Buildings

A concrete skyscraper, a hut of clay bricks, a pyramid of steel and glass and a red-brick house – all these are different kinds of **building.** The style of a building depends on how it will be used, what the climate is like and which building materials are available.

▲ Using materials

The Dayak people of Malaysia build houses from wood and bamboo, called longhouses. They are built on tall poles to keep them dry when the land is flooded.

▼ Domed shape

The O_2 dome in London is the biggest domed building in Europe. It was built specially to celebrate the start of year 2000.

▲ Skyscrapers

A huge skyscraper usually has a frame of concrete or concrete reinforced with metal. The windows and the walls, which are made of concrete, steel or glass, are attached to this frame.

▼ Old buildings

The pyramids in Egypt were built 4,500 years ago as tombs for Egyptian kings and queens. The pyramids are still standing, but some are partly in ruins.

Wow!

The CN Tower in Toronto, Canada stands at 553 metres tall, more than five times taller than the Statue of Liberty in New York, USA!

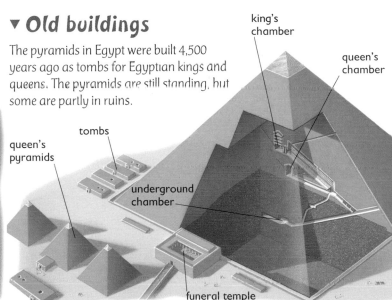

king's chamber

queen's chamber

tombs

queen's pyramids

underground chamber

funeral temple

Butterflies and moths

Find out more:
Insects

Most butterflies are colourful and beautiful. Moths are mainly small, grey or brown – but there are exceptions. There are more than 160,000 kinds of these insects, mostly moths, living mainly in tropical forests and grasslands. They all have two pairs of wide, flat wings covered with tiny scales, and eat plants.

Wow!
The most useful moth is the silkmoth. Its caterpillars (called silkworms) spin a covering or cocoon of silk threads that are made into finest silk cloth.

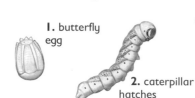

1. butterfly egg

2. caterpillar hatches

3. when fully grown, the caterpillar is ready to turn into a pupa

4. the adult butterfly pushes its way out of the pupa

5. the butterfly spreads and dries its wings

▲ Growing up

All butterflies and moths begin as tiny eggs. These hatch into larvae or caterpillars. When the caterpillar is fully grown it forms a hard body case called a pupa or chrysalis. Eventually, the case splits open and the adult butterfly crawls out. It then dries its wings and can fly after about an hour.

▲ Bright moth

Most moths are small, have hairy bodies, feathery antennae and fly at night. But the zodiac moth of New Guinea is big and bright, with slim antennae and flies by day.

Word box

antennae
feelers found on an insect's head, they are also used to smell

nectar
sweet, sugary liquid made by flowers, to attract insects and other animals

▼ Death's head hawk moth

Most moths hide by day. Their wings are patterned so they blend into their surroundings. But this big, powerful, fast-flying moth has scary markings on its back that look like a human skull!

◄ Pest butterflies and moths

Most adult butterflies and moths sip sweet nectar from flowers. But some of their caterpillars feed on farm crops and cause great damage. White butterfly caterpillars eat cabbages and other vegetables.

Byzantine Empire

In AD324, Byzantium was renamed Constantinople by the Romans. By AD330 it had become the eastern capital of the Roman empire. The city survived long after the fall of Rome in AD410, ruling large areas of southern Europe and western Asia. Yet in 1453, it was captured by the Turks, who called it Istanbul.

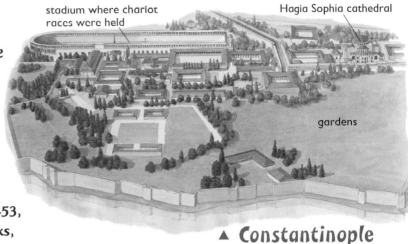

stadium where chariot races were held

Hagia Sophia cathedral

gardens

▲ Constantinople

The city was a rich seaport with high walls. It had markets, workshops, gardens and a beautiful cathedral. The people who lived there were mostly Greeks.

Wow!

Theodora was the daughter of a circus bear-tamer. She married the emperor Justinian in AD525, and became the most powerful woman in the world.

▼ Holy wisdom

The city of Constantinople was an important centre of the Christian faith. It was full of churches and monasteries. The great cathedral, Hagia Sophia ('holy wisdom'), can still be visited today.

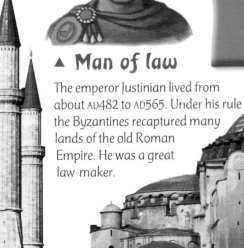

▲ Man of law

The emperor Justinian lived from about AD482 to AD565. Under his rule the Byzantines recaptured many lands of the old Roman Empire. He was a great law-maker.

Camels

Camels have humps on their backs, which some people think contain water. This is partly true, but the hump really contains body fat, which can be changed into energy and water. This is how a camel can survive weeks in its desert home, without water and food. The camel group includes one-humped dromedaries, two-humped bactrians, non-humped llamas and other cousins from South America.

▶ Camel cousins

Like their relatives, the camel cousins of South America have long heads, necks and legs, thick fur, and eat tough plants. Smallest is the vicuna of high grasslands in the Andes Mountains. The guanaco is slightly bigger, and lives lower down the mountains.

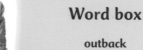

guanaco

Word box

outback
a wild area of land far away from most people and towns

▲ Two humps

The bactrian of Central Asia is well adapted for dry places. It has wide-hoofed feet for walking on soft sand. Its long eyelashes and closeable nostrils keep out dust. It has thick skin and fur to resist hot sun, and tough lips to eat thorny desert plants.

Wow!
Camels are among the few animals that run by moving both legs on the same side forward at the same time. It's called pacing and makes the camel sway from side to side – a rocky ride!

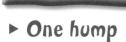

▶ One hump

Dromedaries live mainly in North Africa and the Middle East. Like other camels, they are used for carrying goods and people across dry lands. They also provide milk, meat and skins and are used for racing. Some were taken to Australia for carrying loads and have now become semi-wild in the outback.

Camouflage

Find out more:
Arctic: animals

What makes a polar bear and a vine snake similar? They are both camouflaged – coloured and patterned to blend in with their surroundings. This is common in all kinds of animals, from worms to whales. It helps them to stay unnoticed by predators, or if they are predators themselves, to stay unnoticed by prey (hunted animals)!

▼ Find the flounder

The sea bed can be made up of pale sand, speckled stones or grey mud. Many flatfish have good camouflage. As this flounder swims about, it slowly changes its colours and patterns to match the sea bed. This prevents its wide body showing up clearly to enemies such as sharks.

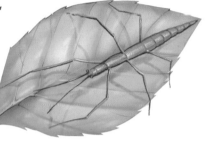

▲ Looks and actions

A creature is often shaped like objects in its surroundings, such as a forest leaf, or seaweed on the shore. The stick insect looks like twigs in trees and bushes, and when the breeze blows, it also sways from side to side, just like them.

▶ Tawny frogmouth

This nocturnal (night-active) bird rests by day out in the open, relying on its camouflage. It stays perfectly still on a tree or log, its feathers patterned to look like an old, rotting branch stump. It watches through narrow eye-slits – opening its big eyes would get it noticed.

Wow!

The fastest quick-colour-change animal is the cuttlefish (cousin of the squid). In a second its whole body can go from almost white to black – or yellow, blue-grey, reddish, even striped!

▶ Spot the chameleon

The chameleon lizard is famed for its ability to change colour. Its eyes see the colours around it. They send a message to the brain, which sends signals along nerves to the skin. This makes tiny grains of pigment (coloured substances) spread out or clump together and change the skin colour.

Canada

The first Canadians were hunters. They may have crossed into Canada from Asia over 30,000 years ago. After about 3000BC, new people came from Asia to settle the frozen north, hunting polar bears and seals. Today, these native people are called Inuits.

animal skins and fur to help keep the ice house warm inside

▶ Arctic survival

The Inuit built houses of stone and turf to keep out the bitter cold of winter. On hunting trips they made shelters out of blocks of snow. These were surprisingly cosy.

blocks of packed snow

tunnel to keep out cold air

◀ European Canada

French and British explorers and settlers moved into Canada in the 1500s and 1600s, trading in fish and furs. Between 1534 and 1541, Jacques Cartier became the first European to explore the St Lawrence River.

Jacques Cartier

▲ Mohawk warrior

The Mohawk people lived in southeast Canada and around the St Lawrence River. They lived in wooden houses and grew beans, maize, squash and tobacco.

◀ Canadian Pacific Railway

In 1885, a new railway was opened. It linked the eastern city of Montreal with Canada's Pacific coast at Port Moody. More and more Europeans travelled westwards and settled the land.

Today, there are more than 500 million motor cars on the world's roads. They come in many different shapes and sizes, from small three-wheeled ones to large four-wheel drive cars for travelling over rough ground. Most cars are powered by an engine, which burns either petrol or diesel fuel.

Wow!

The longest car in the world is so long, it has a swimming pool inside it!

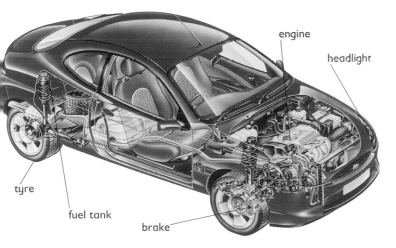

engine

headlight

tyre

fuel tank

brake

▲ Cleaner cars

Electric cars are cleaner because they do not produce waste gases like cars that use petrol or diesel. Waste gases from motor cars pollute the air.

▲ Parts of a car

A car has thousands of different parts. This cutaway view shows some of the most important ones.

▼ Motor racing

Racing cars have a sleek shape to help them go faster. This Formula One racing car can reach speeds of over 320 kilometres an hour.

Word box

mass-produced
made in large numbers

pollute
make dirty

sleek
smooth and shiny

▲ Early cars

One of the earliest mass-produced cars was the Model T, built by the Ford company from 1908–27 in the United States. For about 20 years it was the most popular car and over 15 million of them were sold during this time.

Castles

Find out more:
Castles: life inside • Knights

A castle was a fortress and a home for kings, queens, lords and ladies. It had high towers and massive walls to keep out the enemy. Soldiers guarded the castle and controlled the surrounding countryside.

▶ The first castles

Early castles looked like this. They had a wooden tower, called a bailey, on top of a high mound of earth, called a motte. They were built by the Normans less than 1,000 years ago.

motte-and-bailey castle

▲ Knock it down!

This giant machine was called a trebuchet. It was used to knock down castle walls.

◀ Stronger and stronger

By 700 years ago, castles were being built with more and more round towers and walls. Around them were ditches filled with water, called moats. The walls of this castle, built at Conwy in Wales, went right around the town as well.

▶ Digging underneath

Enemy soldiers would surround a castle and cut off its supplies. This was called a siege, and it could go on for months, or even years. Sometimes enemies tunnelled underneath the castle walls to make them fall down.

Word box

trebuchet
a weapon of war, designed to fire rocks and boulders

fortress
a building or town that has been specially built to protect it from attack

48 a b c d e f g h i j k l m n o p q r s t u v w x y z

Castles: life inside

Castles were places where soldiers were stationed, wrong-doers imprisoned, weapons and armour made and great festivities held. Their main purpose was to provide safety from attackers, which was why the castle lord and his family lived in the keep – the safest part of the castle.

Life in a castle

Lords and their families had very comfortable lives in castles, but servants didn't even have a bathroom. They had to wash themselves in rivers to get rid of any fleas and lice.

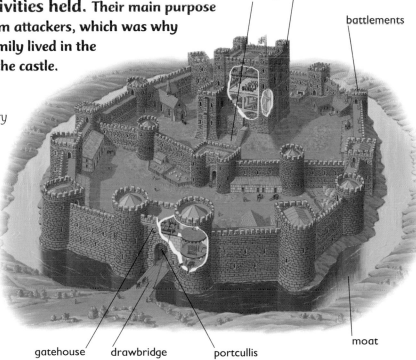

bailey   keep   battlements

gatehouse   drawbridge   portcullis   moat

Lord and lady

The lord of a castle controlled the castle itself, as well as the lands and people around it. The lady and the steward of the castle were in charge of its day-to-day running.

▼ Who worked in the castle?

Many servants lived and worked inside the castle. They cooked, cleaned, served at the table, worked as maids and servants and ran errands. A man called the steward was in charge of all the servants.

steward

Cats are deadly hunters, fast and silent, with strong legs and sharp claws and teeth. All 38 kinds of cats are very similar, differing mainly in size and fur colour. Most wild cats live in forests, have spotted or patched coats and climb trees well. Some survive in deserts. Our pet cats originally came from the African wildcat.

▲ Big cats

The seven big cats are the lion, tiger, cheetah, jaguar, leopard, snow leopard and clouded leopard. The leopard stores a large kill in a tree, away from hyenas and jackals, to eat over several days. It also hunts in towns and raids rubbish for leftover food.

Word scramble

Unscramble these words to find the names of five types of cat:

a. TACLIWD
b. MUPA
c. REGIT
d. TOLECO
e. HATEECH

answers
a. wildcat b. puma
c. tiger d. ocelot e. cheetah

Wow!

The smallest cat is the black-footed cat of southern Africa, which is half the size of many pet cats.

▼ Fast cats

Most cats run fast in bursts, but cannot keep going as dogs do. The cheetah is the world's fastest runner, reaching up to 100 kilometres an hour, but for less than 30 seconds.

◄ Cold cats

Cats shed their fur and grow a new coat once or twice each year. The lynx's winter coat is pale and thick. Like most wild cats, the lynx is now rare. People kill it for its fur, or in case it attacks farm animals or humans.

▲ Lazy cats

The bobcat, named after its short 'bobbed' tail, is a medium-sized cat from North America. Cats tend to live alone, hunt at night and sleep by day. Many have dens in hollow trees, under logs or in caves.

Some cattle graze peacefully in farm meadows — but others may battle with tigers in swamps or with wolves on the prairie. There are about 12 kinds of cattle, such as cows, oxen and buffalo. Half are truly wild. Of the others, such as the yak, gaur and water buffalo, a few are wild but most are kept by people. They are all big, heavy plant-eaters, with horns.

▶ Indian cattle

The gaur or Indian bison has a massive body with humped shoulders. Like most cattle it needs a daily drink and sometimes wallows in mud to get rid of flies and other pests. Other cattle of South and Southeast Asia include the mountain anoa, lowland anoa, banteng, kouprey and tamarua.

gaur

▲ African buffalo

Few wild cattle are as 'wild' as this buffalo, which charges without warning. It often kills the animal that is chasing it. The males bellow, snort, stamp and bang heads during the breeding season. The winner can mate with the females.

Wow!
One of the world's rarest big animals is the kouprey or wild forest ox of Southeast Asia. There are just a few hundred or so left – if that.

▼ Not a 'buffalo'

One of the biggest wild cattle, the male North American bison, stands 2 metres at the shoulder and weighs 1 tonne. These bison were almost wiped out by 'Wild West' European hunters, but herds now roam the range again — although they are far fewer in number.

Cells

Your body is made from billions of tiny living units called cells. Different types of cell are grouped together to carry out particular jobs. Cells divide and multiply as we grow. They are replaced as they wear out.

◀ Oxygen-carriers

This microscope photo of blood shows hundreds of red cells, which take oxygen around the body. The darker specks are white blood cells, which fight infection. They have been stained a dark colour to make them easier to see.

lysosomes are like recycling centres, breaking up old and unwanted substances so their parts can be used again

cell membrane is the 'skin' around the cell and controls what comes in and goes out

mitochondria change food into energy to power the cell's processes

nucleus is the cell's control centre and contains the genetic material, DNA

ribosomes are ball-shaped factories that make useful substances or products

golgi layers wrap up the cell's products so they can be sent where they are needed

Word box

plankton
tiny organisms that float in water

▲ Looking inside

All cells have the same basic form, although there are many different types. The nucleus controls how the cell works. It contains DNA, a material that contains a pattern for the development of the whole body.

axon

axon

signals jump gap

◀ Pass it on

Nerve cells carry messages round the body, in the form of electrical signals. These signals pass along the long, thin axon and then jump to the next nerve cell. Our brain, spinal cord and nerves are packed with millions of these cells.

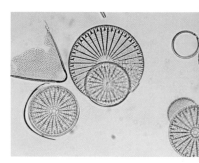

▲ Pond life

Have you seen green haze on a pond? This contains millions of microscopic plants, each made from a single cell. These are diatoms, and they live inside a hard, protective shell. Diatoms are also found at sea, floating in plankton.

Celts

The ancient Celts were farmers and iron workers. Their homeland was in central and western Europe. Between about 700BC and 300BC, the Celtic civilization grew across nothern Europe, bringing new languages and ways of life to many regions. Celtic peoples included the Gauls of northern Italy and France, the Gaels of Ireland and the Britons of Great Britain.

▲ Charioteers

A Celtic charioteer practises his skills. His job was to drive a fully-armed warrior into the thick of battle at high speed.

◄ Furious fighters

Celtic tribes often fought against each other. Many also went to war with the Romans, Greeks and Germans. Their warriors were armed with iron swords, daggers, spears and long shields.

◄ Mirror, mirror

This beautiful bronze hand mirror was used by Celts in southern Britain over 2,000 years ago. The Celts also loved wearing gold jewellery. The Romans complained that they liked showing off too much!

▼ The hill fort

Maiden Castle, in southern Britain, was the chief fort of a Celtic tribe. It was on a high hilltop, defended by fences and steep ditches. It was attacked and captured by the Romans after they invaded Britain in AD43.

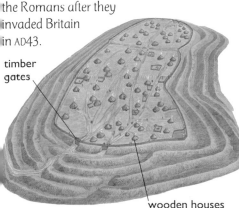

timber gates

wooden houses

► Later Celts

The Celts worshipped various gods and spirits, but during the AD300s and AD400s they embraced Christianity. Ireland became a centre of the faith and produced beautiful religious books, stone crosses and silver work.

In the 1840s, explorers discovered ruined cities deep in the jungles of Central America and Mexico. They had been built by the ancient peoples of the region, such as the Maya, whose history stretches back 5,000 years. The Aztec people built the city of Tenochtitlán in the middle of a lake in 1325. It was the capital of a great empire.

▶ Chichén Itzá

The Maya built a city at Chichén Itzá over 1,100 years ago. It had massive stone temples like this one. When the Toltec people conquered the Maya, they built a new city nearby. Chichén Itzá fell into ruins and the jungle grew up around it.

▲ Score!

The Central Americans loved to play a ball game called *tlachtli*. The players on the court had to get a small rubber ball through a stone hoop. The game was fast, rough and very exciting.

Wow!

The peoples of Central America invented chewing gum. It was made from the sap of a tree and was called *chicle*.

▶ Steps to heaven

Great Temple

The Great Temple towered over Tenochtitlán. It was 60 metres high. Steps led up to two shrines at the top. Here priests worshipped the rain and Sun gods.

▲ Stone giants

Many civilizations grew up in ancient Central America. The Olmec people lived around the Bay of Campeche about 3,000 years ago. They carved huge heads from stone.

Chemicals

Find out more:
Electricity • Energy

Most of what is around us is made up of chemicals.
Plastic, soap, even water, are a mix of chemicals. Some chemicals are dangerous – chlorine for example. However, when chlorine is mixed with another chemical called sodium, salt is formed, which is harmless.

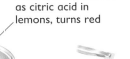
acidic substance, such as citric acid in lemons, turns red

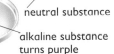
neutral substance

alkaline substance turns purple

Fun and froth!
Make your own chemical reaction.
You will need: vinegar and washing soda.
Add a few drops of vinegar to a spoonful of washing soda in a saucer. They will react with each other by frothing and giving off a gas called carbon dioxide.

▶ Chemical groups

Acids and bases are 'opposite' types of chemicals. They can be tested by using indicator paper, which changes colour when it touches different substances.

▶ Petroleum products

Petroleum, or crude oil, is a natural material that is used to make many different chemicals. Plastics, fuels, paint and soaps all come from crude oil. They are made in an oil refinery, where crude oil is heated in a huge tower. The oil is separated into different substances by condensing it at different temperatures.

oil refinery tower

cooking and heating gases

petrol and vehicle fuels

kerosene for jet fuel, heating and lighting

crude oil turns to gas and rises up tower

diesel oils for truck and train fuel

▼ Chemical colours

Fireworks use chemicals to make wonderful displays. Inside them are tiny metal particles, or chemicals that contain metal. They also contain substances that produce oxygen. When these burn together, each metal produces a different coloured flame – and exciting sparks!

crude oil is heated in a furnace

waxes, tars for road surfaces, polishes

China: beginnings

The ancient Chinese believed that they lived at the centre of the world.
They built great cities and canals and learned how to make beautiful silk, paper and porcelain. Many of the world's most useful things were invented long ago in China.

meeting house in centre of village

hole in roof to let out smoke

thatched roof

wooden wall plastered with mud

supporting poles

▼ Ghostly army

By 221BC, China was a united empire. The first emperor (Qin Shi Huangdi, pictured left), was a powerful man. Only one thing scared him – death. Just before he died, he arranged for an army of life-sized terracotta (clay) soldiers to stand guard around his tomb.

◄ First farmers

This is what a northern Chinese village would have looked like over 5,000 years ago. The farmers living there grew millet and kept pigs and dogs. They made pottery. Rice was grown in central and southern China.

▶ The Great Wall

The first emperor sent hundreds of thousands of workers north to build a great wall. It was meant to stop fierce tribes from invading China. Work on the wall carried on for hundreds of years. When it was finished, it measured over 6,000 kilometres in length.

In ancient times, China was divided into many small states. It was unified in 221BC by the first emperor Qin Shi Huangdi. The Empire lasted more than 2,000 years, surviving wars and invasions until it came to an end in 1911, when China became a republic.

◀ A golden age

During the period AD618 to AD907, China became extremely wealthy. It made the first ever printed books and produced the world's finest pottery, such as this horse figurine.

▶ Forbidden City

Twenty-four emperors made their homes in this splendid palace at Beijing, between 1423 and 1911. It included 800 separate buildings. Ordinary people were not allowed inside its high red walls, so it became known as 'the Forbidden City'.

▲ Silk robes

The emperors of China ruled over a glittering court. They wore robes of silk, such as this one decorated with dragons.

▶ Power to the people

After 1911, there were many wars. The Japanese invaded China during the 1930s. Different political groups fought each other, too. The Communists, led by Mao Zedong, aimed to give power to poor working people. They ruled China after 1949.

Make a Chinese fan

1. Take a sheet of A4 paper.
2. Use colour felt-tip pens to make a Chinese dragon design.
3. Fold the paper into pleats.
4. Staple the bottom end of the fan together.

Cities of ancient times

Find out more:
Cities of modern times

When people lived by hunting, they had to live close to or follow herds of wild animals in order to survive. Only when they began to grow food could people settle in one place, with a sure supply of food. Villages grew into towns and cities where people traded goods. The world's first towns were built in western Asia about 10,000 years ago.

▲ Walls and gates

The city of Babylon was built beside the Euphrates river, Iraq, about 3,800 years ago. It was protected by massive walls. Nine gates led into the city. The Ishtar Gate was covered with blue tiles, decorated with bulls and dragons. Through it, a paved highway led to temples and royal palaces.

▲ A town with no streets

Çatal Hüyük was built by farmers in about 7000BC, beside a river in Turkey. Its houses were made of mud bricks and flat roofs. They were all joined up, with no streets at ground level in between.

▼ Gardens of Babylon

A thousand years after it was founded, Babylon was still a great city. It was famous for its beautiful terraces and gardens, made for a queen called Seramis.

Cities of modern times

Find out more:
Cities of ancient times

In the 1800s, country people began to pour into the cities around the world to work in new factories and offices. Some cities housed as many as four million people. Numbers doubled and doubled again in the 1900s. Today, one in three people in the world lives in a town or a city.

▶ The Eiffel Tower

This 300-metre-high tower was put up in Paris, France, in 1889, to mark the 100th anniversary of the 1789 French Revolution. At that time it was the world's highest building.

◀ City of London

London, the capital of the United Kingdom, became the world's biggest city in the 1880s. Roads, railways and houses soon swallowed up farmland around the city. Factory and household smoke made cities dirty places to live.

▶ Reach for the sky

During the 1890s, skyscrapers were built in the centres of New York City and Chicago. They took up very little space at ground level. They were made possible by new ways of building and by the invention of the lift. These skyscrapers are the Petronas Towers in Kuala Lumpur, Malaysia.

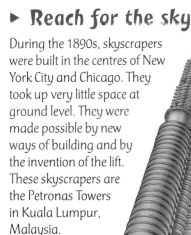

▼ Under the ground

Cities built underground railways from the 1860s onwards. The Moscow Metro, built in the 1930s, has very grand stations, like this one.

Climate

The Earth's rotation and movement around the Sun causes weather patterns that are repeated regularly. These patterns are called climate. A region's climate is affected by many factors such as distance from the Poles or Equator, distance from the ocean, nearby mountains, ocean currents and height above sea level.

▼ All kinds of climate

Earth has several climate regions. Tropical areas around the Equator generally have a hot, rainy climate throughout the year. The lands around the Poles are cold for most of the year. The area between the tropical and polar regions has a temperate climate with warm summers and cool winters.

look at the coloured rings to match the different climate scenes to the main map

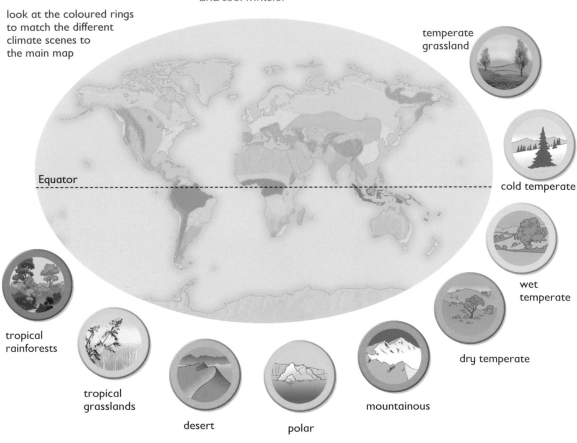

temperate grassland

cold temperate

Equator

wet temperate

dry temperate

tropical rainforests

tropical grasslands

desert

polar

mountainous

Climate change

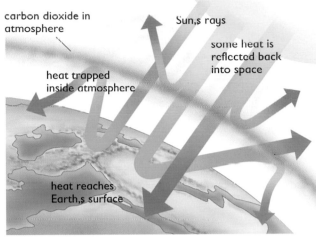

carbon dioxide in atmosphere

Sun,s rays

some heat is reflected back into space

heat trapped inside atmosphere

heat reaches Earth,s surface

Climates can change. This may be caused by a warm ocean current changing position. Humans also cause change, by doing things such as cutting down tropical forests. This may reduce rainfall over a wide area, turning it into desert.

▲ Getting warmer

The Earth's surface absorbs sunlight and turns it into heat. Some of this heat escapes into space. When we burn fuels such as coal and oil a gas called carbon dioxide is released into the air. Large amounts of this gas trap the Sun's heat – the 'greenhouse effect'. This raises the air temperature, just as glass on a greenhouse traps heat inside. This is known as 'global warming'.

▼ Rising waters

As the climate changes with global warming, polar ice is melting. This makes the sea level rise. Some coral islands in the Pacific Ocean have already vanished, and others may follow.

Word box

coral
hard, stony material produced by tiny animals in tropical seas

hurricane
giant storm with high winds

▲ Wild winds

Changes in climate may increase the number of hurricanes that sweep in from the sea. These hurricanes can cause huge amounts of damage to buildings and homes, due to the enormous power of the wind and the great floods that usually follow.

▶ Ice Ages ago

The 'Ice Age' was made up of several cold and warm periods, each lasting many thousands of years. During the last Ice Age, around 15,000 years ago, ice sheets covered Northern Europe. Early humans were well adapted to the cold conditions.

Clocks are instruments that show the time.
The first clocks were developed in the thirteenth century
and had no hands or dial but told the time by ringing a
bell. The word 'clock' probably comes from the French
word 'cloche' and the German word 'Glocke', both of
which mean bell.

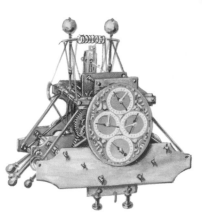

▶ Modern times

A digital quartz watch keeps
time by using a tiny crystal that
vibrates (shakes to and fro)
32,768 times a second when
electricity passes through it.

digital clock

◀ Old and new

Modern digital clocks tell you the
time by simply displaying
numbers. Older-style clocks have
round faces with the numbers
1 to 12 around the edge. Two
hands move round and point
to the correct time.

▲ Sea clocks

Harrison's 'chronometer' was
invented by a clock-maker, John
Harrison, in the mid-1700s.
Powered by a spring, it remained
accurate over long periods of time.
For the first time, it let sailors work
out their exact position at sea, so
they were less likely to get lost.

▶ Very accurate

Scientists keep time
with special atomic
clocks. These are
much more accurate than
ordinary clocks. They keep time
by measuring how fast an atom
(a tiny particle of matter) vibrates.

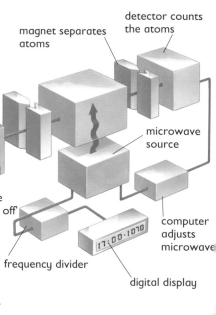

detector counts
the atoms

magnet separates
atoms

microwave
source

oven where
atoms 'boil off'

frequency divider

computer
adjusts
microwave

digital display

Word box

accurate
correct

frequency
the number of radio waves per
second of a radio signal

Clothes in history

The first humans made simple clothes from animal skins, furs and plant fibres. By about 7000BC, people had learned to weave cloth on looms. Wool, linen and cotton were often used for keeping warm or staying cool. Different styles of clothes were worn around the world.

brooch to fix tunic to shoulder

tunic

shift

long dress, or *stola*

toga

thick cloak, or *palla*

Word box

breeches
trousers that reach just below the knees, where they are fastened

fibre
threads of wool, hair, flax, straw, cotton or silk used to make clothing

loom
a frame used for weaving cloth

▲ Viking dress

Viking women wore a shift with a long woollen tunic over the top. The men wore a knee-length tunic over trousers, with a cloak for warmth.

▲ In the Middle Ages

In Europe during the Middle Ages, most poor children wore simple clothes woven from home-made wool. Boys wore short tunics and girls long ones. Hoods and cloaks kept off the rain.

▲ Roman togas

In ancient Rome, important men wrapped themselves in a heavy white cloak called a toga. Senators who passed the laws wore a toga with a purple stripe. Most women wore several layers of clothing.

▼ A true gentleman

This is how European men dressed in the 1700s. They wore a long 'frock-coat' over a waistcoat, knee-length breeches and a three-cornered hat. Both men and women wore wigs, covered in white powder, over their own hair.

◄ Paris fashions

The French were famous for fashion as long ago as the Middle Ages. In the 1800s and 1900s, women all over Europe and North America searched magazines for the very latest Paris designs. These styles date from 1913.

Clothing

We choose our clothing to suit what we do each day. To play sport we wear hard-wearing but comfortable clothes that let us move freely. In cold weather we wear clothing to keep us warm. In some parts of the world, people wear traditional styles of clothing that have been worn for centuries, particularly in country areas.

Wow!

In ancient Rome, only the emperor was allowed to wear an all-purple toga. A toga was a semi-circular cloak worn by men.

▲ Keeping warm

People who live in cold climates, such as Inuits, often wear thick layers of clothing made from natural materials such as wool, fur or leather. Scientists have developed new synthetic materials, which are also extremely warm.

▼ Clothes for the job

Some workers have to wear special clothing for their job. Fire-fighters wear protective suits made of a material that protects their bodies from the heat.

► Egyptian dress

Thousands of years ago, people in ancient Egypt wore clothes made of white linen. Men wore long wrap-around skirts, and women wore long straight dresses. Poor people, children and slaves often wore no clothes at all.

► Uniforms

A uniform tells you that a person does a certain job, or belongs to an organization. You can identify doctors in hospitals from what they are wearing.

▼ Keeping cool

In hot countries, people wear loose-fitting clothing to keep cool. Their clothes are made of cotton or linen. They are usually light-coloured to reflect the Sun's rays.

Word box

climate
the usual weather of a place over a long period of time

reflect
to make light bounce back

synthetic
not natural

Clouds

Clouds are made up of millions of tiny water droplets which are light enough to float in the air. There are several different types of cloud, which form at different heights in the air and in different types of weather. Depending on the temperature and other conditions, clouds bring rain, hail, sleet or snow.

▼ Cloud shapes

Clouds form at different heights, and in different types of weather. These things affect their appearance. Generally, the thin, wispy clouds are high up. Heavy-looking rain clouds are normally nearer the ground.

▲ Frozen drips

Icicles form when snow or ice melts and then re-freezes. The snow starts to melt during the day. Then the dripping water freezes again in the colder night temperatures.

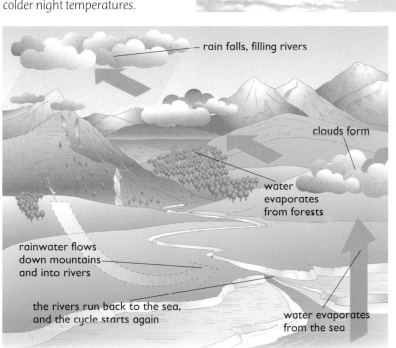

- rain falls, filling rivers

clouds form

water evaporates from forests

rainwater flows down mountains and into rivers

the rivers run back to the sea, and the cycle starts again

water evaporates from the sea

◄ The water cycle

When water from lakes, rivers, seas and vegetation evaporates, it rises into the air as water vapour. The vapours get cooler as they rise and turn into water droplets, which form clouds. Rain clouds form when the droplets merge together to make larger drops. Eventually they become too large and heavy to float and fall to the ground as rain. Then the water cycle, as it is called, begins again. If the air is very cold the water in clouds freezes and forms snowflakes or hailstones.

Colour

Colour is all around you – in the clothes you wear, in the flowers in the park, in a rainbow in the sky and on your TV screen. Even the light from the Sun, which seems to have no colour at all, is filled with colour.

▶ Colours of the rainbow

When white light passes through a glass prism, it breaks up into the different colours of the rainbow: red, orange, yellow, green, blue, indigo and violet. The whole range of bands of colour is called a spectrum.

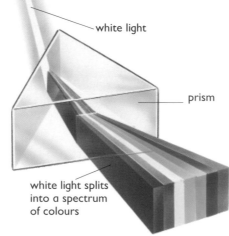

white light

prism

white light splits into a spectrum of colours

a rainbow occurs when raindrops in the air act like prisms

▲ Warning colours

Some animals use colour to warn off their enemies. The bright markings on this butterfly's wings tell its enemies that it tastes nasty!

▶ Mixing colours

We mix colours together to create different ones. Only three colours of light – red, blue and green – are needed to make all the other colours. These three colours, called primary colours, produce all the pictures that you see on your television screen.

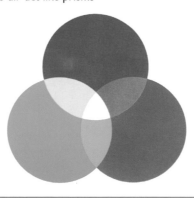

Colour mix

Red, blue and yellow are the primary colours of paint. All other paint colours are made from them. Can you fill in these gaps with the correct colours?

a. red + . . . = orange
b. . . . + red = purple
c. blue + yellow = . . .

answers
a. yellow b. blue c. green

Try this!

Have fun mixing lots of colours with your paints. Blue, yellow and red are the primary paint colours (these are different from the primary light colours). See how many different colours you can come up with. You'll be amazed!

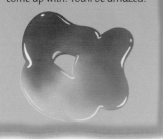

When we look at an object, we do not actually *see* its colour. Instead, we see the light that the object reflects, or bounces off. White light (a mix of all colours) falls on the object, but most of its colours are soaked up or absorbed. The colours that are reflected reach our eyes and give the object its colour. So, we see a leaf as green because it absorbs all other coloured light except green.

▶ Colour wheel

On a colour wheel, one primary colour (red, yellow or blue) will appear opposite the mixture of the two other primary colours. For example, red will appear opposite green, which is a mixture of yellow and blue. These opposites are called complementary colours.

tiny dots of colour

▲ On the page

Colour pictures in magazines and books and on TV screens are actually made up of thousands of tiny dots of colour. Our eyes naturally mix these colours together.

yellow plate

magenta plate

cyan plate

black plate

roller

cylinder

▶ Colour in printing

Lithography is a printing process, used for creating colour pictures. An image is transferred to a surface called a plate. Four of these plates are used to print a full colour picture (see right).
Each plate is placed on a cylinder. A roller then wets all of the plate except the image.
Another roller spreads ink that only sticks to the image. The inked image is then transferred to paper.

Communication

Our whole lives are based on communication. Communication is the sharing of information. People communicate mainly by speaking and writing. We also communicate physically through body language. Animals communicate with each other in a variety of ways.

◄ Noisy monkey

The noisiest land animals are the red and black howler monkeys of South America. They live in troops of 10 to 30 animals, the monkeys howl to define their territory or to send alarm signals to others. The sound comes from the echo chambers beneath their chins, and can be heard 5 kilometres away.

▶ Let's communicate!

As well as words, we use a lot of body language to communicate with people – often to say hello or goodbye. Hand gestures, facial expressions, body positions and eye contact are all ways of communicating with others.

Wow!

One of the longest phone calls ever recorded lasted for 550 hours – nearly a whole month!

Did you write a letter today, make a phone call or send someone a message by email? All these are different ways of communicating with people. Modern technology lets us communicate at very high speeds across the world – by telephone, radio, television or the Internet.

Wow!

There are more telephones than people in the city of Washington D.C., capital of the USA.

Word box

email
short for electronic mail (sending letters by computer)

remote
far away

artificial satellite
a spacecraft that circles the Earth

▲ Faraway places

In remote parts of Australia, the only way to communicate with others is by radio. Some children do their schoolwork by talking to their teacher over a two-way radio.

▼ First telephone

The first telephone was made in 1876 by a Scottish-born inventor called Alexander Graham Bell.

▼ Up in space

When you telephone someone in a distant country, the signal from your call is beamed up to a satellite above Earth. The satellite then sends the signal through space, back down to the Earth and into the other person's phone.

▼ On the move

With the help of mobile phones, people can keep in touch with each other, wherever they are. These phones are small enough to fit in your pocket – or even in the palm of your hand.

satellite

telephone exchange sends messages along the phone network

signal

Computers are complicated machines that can process huge amounts of information in a very short time. They are not intelligent themselves, but they help us to do clever things that we would not be able to do on our own. For example, computers can now beat humans at chess.

Wow!

Special computers are used to calculate the weather forecast. Some can work out a six-day global forecast in just 15 minutes!

▲ Early computers

One of the first proper computers was called *Colossus*. It was built in 1943 to decode (work out) complex messages used by Germany during World War II.

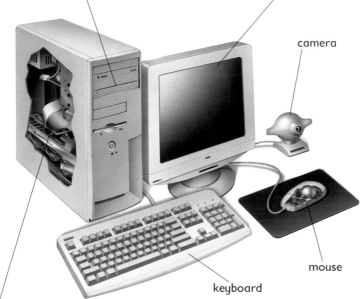

CD-ROM drive reads information from a compact disc

monitor (screen) displays information from the computer

camera

the microprocessor is the computer's main microchip and controls the computer

keyboard

mouse

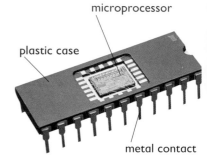

microprocessor

plastic case

metal contact

▲ Tiny chips

Microchips are tiny pieces of a hard material called silicon. We sometimes call them silicon chips. Each chip carries thousands of electrical paths called circuits. Microchips make up the 'brain' of your computer.

▲ What goes where?

Computers have a keyboard, a screen, a mouse and a main box that contains electronic circuits that control computer processes. Most of the latest computers have flat screens. The mouse is a hand-held device that allows you to control the computer.

Over the past thirty years computers have become an enormous part of both our working and our daily lives. **They are used in many jobs to make tasks quicker and more efficient and to enable large amounts of data to be stored and processed.**

◀ Computers in science

Scientists use computers for many things; for example to record data, to write up results of experiments, and to read papers by other scientists that are published on the internet.

▶ Computers in daily life

Computer technology has become such an important work tool that it is now taught in schools. The way we work has changed enormously to take advantage of the new ways we can communicate. Electronic mail (email) is a fast and convenient form of contact. The message is typed into a computer and is sent to another e-mail address along a phone line to a central server. The message is stored here until the recipient connects to a computer to receive it.

Word scramble

Unscramble these words to find the names of four important parts of a computer:

a. somue
b. trepnir
c. romtion
d. cids rvide

answers
a. mouse b. printer
c. monitor d. disc drive

▼ Robot workers

In factories, computers control machines that carry out many jobs automatically. The robot that is spraying paint onto this car body is controlled by a computer.

Word box

circuit
a loop of electricity

microchip
tiny slice of a substance called silicon, containing millions of electronic parts

Conservation

Many animals and plants are in danger and dying out because the habitats in which they live are being destroyed by people. Large-scale building work, farming, tourism and the pollution of rivers and lakes are some of the major causes of habitat destruction. Habitats can only be conserved if governments take measures to protect them and prevent or control these activities.

Word box

deforestation
cutting down large areas of forest

habitat
the type of place where an animal or plant lives

▼ River life

Lots of different types of wildlife depend upon rivers, but they are very vunerable to pollution. Factories often dump waste into them or change their temperature, which can be very damaging.

▶ Rainforests

In many rainforests big areas of trees are being cut down. The correct word for this is deforestation. It is estimated that up to 30 million hectares of rainforest are being cut down each year — that is the same as 80 football pitches every minute. Deforestation removes the habitat of many animals and is a possible cause of global warming.

◀ Saving the panda

China is trying to preserve its giant pandas by breeding them in captivity, and then releasing them into the wild. Pandas only ever nurture one baby at a time, and the birthrate for those in captivity is extremely low. Farming is destroying the places where the pandas live. They are also hunted for their skins and body parts.

▼ National parks

To try and conserve wild parts of the world, large areas have been set aside as national parks. Here, building, tourism and other activities are strongly controlled.

Conservation involves looking after the **plants and animals in our world, and protecting the wild places where they live.** As human beings take up more and more space on the Earth, the places where plants and animals live are in danger. Some species have already disappeared completely.

dodo

◀ Disappearing animals

Some animals and plants have already died out – they have become extinct. The dodo was a flightless bird living on the island of Mauritius in the Indian Ocean. Its forest home was destroyed, and large numbers were hunted.

▼ Working for wildlife

Conservation work may involve planting trees, like the tree farm below, or helping to protect wildlife from being harmed.

▼ Tigers under threat

Tigers have already disappeared from much of Asia. Many have been hunted, or their homes destroyed. They may die out altogether in the next 100 years.

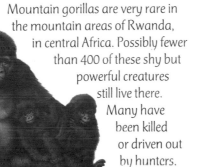

Wow!

The eggs of the extinct elephant bird from Madagsacar were big enough to hold eight litres of liquid – that's the same amount as in 24 soft drinks cans.

▼ Rare plants

In Great Britain, some types of wild plants such as orchids are so rare that it is against the law to pick them or disturb their habitat.

orchid

▼ Gentle giants

Mountain gorillas are very rare in the mountain areas of Rwanda, in central Africa. Possibly fewer than 400 of these shy but powerful creatures still live there. Many have been killed or driven out by hunters.

Word box

illegal
not allowed by law

species
kind of plant or animal

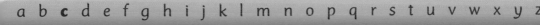

Construction

We have constructed buildings since earliest times to protect us from bad weather, wild animals and sometimes from enemies. The first buildings were made of straw, sticks and mud. Now we use much stronger materials like concrete and steel. Other types of contruction include bridges, roads and railways, which are essential for transport over land.

Wow!
Many castles were built in India between 1500 and 1700. The gateways had iron spikes in the doors to stop war elephants breaking them down.

▲ The longest steel-arch bridge

The longest steel-arch bridge, with a span of 550 metres, is the Hu Pu bridge in Shanghai. Another steel-arch bridge, Sydney Harbour Bridge in Australia, is the world's widest long-span bridge.

▼ Super structures

Modern cities feature several types of construction, including spectacular skyscrapers and bridges, and extensive networks of roads and railways. Skyscrapers are built around a steel skeleton.

▲ Kept in suspense

Suspension bridges span the greatest distances – the longest is the Akashi-Kaiko Bridge in Japan. It spans 1,990 metres.

Courtship rituals

Find out more:
Animals: behaviour

Courtship is what some creatures perform before they mate and produce young. In most animals, a female and male of the same kind come together to breed. In courtship, each checks that the possible partner is fit, healthy and ready to be a parent. Often it involves sights, sounds, smells and actions.

▶ Look at me, peahen!

Usually it's the male animal who puts on a courting display to impress the female. This peacock spreads his long tail feathers as a graceful fan. He shakes this with a rattling noise, calls loudly and struts about.

▲ Getting together

Animals court in many different ways. Grasshoppers chirp, butterflies flap wings, sharks bite each other and crabs lock pincers. This female and male Cape gannet use their long beaks like swords to 'fence'. But the aim is staying together rather than fighting.

dusky titi

Who does which courtship?

Can you match each male animal to his style of courtship?

1. hangs from a branch, shakes his wings and tail and sings loudly
2. swims around the female showing a bright red belly
3. croaks loudly and jumps on the female's back
4. coils around and rubs the female

a. viper **b.** bird of paradise **c.** stickleback **d.** frog

answers
1b 2c 3d 4a

Wow!

The courting 'love song' of the male humpback whale travels more than 100 kilometres through the ocean.

▲ Strong bond

In the Amazon rainforest, the female and male dusky titi stay together, not just during courtship, but all year. Each dawn they sit side by side on a branch, wrap their tails together and sing loudly.

Crustaceans are 'insects of the sea'. Like insects on land, they swarm in the oceans in billions. There are over 40,000 kinds including crabs, lobsters, prawns, shrimps, krill (which look like shrimps), and barnacles on seashore rocks. Copepods and branchiopods are smaller and more rounded, and even more numerous. They include a few freshwater types like the pond 'water flea', daphnia.

Wow!

The largest crustacean is the giant spider crab. Its body is as big as a dinner-plate and its long legs and pincers would hang over the edge of a double bed!

▶ On the march

Some crustaceans migrate (travel) with the tides or seasons. These spiny lobsters are marching to deeper water to breed.

▼ Crustaceans on land

A few crustaceans, like the wood-louse (sowbug), survive on land, far from the sea. Even so, they need to stay in cool, damp places, such as under bark or logs, or they dry out and die.

▼ Tough customer

The robber crab is big, strong and fierce, with pincers the size of your hands. Like many crabs and other crustaceans, it feeds by scavenging on old, rotting bits and pieces of almost anything. This crab lives mainly on the shore, and can even climb trees.

◀ Non-crusty crustacean

Most crustaceans have a hard outer body casing, one or more sets of antennae (feelers), at least four pairs of legs, and perhaps strong pincers. The hermit crab is unusually soft-bodied. It finds an empty whelk or similar shell and hides safely inside it.

Crocodiles and alligators

Crocodiles have survived from the age of dinosaurs – but in some cases, only just. There are 23 types of crocodiles and their cousins – alligators, caimans and gharial (gavial). All are powerful meat-eaters, catching prey or scavenging on dead meat. But some have been hunted by people for meat and skins, or because they threaten us or our animals.

Word box

estuarine
in or from an estuary (river mouth), where a river widens and flows into the sea

hibernate
sleep very deeply for weeks, usually to survive a long winter

▼ Biggest reptile

The largest crocodile, and biggest reptile, is the saltwater or estuarine crocodile. Most crocodiles live in fresh water along rivers, lakes and swamps, but this massive beast swims along coasts and even out to sea. It lives along the shores of South and Southeast Asia and Australia.

▲ Chinese alligator

One of the smallest and rarest types, the Chinese alligator is only 2 metres long. Its prey is also small – water snails, worms and the occasional water rat or duck. During the winter it hibernates out of water, in a cave or den, waking up in the warmth of spring.

Wow!

Crocodiles are among the longest-lived animals. Some survive to well over 100 years of age.

▶ Teeth and scales

A crocodile's pointed, well-spaced teeth grip all kinds of prey, including fish, birds and mammals. The body is covered with hard, bony scales. As old teeth and scales wear and fall off, new ones take their place.

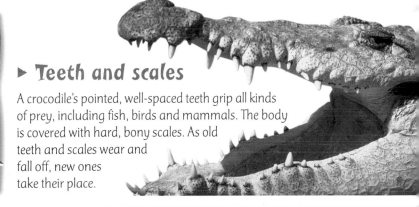

Crusades

Find out more:
Turkey

In 1075, the Seljuk Turk Muslims captured the holy city of Jerusalem. In 1096, after the Seljuk Turks declared that pilgrims could no longer visit Jerusalem, Christian knights living in Europe began a series of religious wars called the Crusades. Most of these were fought against Muslims in the Near East, but others took place in Spain and Central Europe.

▶ Saladin

One Muslim leader was admired and respected even by his enemies. His name was Saladin, or Saleh-ed-din Yussuf, and he lived from 1137 to 1193.

▶ Sword on sword

Terrible wars were fought in the Near East until 1291. The Christian knights wore heavy armour, even in the heat of the desert. Their Muslim enemies were armed with steel swords, round shields and bows and arrows. The Europeans called them 'Saracens'.

Word box

Crusades
'wars of the Cross', the Cross being the symbol of Christianity and the badge of the Christian knights

Near East
the lands of southwest Asia, today occupied by Turkey, Syria, Lebanon, Israel and the Palestinian Territories

Crystals

**Most crystals are formed from minerals –
natural substances found in the Earth's crust.**
They come in different shapes, but all have straight edges
and flat surfaces. Some crystals, such as salt, are simple
cubes. But other substances produce crystals with more
complex shapes.

▼ Sugary crystals

The sugar you use at home is
actually tiny crystals. Water is
slowly made to evaporate
(disappear into the air) from sugar
syrup, so that
solid sugar
is left
lumpy as
crystals.

▲ Spiky shapes

Amethyst crystals are formed from
a mineral called quartz. With its
many different surfaces and angles,
this is a good example of crystals
with a complex shape.

▲ Inside snow

Snow is made up of millions of tiny
ice crystals. These form inside cold
clouds, where they collide and stick
together to produce snowflakes.
Some snowflakes have star shapes
with six sides like this, others look
like long needles of ice.

Try this!

Put hot tap water (careful!) in a jam
jar. Now pour in salt, stirring until it
has all dissolved. Let the water cool.
Tiny salt crystals will slowly form on
the bottom of the jar. Use a spoon to
remove most of the crystals, leaving
just one or two of the largest. Put the
jar somewhere warm and check it
every week. As the water evaporates,
the salt crystals will grow in size.

◄ Liquid crystal

The LCD (liquid crystal
display) screen of this
hand-held television
is made up of
'liquid' crystals.
These are crystals
that have been heated
up so they become cloudy.
Thousands of liquid crystals
build up to make the image you
see on the screen.

Dance

All over the world people dance, usually to music, as part of ceremonies or celebrations, to express themselves, to entertain others – or simply to have fun. We know that people danced thousands of years ago, because paintings on cave walls show prehistoric people dancing before hunting trips.

Wow!

Every August, men of the Hopi tribe from Arizona, USA perform a sacred dance with live rattlesnakes in their mouths.

▲ Traditional dances

In African villages, dances are usually performed to celebrate important events such as births, weddings and good harvests. These dancers stamp their feet as they move in time to the beat of drums.

▼ Dragon dance

The Chinese celebrate each Chinese New Year's Day with a special parade. People dance through the streets wearing a large dragon costume. Chinese people believe that the dragon will keep away evil spirits during the year ahead.

▼ Learning ballet

Ballet dancers start their training from a very early age. They have to practise hard to develop their strength and to learn all the movements perfectly.

▼ Carnival dancers

In Brazil, people dance in the street during carnival time.

Word box

carnival
a street celebration with music and dancing

prehistoric
before written history

sacred
holy, related to religion

Deep-sea animals

Find out more:
Fish • Oceans: life

At the bottom of the sea, every day is the same – and night too. It's always dark, cold and still, with huge water pressure. Below about 500 metres there is no light, and so no plants. Animals survive on bits of food sinking down from above – or eat each other. There are glow-in-the-dark fish, squid, strange-shaped crabs, shellfish, starfish, sea urchins, sea cucumbers, sea lilies and giant worms galore!

▲ Big-mouthed eel

The gulper eel, about 60 centimetres long, is also called the black swallower. Its flexible mouth can swallow an animal twice its size. Many deep-sea creatures are black. Colours and patterns are of no use in the darkness. Some animals have no eyes at all.

▶ Fanged fish

The deep sea is the world's biggest habitat. But food is quite scarce, so relatively few animals live there. Most are small – the viperfish is hardly longer than your hand. It has long fangs, like a snake, to grab any possible passing meal.

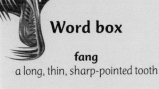

Word box

fang
a long, thin, sharp-pointed tooth

pressure
a pushing or pressing force, measured over a certain area such as a square centimetre

◀ Deep-sea anglerfish

This wide-mouthed, sharp-toothed hunter 'fishes' for prey with its long front fin spine, which has a glowing tip. Small creatures are lured by this light in the darkness, and the angler swallows them whole.

▶ Deep-sea tubeworms

Here and there on the sea bed, hot water rich in minerals, from deep in the Earth, spurts out through cracks. Microbes and tiny creatures thrive on the minerals, and they become food for bigger crabs, blind fish and tubeworms larger than your arm. It is a warm, food-rich 'island' on the vast, cold, muddy ocean floor.

tubeworms

Deer

Male deer spend most of the year growing their impressive antlers on the head. When these fall off, a new set starts to grow. Deer are hoofed, plant-eating mammals with keen senses. Most of the 45 different kinds live wild in woods and forests. Some deer are kept in parks or as herds for meat, milk or skins and become quite tame. Others are hunted in the wild.

Wow!

The reindeer, or caribou, is the only kind of deer where the female has antlers, as well as the male.

Chinese water deer

moose or elk

red deer

◀ Big deer

The biggest deer is called a moose in North America and an elk in Europe. A large male stands 2 metres at the shoulder and has antlers 2 metres across. Another large deer is called a red deer in Europe and a wapiti in North America and East Asia.

▲ Small deer

The smallest deer include muntjac, Chinese water deer (where neither sex has antlers) and chevrotains or mouse deer. Some are hardly bigger than rabbits. They lead secretive lives in thick forests, either alone or in small groups.

Word scramble

Unscramble these words to find the names of five types of deer:

a. WOLLAF
b. ERO
c. KISA
d. MABRAS
e. KEL

answers
a. fallow b. roe
c. sika d. sambar e. elk

▼ Deer herd

Most deer live in herds (groups) made up of hinds (females) with fawns (young) and separate stags or bucks (males). These white-tailed bucks are from North America. At breeding time the males bellow, stamp and clash antlers (rutting). The winner takes over the female herd for a time, to breed.

Deserts

Deserts are dry places where very little rain falls each year. Sometimes heavy rains in one year are followed by no rain at all for the next few years. Life for desert people can be very difficult. Many, such as the San people of Africa's Kalahari desert, are nomads. They move from place to place in search of water.

Wow!

The Atacama Desert in Chile, South America had no rain for 400 years. The rains finally arrived in 1971.

▶ Desert water

Oases lie near sources of water, such as springs or underground streams. Plants can grow here, so people often settle in these areas.

▲ Clever plants

Most deserts are near the Equator, the imaginary line that runs around the centre of the Earth. These deserts are hot and dry and few plants can survive. One type of desert plant, the cactus, stores water in its thick, fleshy stems.

▲ Polar deserts

Deserts are not always hot. The icy lands around the North and South Poles are known as cold deserts.

▶ Keeping cool

Animals in hot deserts try to avoid the extreme daytime heat by hiding beside rocks or underground. They come out in the cool night-time air to look for food.

Key

1 kangaroo rat
2 rattlesnake
3 tarantula
4 ringtail
5 chuckwalla
6 fennec fox
7 long-nosed bat
8 mule deer

Deserts: animals

Find out more:
Birds • Cats • Frogs and toads

The world's deserts are dry, harsh places, but only about one-fifth are scorching sand. Most are stony or rocky, and some are freezing cold, especially at night. Yet animals survive here – especially scorpions, beetles and other insects, reptiles like lizards and snakes, and birds that can fly far to find water and food.

▲ Thorny devil

The moloch, or thorny devil, lives in Australia's 'Red Centre'. It walks slowly and unafraid, protected by its totally prickly body, and licks up ants and termites. At night, it dips its head low, and dew collects on its body and trickles into its mouth.

▼ Caracal

The caracal or desert lynx survives in the world's biggest desert, the Sahara of Africa. It hunts ground animals such as wild pigs and can spring 3 metres into the air to grab low-flying birds.

▼ Eat anything

The tall, flightless emu is Australia's 'eat-anything' bird. It pecks up leaves, thorny plants, dry grass, seeds, roots, grubs and small animals. Emus live in groups, deep in the dry outback. Sometimes they raid farm fields and have to be culled.

▲ Tough toad

Most amphibians need water, but a few are adapted to dryness. Spadefoot toads live in many deserts. They have thick skin and a wedgelike part on the foot, for digging. By day they hide in the soil, where it is cooler and damp. When the rare rains arrive, they breed quickly in puddles.

Word box

cull
controlling the number of animals by killing them for a very good reason, such as preserving their own habitat

Dinosaur ages

Find out more:
Dinosaurs • Reptiles: habitat

Dinosaurs lived between 230 million and 65 million years ago. This vast length of time is called the Mesozoic Era. Dinosaurs were around for about 80 times longer than people have been on Earth!

▼ Timeline

This timeline shows some of the animals and dinosaurs that lived between 286 million and 2 million years ago.

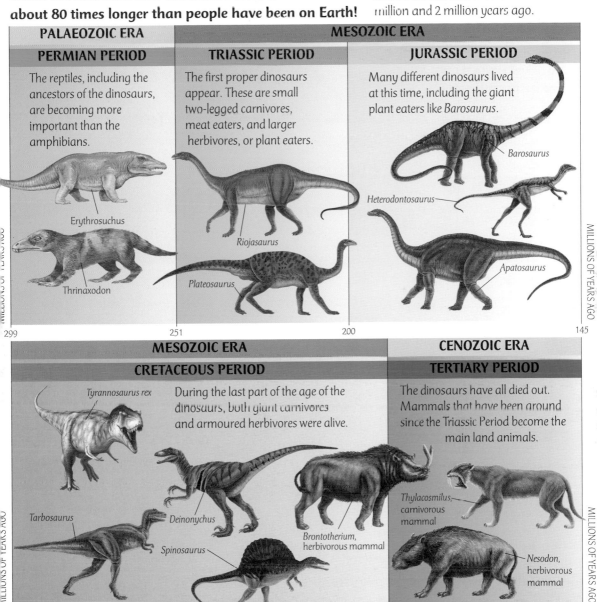

PALAEOZOIC ERA	MESOZOIC ERA	
PERMIAN PERIOD	TRIASSIC PERIOD	JURASSIC PERIOD

The reptiles, including the ancestors of the dinosaurs, are becoming more important than the amphibians.

Erythrosuchus

Thrinaxodon

The first proper dinosaurs appear. These are small two-legged carnivores, meat eaters, and larger herbivores, or plant eaters.

Riojasaurus

Plateosaurus

Many different dinosaurs lived at this time, including the giant plant eaters like *Barosaurus*.

Barosaurus

Heterodontosaurus

Apatosaurus

MILLIONS OF YEARS AGO

299   251   200   145

MESOZOIC ERA	CENOZOIC ERA
CRETACEOUS PERIOD	TERTIARY PERIOD

Tyrannosaurus rex

During the last part of the age of the dinosaurs, both giant carnivores and armoured herbivores were alive.

Tarbosaurus

Deinonychus

Spinosaurus

Brontotherium, herbivorous mammal

The dinosaurs have all died out. Mammals that have been around since the Triassic Period become the main land animals.

Thylacosmilus, carnivorous mammal

Nesodon, herbivorous mammal

MILLIONS OF YEARS AGO

145   65   2

a b c **d** e f g h i j k l m n o p q r s t u v w x y z   **85**

Dinosaurs

Dinosaurs were reptiles that roamed the Earth millions of years ago. The giant ones were the largest creatures ever to have lived on land. One of the smallest dinosaurs, *Compsognathus*, was the same size as a chicken. Some dinosaurs were fierce meat eaters and some only ate plants.

Compsognathus

Wow!

Argentinosaurus, one of the heaviest dinosaurs, weighed up to 100 tonnes – that's 20 times heavier than a fully grown African elephant.

▶ Fierce hunters

Tyrannosaurus rex was one of the fiercest, largest meat-eating dinosaurs. It was 12 metres long and hunted large, plant-eating dinosaurs.

▲ Flying reptiles

Pterosaurs were large prehistoric flying reptiles, not dinosaurs. They had enormous wing spans of up to 12 metres, and were very good fliers. Their wings were made of skin and their bodies were usually furry.

▼ Finding fossils

Much of what we know about dinosaurs comes from fossils, the hard remains of animals and plants found in rocks. People began to study dinosaurs after an English doctor and his wife found a huge tooth in a pile of road gravel in 1822. He realized that the tooth probably came from a giant reptile that looked like an iguana.

Word box

iguana
a kind of lizard

prehistoric
a very long time ago

▲ Dinosaur defences

Stegosaurus was a plant-eating dinosaur that walked on all four legs. A row of bony plates along its back may have protected it from attack. These plates probably helped to cool the dinosaur's body too.

Disasters

Find out more:
Diseases • Medicine • Volcanoes

In the past, natural disasters and illnesses were often believed to be punishments sent from God. People suffered, as we do today, from floods, fires, volcanoes and earthquakes, but in those days they had no fire engines or rescue teams. There was little understanding of disease and little effective medicine.

▲ The plague

Between 1347 and 1351, a terrible illness called the Black Death raged across Asia and Europe. It was passed on to humans by rat fleas and killed about 75 million people. This deadly disease, or plague, returned again and again. It killed tens of thousands of people in London in 1665.

▲ Great Fire of London

When houses were mostly built of wood, there was a great risk from fire. In 1666, a fire at a London bakery spread across the city, destroying over 13,000 homes.

Wow!

In AD472, so much ash erupted out of the volcano Mount Vesuvius that some of it was carried as far away as Turkey!

▶ Volcano disaster!

Almost 2,000 years ago, the entire Roman town of Pompeii was buried under hot ashes when the volcano Mount Vesuvius erupted in AD79. Since then, it has erupted several more times, with great force.

Discoveries

Scientific discoveries help us to understand how the world works and to invent new technologies and materials that make our lives easier. They also enable us to understand how our own bodies work and develop ways of combating illness and diseases.

◀ Eureka!

A scientist called Archimedes lived in Greece over 2,000 years ago. He made some important discoveries in physics and mathematics. He made one discovery while in the bath. Archimedes is said to have jumped out of the bath and run into the street without any clothes, shouting the word 'Eureka!', which means 'I have found it!'.

◀ Important ideas

Isaac Newton was an English scientist who lived in the 1600s and early 1700s. He made many important discoveries about light, colour and gravity. Newton realized that gravity keeps the Moon travelling on its path around the Earth.

Wow!

A popular story claims that Isaac Newton made his discovery about a force called gravity when in the 1600s, he saw an apple fall to the ground in an orchard.

▼ Fighting disease

In 1867, English doctor Joseph Lister helped make surgery safer with the introduction of carbolic acid spray. He realised that many deaths in hospital were caused by infection, and came up with a solution that could be used to kill germs. The use of his spray meant that deaths among hospital patients plummeted from 45 percent to 15 percent.

▼ Dangerous work

Marie Curie and her husband Pierre were scientists who worked in France in the late 1800s and early 1900s. Marie Curie was a clever and hard-working physicist who discovered a dangerous but useful chemical substance called radium.

Find out more:
Jobs • Sciences • Scientists • X-rays

▲ Hospitals

Some diseases require a visit to the hospital so the doctors and nurses can carry out tests, give a course of treatment, provide specialist care or perform an operation.

A disease is a sickness of the body or mind.
There are thousands of types of disease, ranging in seriousness from the common cold, which is usually quite harmless, to heart disease and cancers, which can be very serious. Diseases have many different causes, including harmful germs and bad living conditions, and some conditions are passed from parent to child. Scientists are working hard to find ways of preventing and curing diseases and are developing new drugs and treatments all the time.

aloe vera

garlic

▲ Healing plants

Herbs and other medicinal plants have been used for centuries to treat diseases. Eating garlic is good for general health and can help to keep your blood healthy. Aloe vera is used to treat skin conditions.

▼ Black Death

In the 1300s a terrible illness called the Black Death swept from one country to the next. It killed almost one-third of all the people in Europe. The disease was spread by fleas from black rats.

▼ Ancient medicine

Doctors have been treating sick people for thousands of years. In ancient Egypt, for example, doctors knew how to treat stomach illnesses and eye infections. This doctor is treating a patient who is suffering with a skin complaint.

mosquito

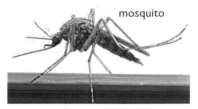

▲ Stopping disease

Mosquitoes can spread a dangerous tropical disease called malaria, by biting human beings. Taking tablets can prevent the disease from developing. Other diseases can be prevented by giving special injections which are called vaccinations.

Word box

malaria
a disease that causes bouts of fever and is caused by a parasite which is carried by mosquitoes

Dolphins

Find out more:
Oceans: life • Zoo

Dolphins seem to have great fun as they swim, leap and play among the waves. But each year millions get caught in fishing nets and drown. There are 32 types. These include pilot whales and six river dolphins, which live in fresh water. The six types of porpoises have much blunter snouts. They all have teeth and hunt fish or squid. Most live in schools or pods (groups), and communicate with squeals and clicks.

Wow!

Hector's dolphin is sometimes called the Mickey Mouse dolphin, because its dorsal (back) fin is shaped like this famous cartoon character's ears!

◀ The largest dolphin

The largest dolphin is one of the world's biggest predators – the killer whale, or orca. A big male is almost 10 metres long and 10 tonnes in weight. Some pods of orcas hunt mainly fish in one area, while others wander and prefer seals.

▲ Blunt-beaked dolphin

Risso's dolphin is one of the larger types, measuring about 4 metres in length. Like most dolphins it has smooth, sleek skin, two flippers, a dorsal fin and curved tail flukes. It also has an unusually short beak.

▶ Baby dolphins

Dolphins are mammals and breathe air through the blowhole on the top of their head. A baby dolphin is born underwater and nudged to the surface by its mother, for breaths of air. A calf, like this spinner dolphin, swims close to its mother.

Drawing and painting

Thousands of years before the very first civilizations developed in Mesopotamia, Egypt and China, artists had begun to decorate the world in which they lived. Artists draw and paint for many reasons, but one is to make our surroundings look more interesting and beautiful.

◀ Cave painting

In 1940, four French boys were searching for treasure in a cave near the Dordogne River in France when they discovered some amazing cave paintings. Made over 15,000 years ago, the paintings show bison and deer.

▼ Simple beauty

Japanese art of the 1500s and 1600s was simple and patterned. Artists painted bold, flat shapes, using bright colours and gold leaf (a thin sheet of metal). This picture shows part of a painting used to decorate a paper screen.

▼ Splish! Splash! Splosh! Splat!

Jackson Pollock lived in the USA. In the 1950s he used to make paintings with swirling colours by hurling, splattering and dribbling paint across the canvas.

▲ Light and colour

Claude Monet was a French painter who lived from 1840 to 1926. He chose to paint realistic impressions of light and colour. He was called an Impressionist.

◀ Leonardo da Vinci

Although celebrated as a painter, Italian artist Leonardo da Vinci (1452–1519) only completed about 25 paintings. He made drawings in much greater numbers than any artist before him.

Ducks and swans

Find out more:
Birds • Freshwater animals

In almost any river or lake, you will find colourful, quacking, flapping, paddling waterfowl – ducks, geese and swans. There are 150 different kinds, all strong fliers with webbed feet. They peck, dabble or up-end with their wide beaks, feeding on water plants, grass, seeds, and sometimes small animals such as pond snails, worms and grubs.

Word box

dabble
when waterfowl feed by opening and closing the beak quickly at the water's surface

up-end
when waterfowl feed by poking the head and neck under the water, with the tail sticking up

▼ Canada geese

People have taken these geese from their North American home, across Europe and even to New Zealand. Like many geese, in some regions they journey or migrate northwards to breed in summer. They then return south to warmer regions in winter.

▲ Black swan

Waterfowl, also known as wildfowl, can be quite tame. The black swan, originally from Australia, has been taken to many new regions to brighten up lakes and parks. Its wings are more than 2 metres across and it has a very long neck – even for a swan!

▼ Mute swan

Most waterfowl build large, untidy nests along river and lake banks. The mute swan hen (female) gives her babies piggyback rides from the nest, as they quickly learn to swim and feed. The cob (male) stays nearby to guard them.

◄ Shelduck

Shelducks like shallow, salty water along seashores, coastal lagoons and salt pans. They search in the mud for shellfish and worms. The most common duck is the mallard. Others include eiders, scoters, teals, wigeons, pintails, shovelers, scaups and smews.

92 a b c **d** e f g h i j k l m n o p q r s t u v w x y z

Eagles and hawks

Eagles, hawks and falcons are the great predators of the skies.
There are more than 300 kinds of birds of prey, or raptors, from huge American condors with 3-metre wings to tiny falconets and kestrels hardly bigger than blackbirds.

Wow!
The peregrine falcon moves faster than any other animal when it power-dives or 'stoops' onto prey at 220 kilometres an hour.

▲ International hunter

The osprey or fish-eagle is the most widespread raptor, found on all lands except the far north and Antarctica. Like most raptors, it hunts by day using its incredible eyesight, soaring and gliding until it spots a fish just under the surface.

▶ Feet for fishing

All birds of prey have sharp, hooked beaks and sharp, curved talons (claws). The osprey's talons are especially sharp, and its toes are spiny underneath, to grip slippery fish as it hurls itself feet-first into the water.

osprey talon

▼ Gyrfalcon

The largest falcon is the gyrfalcon, which hunts over Arctic ice and snow. It swoops low and catches mainly birds, such as ptarmigan and willow grouse, plus occasional lemmings and voles. As with many raptors, the male and female make amazing courtship flights as they dive, climb, roll and loop in the air.

◀ Golden eagle

The female and male golden eagle build a big, untidy nest of twigs, high on a tree, cliff or crag. They may have several nests, called eyries, using one each year and adding more twigs each time.

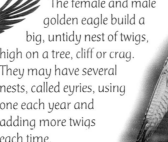

Early kings and queens

Find out more:
Kings • Queens

Kings and queens have ruled over people and kingdoms for hundreds of years. Sometimes, they claimed to rule by the will of God. When they died, their children often became king or queen and ruled the country after them.

Word box

legend
a traditional story often linked to a place or historical character

◀ Poisoned queen

Cleopatra was the last queen of independant Egypt, in North Africa. According to legend when the country was invaded by the Romans, she killed herself by allowing a poisonous snake to bite her arm.

▲ King Offa

Offa ordered that a wall be built between his kingdom and Wales, to guard the border. He ruled Mercia, in the English Midlands from AD757 to 796. He is remembered for minting the first silver penny coins and for Offa's wall, much of which still stands today.

Wow!

Louis XIV's palace at Versailles, outside Paris, is almost half a kilometre long and has around 1,300 rooms.

▶ Warrior queen

Around AD60 a queen called Boudicca ruled the Iceni tribe in Britain. She led her army against the Romans. Boudicca and her soldiers destroyed Roman towns and killed many soldiers. She poisoned herself to avoid being captured.

Earth

South America

The Earth is a huge, rocky ball spinning around in space. It is around 4.6 billion years old. Its surface is covered with large areas of land surrounded by sea. The layers of air around the Earth make up its atmosphere. In the atmosphere are the gases that all living things need to stay alive.

▲ Earth from space

This view was taken from a spacecraft high up above the Earth's surface. You can clearly see the shape of the continent of South America, surrounded by dark-blue water. The wispy white areas are patches of swirling clouds.

▼ Moving Earth

About 220 million years ago, all the continents were joined as one super continent, called Pangea. Very slowly, this continent began to break up.

Pangea

200 million years ago, Pangea had split into two huge continents called Laurasia and Gondwanaland

even today the continents are still moving – North America is moving very slowly away from Europe

◄ Hot rocks and metals

The outer layer of the Earth is called the crust. It is between 30 and 50 kilometres thick below the land but only 5 to 10 kilometres thick below the oceans and seas. The very centre of the Earth lies about 6,400 kilometres below the surface – that's about the same distance as crossing North America from one side of the continent to the other.

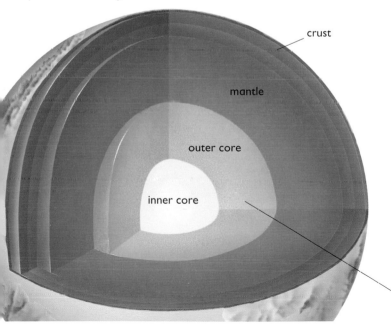

crust

mantle

outer core

inner core

in places the temperature is so hot that the rocks and metals have melted and become liquid

Earth features

There are many wonderful sights on the surface of our amazing planet. They include thundering waterfalls, steep cliffs by the seashore and huge caves deep underground. Some of these features took millions of years to form.

▼ Natural disaster

An earthquake is a natural disaster. It can cause serious damage in just a few seconds. It is the violent shaking of the rocks inside the Earth.

▼ On the surface

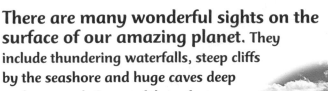

Lots of different features cover the Earth's surface, such as snowy mountains, deep valleys, rocky deserts and enormous ice sheets.

sliding plates

huge cracks can appear in the Earth's surface and can cause damage to buildings and roads.

centre of earthquake

continental shelf

material left by river currents

▼ Deep down

Far below the surface of the oceans lies another landscape – on the floor of the ocean. Here there are mountains, wide plains and slopes and deep sea trenches.

continental slope

ocean ridge

deep sea trench

Egg-laying mammals

Find out more:
Eggs • Mammals and their babies

Most mammal females give birth to babies.
But there are five kinds of mammals that are egg-layers
– these are called monotremes. One of these is the
duck-billed platypus from eastern Australia. The other
four are echidnas (spiny anteaters) from Australia
and New Guinea. Echidnas have sharp spines as
well as fur. They have huge claws to dig for
ants, termites, grubs and worms, which they
lick up with their spiny tongues.

egg in pouch

▼ How the platypus lives

The platypus lives along rivers and
billabongs. At night it noses in the
mud for worms, shellfish and other
small animals. The male has a
spur on his rear ankle, which he
uses to jab poison
into enemies.

Wow!

The young platypus has a long
journey as it leaves its nursery
burrow to see daylight for the first
time – the burrow may be more
than 30 metres long.

▲ Echidna and egg

The short-beaked echidna rests
in her burrow, holding her egg
warm and safe in a slitlike pouch.
This develops on her belly only at
breeding time. The egg grows in
her body for 23 days, then develops
in her pouch for 10 days. After
hatching, the baby stays in the
pouch for another seven weeks, then
in a nest burrow for six months.

Word box

billabong
Australian native word meaning
'dead water', used for a natural
pool or small lake

spur
sharp claw or clawlike part on
the foot or ankle of some animals,
especially birds

Eggs

Most female animals lay tough-shelled eggs.
This includes all birds, nearly all reptiles, fish, insects,
spiders and other creatures. Each egg contains a tiny
young animal, called an embryo, which grows and
develops into a baby. When
ready, it bites or tears its
way out of the shell –
and then often faces
the world alone.

ostrich egg

bee hummingbird egg

shell membrane (lining)

embryo

yolk

shell

fluid

tiny pores (holes)

▲ Inside an egg

A typical egg has a tough outer case or shell for protection. Inside is a store of yolk to nourish the tiny developing animal, or embryo, which floats in a pool of fluid for protection. Oxygen, the substance that all animals need to breathe, passes to the embryo through tiny pores in the shell.

▲ Size and number

The ostrich lays the largest eggs – 16 centimetres long and over 3,000 times heavier than the tiny egg of the bee hummingbird. The kiwi lays a single egg, one-quarter the size of its body. The ling fish lays more than 20 million tiny eggs.

Wow!

Small creatures called fairy shrimps have hatched out of eggs that were wetted again, after being dried and preserved for more than 2,000 years.

▼ Slimy eggs

Bird eggs have hard, rigid shells. Most other eggs have slightly flexible, leathery shells. Frog and toad eggs, called spawn, are covered with slimy jelly. Frog spawn is clumped, while toad spawn is in long strings or 'necklaces'.

frog spawn   toad spawn

▼ Hidden eggs

Many reptiles, such as this African dwarf crocodile, dig a hole and then cover the eggs with old plants. The hole is often close to water. As the plants rot they create heat. This incubates the eggs (keeps them warm) and helps them develop.

Egypt

Egypt became a powerful kingdom about 5,000 years ago. Its rulers were called pharaohs. The ancient Egyptians built great cities, pyramids, statues and temples. Some of them can still be seen today. The ancient Egyptians used a kind of picture-writing and made paper called papyrus from reeds.

▲ Marvellous mud

Floods from the river Nile left behind thick, black mud. This was the perfect soil for growing wheat, barley and vegetables. Egyptian farmers also raised cattle, sheep, pigs and geese.

▶ Water works

This machine is called a *shaduf*. The ancient Egyptians used it to lift water from the river Nile. They needed water for their crops, because there was hardly any rainfall. Egypt is a hot land with rocky deserts.

▼ Buried treasure

The Egyptians believed that dead people went on to another life. They filled their dead rulers' tombs with things they thought they might need in the next life like jewels and food. This gold mask was found in the tomb of Tutankhamun.

wall carvings of battle scenes

decorated columns

hypostyle hall where processions took place

▶ Pharaoh power

This pharaoh was called Rameses II (c. 1292–1225). He ruled Egypt over 3,000 years ago. People believed that the pharaohs were gods living on Earth.

▲ Praise to Amun-Ra!

The temple of Karnak is massive. Its priests worshipped a god called Amun-Ra around 4,000 years ago. Each New Year they held a big festival there. They killed oxen and offered them to the god.

Egyptian life

Find out more:
Egypt • Egyptian tombs

Ancient Egypytian society was highly developed and many aspects of Egyptian daily life are familiar to us today. Most people lived in houses made of sun-dried mud and cooked bread in clay ovens. The wealthy sent their children to school, but most Egyptian children worked with their parents in the fields or learned a trade or craft from their father.

◀ Fashion and beauty

Ancient Egyptian men wore a simple tunic or kilt, while women wore long dresses of white linen. Wealthy people wore wigs made from human hair or sheep's wool. Wigs needed a lot of attention and Egyptians cared for their wigs with combs made of wood and ivory.

▲ The river Nile

Without the water of the Nile, the civilization of Ancient Egypt might never have existed. Travel by boat on the Nile was the most common way of getting around in ancient Egypt. The first boats were made of reeds from the papyrus plants that grew along the riverbank.

▼ Picture writing

The Egyptians used a kind of picture writing called hieroglyphics. Each picture stood for a different word or sound. The pictures were painted onto walls.

Word box

falcon
a fierce hunting bird

fertile
produces good crops

tomb
a special place where somebody is buried

◀ Dressing up

In Egypt, men and women both wore make-up. Of particular importance to them was kohl, a special black eye make-up, which was made from ground-up raw metals mixed with oil. The Egyptians believed it had magical healing powers, and even thought it could restore bad eyesight and fight eye infections. Egyptians also used rouge for the cheeks and lips, face powder, paint for fingernails and hair dyes. Many of the more wealthy Egyptians also wore elaborate jewellery called amulets which were thought to protect the wearer from evil spirits.

Egyptian tombs

Find out more:
Egypt • Egyptian life

Magic spells and curses were used to protect ancient Egyptian tombs. At first, the pharaohs were buried inside huge stone tombs called pyramids, which pointed up to the sky. Later, they were buried secretly in rock tombs, hidden in the Valley of the Kings, near the ancient city of Thebes.

▲ The pyramids

The Egyptians built spectacular tombs for their dead rulers, who were called pharaohs. The biggest tombs were the three huge pyramids at Giza. The Great Pyramid, which contains more than two million blocks of stone, took over 20 years to build.

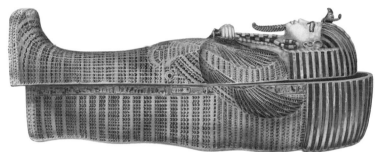

Isis
Osiris
Horus

Wow!
The Egyptians made mummies of animals, including cats, birds and crocodiles.

▲ King Tut's tomb

A young pharaoh called Tutankhamun died in 1327BC. He was buried in three separate coffins that fitted inside each other. This is the middle coffin, which is made of gold and decorated with precious gems.

▲ Gods and death

The ancient Egyptians worshipped thousands of different gods and goddesses. Three of the most important ones were Osiris, the god of death and his wife Isis, maker of the first mummy. Horus was their son, and protector of the pharaoh.

▶ Making mummies

Egyptians made mummies, because they thought that the dead needed their bodies in a new life after death. Trained people removed the internal organs first. Then they dried out the body, rubbed it with oils and wrapped it in bandages. The body was placed inside a wooden coffin.

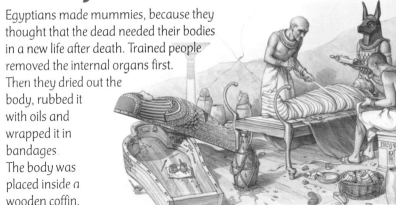

Electricity

Electricity is one of our most useful kinds of energy. It lights up our streets and homes and powers our computers, televisions and washing machines. Even some trains are powered by electricity. Most of our electricity comes along cables from power stations to our homes.

◄ Giant spark

The lightning you see in a stormy sky is really an enormous spark of electricity. The heat from lightning is so powerful that it can set trees and houses alight.

metal strip
switch
bulb
coil
battery
plastic casing

Word box

attract
to pull towards

cable
a thick wire that carries electricity

a battery contains chemicals that make electricity when the switch is turned on

a switch turns electricity off and on by breaking the circuit and joining it again

▼ Battery power

Machines such as torches and hand-held computer games are powered by batteries. Inside a battery are chemicals, which react with each other to produce electricity. Cars use huge batteries to start up their engine.

bulb glows when electricity passes through it

▲ On and off

When you switch on a torch, electricity flows from the battery to the bulb and lights it up. The electricity flows along a path called a circuit. When you switch the torch off, you break the circuit. The flow of electricity stops and the torch goes out.

▲ Plus to minus

In an electric circuit, current flows from the positive (+) pole of a battery to the negative (-). If the current flows through a light bulb, the 'resistance' of the thin metal filament (thread) inside the bulb produces light.

What is static electricity?

Comb your hair quickly for about 15 seconds on a dry day. Now hold the comb close to your head — your hair will stand on end. Comb your hair quickly again and hold the comb over some small pieces of paper. What happens? The combing action fills your comb with static electricity. Your hair, and the pieces of paper, are attracted by this static electricity.

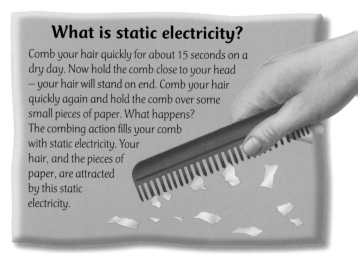

Electricity: creation

Many machines are powered by electricity, because it is clean and cheap. Electricity is produced in power stations, sometimes by burning coal, oil or gas, and sometimes by nuclear power or by the use of water to turn huge turbines. It is sent along a network of cables supported by metal towers called pylons.

▲ Water power

A hydroelectric power station uses the energy in water from a fast-flowing river or a dam to produce electricity. Flowing water is a source of energy that will never run out. We call it a renewable source – one that can be used again and again.

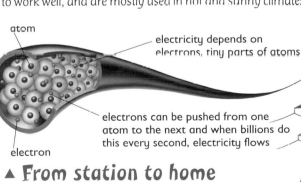

▲ Solar panels

The light or heat energy from the Sun can be turned directly into electricity by devices called solar panels. A panel does not produce much power, so many are usually joined into banks of panels. They need strong sunlight to work well, and are mostly used in hot and sunny climates.

atom

electricity depends on electrons, tiny parts of atoms

electrons can be pushed from one atom to the next and when billions do this every second, electricity flows

electron

power station

transformer

cables carry electricity

pylon holds cables safe, far above the ground

the battery or generator at a power station gives the 'push' that starts the electrons on their journey

▲ From station to home

From the generator, electricity passes to 'step up transformers', which produce high voltages (how the strength of electricity is measured). This electricity is then put through 'step down transformers' and carried by cables into homes and factories.

Find out more:
Electricity • Energy • Machines

Electricity is constantly at work around you.
You switch lights on and off or watch the television. Cars need electricity to start their engines, and most trains are powered by electricity. Electricity is also produced by natural things, such as lightning, and is even present inside our own bodies.

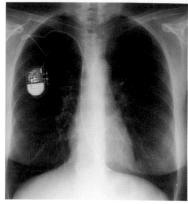

◄ Hair-raiser

Static electricity is the same as flowing electricity except that it does not move. It can make a push or pull effect like a magnet – which can be very hair-raising!

► Charge!

A mobile phone's battery is rechargeable. This means that when the battery runs down, the chemicals inside can be recharged by sending electricity through them.

▲ Beating heart

In some heart problems, the impulses of electricity that control the heart's beating are not produced properly. So an artificial pacemaker may be put under the skin to generate electrical signals for the heart.

▼ Electric fun

Electricity can be used for decoration and for fun. Fairgrounds rely on plenty of coloured lights and rides powered by electricity.

Make a circuit

You will need: a lightbulb, some wire, a 3-volt battery, a plastic ruler, a metal spoon, some dry card

Ask an adult to help. Join the lightbulb to the battery with pieces of wire, as shown below. Electricity flows round the circuit and lights the bulb. Make a gap in the circuit and put various objects there instead, such as the ruler. See if they allow electricity to flow again.

Elephants

No other animal looks like the elephant, with its long trunk, large tusks and huge ears.
Asian elephants and African forest elephants live mainly in woods, while African savanna elephants live on grasslands. All are under threat, shot for their ivory tusks or because they destroy farm crops. Some Asian elephants are tame and carry logs for people or let them ride on their backs.

▶ Asian elephant

This elephant is slightly smaller than the African types and has smaller ears. An elephant's trunk is its nose and top lip joined together. It uses it to grasp food, suck up water to squirt in its mouth, sniff the air and stroke babies and friends in the herd.

▲ African elephant

Most African savanna elephants have tusks. Tusks are huge incisor teeth, made of ivory. They are used to dig for food, push down trees for their leaves, fruits and bark, for defence against enemies and to fight rival males at breeding time.

rock hyraxes

◀ Small cousins

The closest relations to elephants are the hyraxes of Africa and the Middle East. Rock hyraxes are found in dry, rocky places. Tree hyraxes are found in branches. They all live in groups and eat plants.

Word scramble

Unscramble these words to find the names of five types of elephant food:

a. SAGRS
b. KARB
c. SEVLEA
d. STURIF
e. STORO

answers
a. grass b. bark
c. leaves d. fruits e. roots

▼ Living in herds

A herd contains mothers and calves (young). 'Aunts' without young help with calf-care. An older female, the matriarch, leads the herd to traditional feeding places and waterholes.

Empires and colonies

Find out more:
Britain and Ireland

In the 1500s and 1600s, the Europeans explored new lands in Africa, Asia and the Americas. They wanted to take away the riches of these countries and rule the people who lived there. From the 1500s onwards Britain, France, Germany, the Netherlands, Belgium, Portugal and Spain controlled vast empires.

▲ Queen and Empress

During the reign of Queen Victoria, from 1837 to 1901, Britain conquered the world's largest ever empire. Over time it included Canada, India, Africa and Australia.

▼ Cruelty in the Caribbean

Spain, Britain and France ruled the Caribbean islands. They grew sugar cane there, using slaves from Africa. The slaves were treated with great cruelty. Slavery continued in the Caribbean until the 1830s.

▲ Bolívar of Bolivia

Spain ruled much of South America. By the 1800s, many colonists (settlers) wanted to break away from the old country. In 1811, a soldier called Simón Bolívar began to fight for the freedom of Venezuela, Colombia, Ecuador, Peru and Bolivia.

▶ Freedom for India

By the 1900s, nations were demanding their freedom. Sometimes they went to war against their colonial rulers. The great Indian leader, Mohandas K. Gandhi, believed in peaceful protests. The British left India in 1947.

Find out more:
Conserving wildlife • Pollution

Hundreds of mammals, birds, reptiles and other animals are under threat. They are killed for their meat, fur, feathers or skins, or killed as 'sport' trophies. They are also accidentally harmed by pollution, or caught in nets and traps. But the single greatest threat they face is habitat destruction.

▼ Tourist trouble

Dolphins, and sea turtles such as leatherbacks, get trapped in fishing nets and drown. Turtles are also threatened by tourism. Quiet beaches, where they lay eggs under cover of darkness, are invaded by hotels, bright lights and noisy nightlife.

leatherback turtle

Word box

conservation
protection of the natural world

habitat destruction
ruining the natural places where animals live by using them for farming, houses, roads, industry and other purposes

Conservation – how we can help

- Support organizations that help wildlife
- Join campaigns to save natural regions and wild places
- Help research and captive breeding projects – for example, 'adopt an animal'
- Buy products that are environmentally friendly
- Waste less and recycle more
- Encourage people to care for wildlife

▲ Ancient fish

The coelacanth became famous in 1938, when a specimen was caught off east Africa. Until then scientists had thought it had died out 70 million years ago. The coelacanth is still considered critically endangered.

▶ Giant panda

The giant panda is a famous symbol of conservation, and its numbers are slowly increasing after a great conservation effort. Like other large animals, pandas breed slowly, having only one or two young, several years apart.

The engine inside a motor car needs energy to work. It gets this energy by burning a fuel such as petrol or diesel. Something that has energy is able to do work. Your body also needs energy – to run, skip, think and even to sleep. Your energy comes from the food you eat – it's your body's fuel.

▼ Heat and light

Energy from the Sun reaches the Earth as heat and light. Some of that energy is stored inside fuels such as coal, oil and gas.

oil

coal   gas

Word box

active
busy, full of energy

coiled
wound up into rings or spirals

▶ How much energy?

A young, active person whose body is still growing needs lots of energy. So does an athlete, or a builder doing heavy work. Older people and office workers need less energy because they are not so active.

▼ Stored energy

What has a coiled spring to do with energy? The answer is that energy is stored inside the coiled spring, ready to do work. Some watches have a spring inside. When you wind up the watch you are storing energy inside the spring. As the spring unwinds, it turns the hands of the watch.

the spring is wound and energy is slowly released

the spring is hidden beneath this wheel

bread and cereals

fish and meat

cheese, butter and oil

▶ Energy foods

All the energy we get from food starts out as green plants. Humans eat plants (vegetables and fruit) and animals (meat and fish). The animals we eat have received their energy from eating green plants. Here are some of the foods we get our energy from.

fruit, vegetables and dairy products

Wow!

A 100-gram serving of peanut butter contains 2,600 times more energy than 100 grams of lettuce.

Most of the energy in our world comes from the Sun. Without it, the plants that provide us with food could not grow. Fuels such as coal and oil are made from the remains of plants and animals that lived long ago. These living things used the Sun's energy to grow.

▲ Harmful air

When we burn oil it produces harmful waste gases and dirt that enter the air. The air in many cities is filled with these waste gases from motor cars and factories.

▼ Nuclear energy

Some of our electricity comes from nuclear power stations. Instead of using the heat from burning oil or coal, a nuclear power station uses the heat energy released when atoms of nuclear fuel are split. The splitting process is carefully controlled in order to be safe.

▲ Sun energy

Did you know you can get energy from sunshine? The solar panels shown above turn light from the Sun into electricity. The electricity is used to provide power for remote telephones and parking meters.

▼ Important fuel

Oil is one of the world's most important fuels. We take oil from deep under the sea or the ground, where it lies trapped between layers of rock. Oil drilling machinery is kept on special platforms out at sea, like the one shown here.

Word box

atom
a very tiny part of something

dam
a barrier specially built to hold back water

▶ Wind power

The energy in wind has been used for hundreds of years to turn the sails of windmills. We now use this wind energy to produce electricity. A large group of wind turbines is called a wind farm.

Engines

The invention of engines allowed us to control and change the world around us. Engines let us travel. They let us transport very heavy materials around the world. Engines also power the machinery we need to mine coal and important minerals.

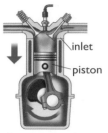

1. piston moves down to suck in fuel and air

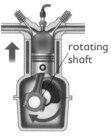

2. the piston moves up to squeeze the fuel and air

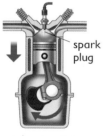

3. spark sets mixture alight pushing piston down

4. the piston moves up to push out waste gases

◄ How petrol engines work

Air and fuel is pushed into a cylinder. Tiny explosions caused by 'spark plugs' keep the piston moving up and down. This makes the shaft rotate, which connects to gears so that the wheels go round. Most cars have petrol engines.

Word box

cylinder
tube in which fuel is burned

diesel
an engine fuelled by diesel oil instead of petrol, that has no spark plugs

▶ Electric motors

Some of the fumes given out by petrol and diesel engines can harm the environment. For this reason, electric motors are now becoming more common in vehicles. They are powered by batteries and are cleaner, quieter and more reliable.

▲ The power of steam

Steam engines helped to develop our modern civilization. Early locomotives were steam-driven, powered by coal or wood. They have mostly been replaced by diesel or electric trains. However, steam trains are still used in some poorer countries.

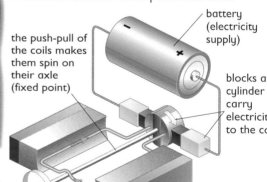

the push-pull of the coils makes them spin on their axle (fixed point)

battery (electricity supply)

blocks and cylinder carry electricity to the coils

current flows along coil of wire

a magnet pushes the electricity-carrying coils, which have their own magnetism

Europe

Europe is the smallest of the seven continents.
It is a land of pine forests, grassy plains, snow-topped mountains and hot, sunny coastlines. The northern part of Europe has cold winters and warm summers while the countries around the Mediterranean Sea have hot, dry summers and mild winters.

▲ The far north

The far north of Europe has many small islands and deep sea-filled valleys called fjords, like the one above. Places in the far north have long, cold winters where it stays dark for much of each day.

▲ Flat lands

Land beside the North Sea coast is extremely flat – some of it is even below sea level. Because of this, Belgium and the Netherlands are called the 'Low Countries'.

▼ Snowy mountains

The Alps stretch in a curve from southeast France across northern Italy, Switzerland and into Austria. In winter, thousands of tourists come to ski on the snowy slopes.

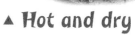

▲ Hot and dry

In the dry, sunny climate of southern Europe, groves of olive trees and orange and lemon trees are a common sight. Vineyards produce grapes for the wine industry. Tourists spend holidays along the Mediterranean coast.

▲ Busy river

The Danube river crosses central Europe, from its source in Germany to its mouth on the shores of the Black Sea. Ships and barges carry agricultural products, steel and chemicals on the busy waters.

European people

Find out more:
Europe • Greeks • Atlas: Europe

Europe is a continent of many different peoples, cultures and languages. It is also very crowded, particularly the towns and cities of countries such as the Netherlands and Belgium. Since the time of the ancient Greeks, Europeans have probably changed the world more than any other group of people. They have taken their languages, inventions, religions, ideas, art and music to almost every corner of the world.

Word box

boundary
a place where one country's land ends and the next country's land begins

◀ Historic cities

Europe has many historic cities, with magnificent sights. In the 1400s and 1500s the Italian city of Florence was a meeting place for painters, musicians and writers.

▲ East and west

At the end of World War II Germany was divided, but in 1990 East and West Germany were united again. Berlin became the capital of the new Germany. The city's Brandenburg Gate used to mark the boundary of the divided city.

▶ United countries

This is the flag of the European Union. Currently 27 countries belong to the European Union, an organization that involves countries working together closely on important matters such as money, jobs, industry and farming.

▶ Industry at work

Important industries in Europe include car manufacturing, food processing and chemicals and plastics. Many of the world's big car companies, for example Ford, have factories in several European countries.

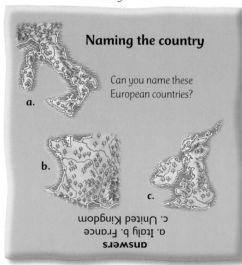

Naming the country

Can you name these European countries?

a.

b.

c.

answers
a. Italy b. France
c. United Kingdom

Christopher Columbus

In the past, explorers set off for distant lands to look for riches, other people to trade with and places to settle. Some of the earliest explorers were Greek traders who explored the lands around the Mediterranean Sea. With the invention of stronger ships and better maps, many European explorers set sail to discover new lands in the 1400s. It was in 1492 that Christopher Columbus first sailed to America.

▲ Marco Polo

A young Italian called Marco Polo explored China and parts of Asia during the 1200s. He was a popular visitor at the court of the Mongol emperor, Kublai Khan.

▼ Heading west

In 1804, Americans Meriwether Lewis and William Clark set off to explore the northwest United States. During their two-year expedition they travelled over 12,000 kilometres.

Lewis and Clark travelled with the help of a female Native American guide

▼ Around the world

Ferdinand Magellan led the first sea voyage around the world. He set sail in 1519 but was killed halfway through the journey. Only one of his five ships completed the journey.

▼ Deep sea diver

In 1960, two men inside the diving vehicle *Trieste* descended more than 10 kilometres into the Marianas Trench, the deepest part of the Pacific Ocean.

▲ Antarctic disaster

Captain Robert Scott's second expedition to reach the South Pole ended in tragedy. When his team finally reached the South Pole on January 18, 1912, they found that a Norwegian team had arrived there one month earlier. Scott and his men died from hunger and cold on the way home.

Wow!

In 2000, British explorer David Hempleman-Adams attempted to fly over the Arctic Ocean to the North Pole in a hot-air balloon. He flew to within a few kilometres of the North Pole.

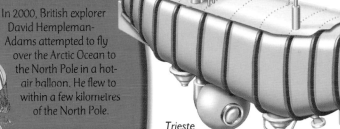

Trieste

Explorers at sea

In the days of sailing ships, sea voyages could last many years. Sailors had to find their way across the oceans, battle with storms and survive shipwrecks. When they did land on unknown shores, they risked being attacked by the local people.

▲ Leif the Lucky

The Vikings were great seafarers. Their ships, called longships, reached Iceland and Greenland. In 1000, a sailor called Leif 'the Lucky' Eriksson reached North America.

▲ A vast fleet

Between 1405 and 1433, the Chinese admiral Zheng He made seven voyages, exploring the Indian Ocean. On his first voyage there were 62 big boats called junks, 225 small boats and 27,000 men!

▶ Captain Cook

James Cook was an English sea captain who was a brilliant navigator. In the 1760s and 1770s, he explored the Pacific Ocean and the coasts of New Zealand and Australia.

▶ Great voyages

This map shows some of the great voyages of exploration. Look at the map key to find out which explorer sailed which route.

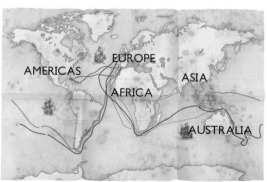

AMERICAS

EUROPE

ASIA

AFRICA

AUSTRALIA

Map key

Red: Christopher Columbus, 1492
Yellow: Vasco da Gama, 1497–98
Green: Magellan, 1519–22
Blue: James Cook, 1768–71

Explorers on land

Find out more:
Explorers • Explorers at sea

Today, every place on Earth has been mapped.
Only 200 years ago, some civilization's maps included
blank areas, showing lands which they had not yet
explored. Travel was slow and often dangerous, but
many brave men and women set out to
explore the world.

▼ Tireless traveller

Ibn Batuta came from Tangiers in North Africa. He travelled from 1325 to 1354, reaching the Middle East, India, China and Southeast Asia. He also journeyed south across the Sahara Desert to the city of Timbuktu

▼ Africa explored

From the 1850s, a Scottish explorer called David Livingstone made many journeys across Africa. By 1869 he was believed lost, so a British journalist, Henry Morton Stanley, set out to look for him. He found Livingstone in 1871.

Word scramble

Can you unscramble these words to find destinations for explorers?

a. ELOP THRON
b. EVIRR NOAMAZ
c. AHARAS DETRES
d. WEN AGUINE

answers
a. North Pole b. river Amazon
c. Sahara Desert d. New Guinea

▼ To the South Pole

Howling winds and bitter cold failed to stop explorer Roald Amundsen, a Norwegian, from crossing icy Antarctica to reach the South Pole in 1911.

Roald Amundsen

Alexander von Humboldt

◄ Jungle journeys

From 1799 to 1804, Alexander von Humboldt, from Germany, and Aimé Bonpland, from France, surveyed the steamy rainforests of South America. They came across electric eels and alligators and brought back 12,000 samples of plants.

Farm animals

Find out more:
Cattle • Horses and zebras • Pets

Animals are kept on farms for doing work and providing milk, skins, fur, feathers, scales and meat. Farm animals include chickens, cows, sheep, goats and pigs, and more unusual ones, such as llamas, camels, reindeer, rabbits, guinea-pigs, pigeons, ostriches, salmon, and even snakes and crocodiles!

▶ Chicken

The world has more chickens than people. There are at least 500 different breeds and they provide one-third of all our meat, plus trillions of eggs. But some are not kept for practical use. They are 'fancy fowl' with bright colours and extraordinary feathers, bred to win prizes at shows.

▼ Milk for all

People have kept farm animals, such as cows, by selective breeding from their wild ancestors to produce the things we need. The cow gives tasty meat, tough skin for leather, and plenty of milk — not only to feed her calf, but for us, all year round.

▼ The 'recycling' pig

About half the world's one billion pigs are in south and east Asia. They eat anything from roots and fruits to grubs, worms and scraps, and are farmed for their meat — pork, bacon and ham.

Word box

ancestor
a relative from long ago, like a great-great-grandparent

selective breeding
choosing animals with certain features (like long fur) to breed together, so the features are greater in their offspring (such as even longer fur)

◀ Special breeds

Goats were first herded almost 10,000 years ago. There are dozens of different breeds, each with special features. Angora goats have fleeces (woolly coats) of fine, white, silky fur. It is shorn (cut off) and woven into mohair cloth.

Long ago, people gathered wild plants and ate roots, leaves and seeds. They found that seeds they collected sprouted, so they planted some of the seeds each year, and were able to grow crops for food. They also learned to tame wild animals, such as goats and sheep. Farming began in the Middle East, about 10,000 years ago.

▲ The first farmers

By choosing only the best seed each year, farmers turned wild grasses into useful grain crops such as wheat or barley. They harvested them with tools made of stone, wood and bone.

steam-powered tractor, late 1800s

▲ Nice rice!

Farming started in different parts of the world at different times. Rice was grown in China 7,000 years ago. It was often sown in flooded fields like these ones. Rice became the most important crop in Asia.

▼ Sowing seed

In Europe during the Middle Ages, horses or oxen were used to cultivate (stir up) the soil and prepare it for sowing. Seed was scattered by hand.

▲ Soil-buster

Steam power began to be used to drive farm machinery in the 1800s. In the 1900s, the first petrol-driven tractors were made.

Word box

crops
plants that can be grown for food, such as rice or wheat, or for making cloth, such as cotton

tame
make a wild animal used to living and working with people

b c d e **f** g h i j k l m n o p q r s t u v w x y z

Farming today

Find out more:
Farm animals • Food through the ages

Farmers across the world grow crops and rear animals to provide food for people to eat.
In poorer countries, farmers usually work on small plots of land using simple tools and traditional methods. In countries such as the United States, farming is carried out on a large scale and huge machines do much of the work.

Wow!
A cotton-picking machine harvests the same amount of cotton as 80 people picking the cotton by hand.

◄ Plains of wheat

The Prairies are the wide, grassy plains of North America. They are one of the world's largest wheat-producing areas. Large herds of cattle are reared here, too.

▲ Sheep-rearing

Farming differs from place to place, depending on the soil, climate and the shape of the land. The mild, wet climate of New Zealand is well suited to rearing sheep, because there is plenty of good grazing land. More sheep than people live in New Zealand!

► Giant combine harvesters

In richer countries, giant machines called combine harvesters gather in the ripe crops at harvest time. In poorer countries the harvest is cut by hand.

Word box

millet
a plant crop producing tiny seeds that are crushed to make flour

plough
a bladed farm tool used to prepare ground for planting

◄ Ploughing land

This Asian farmer is ploughing land with a plough pulled by oxen. He will use this land to grow crops such as rice.

Film and television

Film and television are two of the most important forms of communication, or media. Films provide us with entertainment and are often based on an issue close to the director's heart. Television brings news, sport, cartoons, music and factual documentaries into our homes. In the world's wealthier countries almost every home has a television.

◀ Early TV

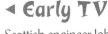

Scottish engineer John Logie Baird developed an early form of TV in the 1920s and 1930s. This system used lenses set into revolving discs.

▼ Making pictures

Television programmes are electrical signals sent to your home as electro-magnetic waves by way of satellites or underground cables. Your television set converts the signals into sound and pictures using electron guns and beams.

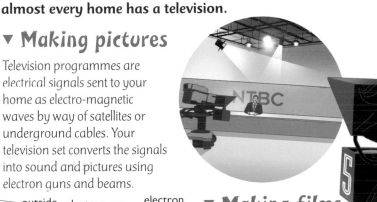

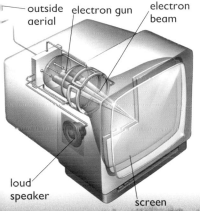

outside aerial — electron gun — electron beam

loud speaker

screen

▼ Making films

In 1911, US film makers went to a remote settlement called Hollywood, near the city of Los Angeles. They wanted to film westerns and the area was dry and scrubby. Within two years Hollywood had become the centre of American film-making, and it has dominated the industry ever since.

▲ In the studio

This picture shows a newsreader being filmed inside a TV studio as he reads the news. Other parts of the news programme are filmed 'on location' – out and about wherever the story takes place.

Fish can live anywhere there is water – icy oceans, freshwater lakes, fast-flowing rivers and tropical seas. Some fish, such as the walking catfish, can even survive for a few days on land. Fish come in many different sizes, from the tiny pygmy goby, which is smaller than your fingernail, to the 12-metre-long whale shark.

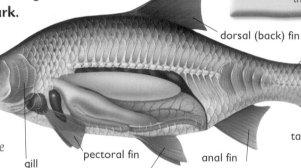

dorsal (back) fin   scales

tail fin

anal fin

pectoral fin

pelvic fin

gill openings

▶ Fishy parts

A fish has special parts called gills to let it breathe underwater. It uses its gills to take in oxygen from the water. Fish use their fins to help them swim.

> **Word box**
>
> **freshwater**
> non-salty water in lakes and rivers
>
> **tropical**
> the hot parts of the world around the Equator

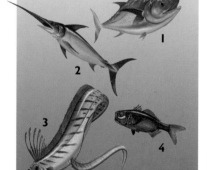

◀ Surface to floor

More than 13,000 kinds of fish live in the oceans and seas. Most swim at the surface, like the tuna (1) and the blue marlin (2). Others, such as the oar fish (3) and the lantern fish (4), live deeper down. A few, such as the tripod fish (5) and the gulper eel (6), live close to the ocean floor.

▼ In fresh water

Freshwater fish such as perch and trout live in rivers, streams and lakes. Some fish live in streams that flow deep under the ground. Most freshwater fish cannot survive in the salty oceans and seas.

perch

> **Word scramble**
>
> Unscramble these words to find the names of four saltwater fish.
>
> **a. grenhir**
> **b. dakcodh**
> **c. utan**
> **d. tiblahu**
>
> d. halibut
> a. herring b. haddock c. tuna
> **answers**

▲ Fishy killers

Many sharks are fierce hunters. They have strong teeth and jaws and can attack fish and dolphins with great speed. This blue shark can grow up to 3.8 metres in length.

Flamingos and wading birds

Find out more:
Birds

As you paddle in the sea or lake, there are probably birds doing the same. There are over 400 types of waders or shorebirds. Most have very long legs, to walk in deep water without getting too wet, and long necks and bills, to reach down and peck in sand or mud for food such as worms.

Wow!
Flamingos can wade and feed in very salty, shallow lakes where the water is hotter than in our bathtubs.

◄ Scarlet ibis

In northern parts of South America, these brilliant birds gather in huge flocks and, unusually for waders, build their nests in trees. They probe deeply in mud with their long bills, finding food mainly by touch.

▼ Catching oysters

Waders, such as the oystercatcher, do not have webbed toes. Oystercatchers are widespread across Europe and Asia, along lakes and seas. The bill has a chisel-shaped end which can easily crack open tough-shelled sea food.

Word box

bill
a bird's beak (other animals like dolphins and octopus have 'beaks' but these are not called bills)

webbed
toes (or fingers) joined by flaps of thin skin, usually for swimming

▲ Going fishing

Most herons stand tall, wade slowly, then stay very still as they watch for fish, frogs and insects. But some, like this green-backed heron, 'go fishing'. They drop small bits of food into the water to attract fish, which the heron then grabs with its dagger-sharp bill.

▲ Longest legs and neck

Flamingos are the tallest waders, about 150 centimetres high. They live in large flocks. A flamingo feeds in water by holding its bill upside down and 'combing' tiny animals and plants with brushlike parts inside its bill.

Fliers and gliders

Only bats, birds and insects can truly fly.
Many other groups of animals have a few types that can glide, swoop, soar or float. There are 'flying' spiders, fish, frogs, snakes, lizards, possums and squirrels. Most have wide, flat body surfaces that work like parachutes, but cannot be flapped like real wings.

Word box

pectoral
to do with the shoulder region, at the front or upper side of the body

Wow!

Sometimes a gust of wind lifts a flying fish so high, it lands on the deck of a boat – and cannot take off again.

▼ Furry gliders

American flying squirrels have a furry flap of skin along each side, stretched by holding out the legs. The squirrel steers by tilting its flattened tail. Like other squirrels, it is an expert climber and eats nuts, fruits and juicy bark.

▲ Flying fish

These fishes' 'wings' are its pectoral fins. The flying fish leaps out of the water at up to 50 kilometres an hour. It swoops for up to 100 metres, usually to avoid a predator such as a marlin or shark.

▲ Flying frog

The amazing flying frog of the Southeast Asian rainforests has large webs of skin between its toes, for gliding and swimming. It also has narrow skin flaps along its legs. It lives in trees and lays its eggs in a leaf.

◀ Super glider

The 'flying lemur' is not a lemur but a colugo, a plant-eating mammal from the Southeast Asian rainforest treetops. It is the best mammal glider and has thin, stretchy skin flaps all around its body. It can easily glide 100 metres, and on a breezy day, land higher up than it took off.

Flies

It's hard to ignore a buzzing housefly, blood-sucking mosquito, hovering hoverfly or painful-biting horsefly. There are over 120,000 kinds of fly. A fly has only two wings, unlike most other flying insects, such as bees and butterflies, which have four. Flies live in almost every habitat and eat every kind of food, from flowers and fruits to blood, rotting flesh, dung and other flies.

▶ Housefly

Some flies have sharp, pointed mouths for sucking up liquids. The housefly has a spongy tip to its tubelike mouth. It dribbles saliva onto food, which turns it into a 'soup', then sucks it up. Like most flies, it has small feelers and big eyes.

◀ Scorpion fly

The scorpion fly does not have a tail sting. The tail end is specialized for mating in the male or laying eggs in the female. Nor is it a true fly. It is one of many insects called a 'fly' – because it does just that.

▶ Fruit fly

Some flies are pests. Fruit flies gather around ripe and rotting fruit in autumn and can ruin farms and orchards. But these flies can be useful, too. Much of what we know about our genes, has come from studies of fruit flies.

> ### Wow!
> Some midges, which are tiny kinds of true flies, beat their wings over 1,000 times every second.

▼ Dragonfly fly-eater

With four wings, the dragonfly is not a true fly. It is very fast and acrobatic as it hunts gnats and midges (which are true flies). Other insect fliers that are not real flies are stoneflies, alderflies, caddisflies, mayflies and sawflies.

dragonfly

mayfly

mosquito

Flowers

Find out more:
Deserts • Plants

Flowers are the brightly coloured, sweet-smelling parts of plants such as roses, tulips, orchids and lilies.
Yet not all flowers are colourful and fragrant. Some plants, such as grasses, produce small flowers with no smell at all. All flowers produce seeds that grow into new flowering plants.

◀ Busy bees

This bee is collecting pollen in tiny 'baskets' on its back legs. It will carry the pollen to another flower.

Word box

bloom
to produce flowers

fragrant
sweet-smelling

sprout
to begin to grow

▶ Flowery parts

Each flower has male parts called stamens and female parts called carpels. Stamens produce tiny grains of pollen. Usually, pollen from one flower has to reach the female parts of another flower before seeds can start to grow.

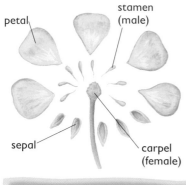

petal
stamen (male)
sepal
carpel (female)

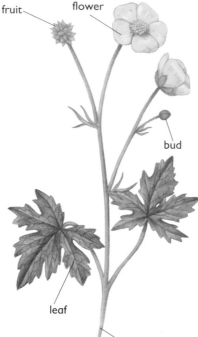

fruit
flower
bud
leaf
stem
roots

▼ Flower gardens

You can see displays of flowers in parks and gardens everywhere. People have enjoyed growing and arranging flowers since the time of the ancient Egyptians.

A wildflower garden

It's really easy to grow flowers. Why don't you try planting your own wildflower garden in a spare patch of land (don't forget to ask an adult first)? Your wildflower garden will attract insects such as butterflies and bees. You could dry and press the flowers and use them to decorate your own stationery.

▼ In the desert

Desert flowers usually bloom after a burst of rain. The seeds lie in the ground when it is dry, and then start to sprout as soon as the rain arrives.

The first flying machine, or aircraft, to carry people through the air was a hot-air balloon. It was built by the French Montgolfier brothers, and in 1783 it flew for about 8 kilometres. Two hundred years later, people could fly at supersonic speeds (faster than the speed of sound) in specially designed jet aircraft.

◀ Hot air

Two passengers travelled in the Montgolfier balloon in the skies above Paris, the capital of France. The linen balloon was filled with air heated by burning straw and wool.

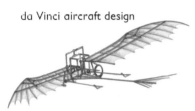

da Vinci aircraft design

▲ Early plane

An Italian artist and inventor called Leonardo da Vinci (1452–1519) produced one of the first aircraft designs, in the 1500s. The aircraft's wings flapped like a bird's wings.

▶ War planes

During World War I, the design of aircraft improved. By the end of the war, planes could fly more quickly and most were made from metal, not wood.

▼ Airships

Like balloons, airships are filled with gas, but they also have engines and steering equipment. Travel by airship was popular until 1937, when the *Hindenburg*, a huge airship filled with hydrogen gas, exploded near New York, USA. Thirty-six people on board were killed.

flying boat

▲ Flying boats

In the 1920s and 1930s a few people travelled abroad in large aircraft that landed on water. These seaplanes were called flying boats. From 1938 they made flights across the Atlantic Ocean between Europe and North America.

the *Hindenburg*

▶ The first flight

Two American brothers, Orville and Wilbur Wright, were the first people to make a powered, heavier-than-air aircraft fly. In 1903 their *Flyer* aeroplane flew over Kitty Hawk in North Carolina, USA, for 12 seconds.

a b c d e **f** g h i j k l m n o p q r s t u v w x y z **125**

Today, the biggest passenger airliners are known as wide-bodied jets. Wide-bodied aircraft such as the latest 747s can carry over 600 passengers for very long distances without stopping to refuel. Small planes that carry just a few passengers are known as light aircraft. We use them to deliver mail, to carry small groups of passengers on short journeys and to make special flights such as the delivery of emergency supplies. Most pilots learn to fly in light aircraft.

▼ Jumbo jets

This modern passenger plane is a Boeing 747. These planes are nicknamed 'jumbo jets' because of their enormous size.

a helicopter has long, spinning blades, called a rotor, instead of wings

the smaller rotor on the tail stops the helicopter from spinning round in the opposite direction from the rotor on top

Wow!

In 1999 *Breitling Orbiter* became the first hot-air balloon to fly non-stop around the world. The journey took 20 days.

▼ Crop sprayer

This light aircraft is used for spraying chemicals over a field of crops. The chemicals kill harmful insects and other pests.

▼ Power and speed

These powerful jet fighters can perform twists and turns in the air at the same time as each other. This is called flying in formation.

▲ Helicopters

Helicopters carry people or supplies to places that are difficult to reach.

Word box

pests
small animals that can cause damage to crops

spinning
turning around very fast

Food

Food gives us energy to move and keep warm. Without it, we could not survive. People used to gather or farm their own food. Today, big businesses and complex scientific processes are needed to provide enough food for lots of people and to send it long distances.

Look inside food

Look at the labels on some food packages. They tell you how much carbohydrate, protein, fats and sugar the foods contain. Some also tell you how many vitamins and minerals there are in the food.

◄ Totally tropical!

Tropical fruits grow mainly in the tropics where it is warm, as they cannot survive frost. The best known are bananas, pineapples and melons. Large quantities of these are exported (shipped to other countries). Other tropical fruits include guavas, breadfruit, mangoes and papayas.

◄ Italian favourite

Pizza was invented by the Italians. The word 'pizza' is Italian for pie. It is thought to have first been made by a baker at the royal court in Naples, southern Italy, during the 1700s. Pizza is now a favourite food around the world.

► What's in food?

Food contains special substances called nutrients. There are five main kinds of nutrients – carbohydrates, fats, proteins, vitamins and minerals. You need the right amounts of all these nutrients, as well as water and fibre to stay healthy.

milk contains calcium, a mineral that gives you strong bones

carbohydrates are found in bread, pasta, potatoes and rice – they give you energy

fresh fruits and vegetables contain lots of vitamins and minerals. They help you fight disease, keeping you fit and healthy

proteins in cheese, meat, eggs, nuts and fish help you grow and keep your body strong

fats from foods such as butter, oil and cheese give you energy and healthy nerves

fibre is important for helping the digestive system to work properly. Fruit and vegetables are fibre-rich

Food production

Most of the food we eat is produced using mechanized farming methods. These are very fast and efficient and allow prices to be kept down. However, some of these methods involve harmful fertilizers and pesticides or cruelty to animals. People are becoming worried about this and are increasingly buying foods produced organically, without chemicals, or using methods that do not cause suffering to animals.

▼ Fast food

Hamburgers, hot dogs and French fries are known as fast food. This kind of food can contain a lot of fats. Eating too many fats can be unhealthy.

▼ Growing food

Huge areas of wheat and other crops grow in Canada and the USA. Some of this food is sold to countries that do not grow enough food of their own.

▶ Different milk

In Great Britain and North America, most of the milk that people drink is from cows. In other parts of the world, milk comes from sheep, goats – and even camels.

◀ After the harvest

We buy fruits and vegetables soon after they have been harvested (picked). Fresh foods like these can be bought at markets and supermarkets. Other foods, such as wheat, are sent to factories to be made into bread and pasta.

▼ Not enough food

A famine occurs when there is not enough food. People can starve and die. A lack of rain is the usual cause of a famine.

no rain means that plants die

Food match

Can you match each of these foods with the correct plant or animal?

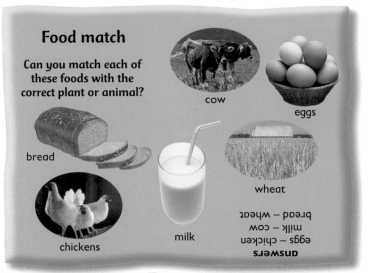

bread

cow

eggs

wheat

milk

chickens

answers
bread – wheat
milk – cow
eggs – chicken

Food through the ages

Find out more:
Farming through the ages

Until explorers reached the Americas in the 1500s, no Europeans had ever seen potatoes or tomatoes. For thousands of years, people mainly ate food that was grown locally. From the 1600s, foods were traded around the world. Australians were drinking tea from China and Europeans were eating beef from Argentina.

tomatoes   chillies

▲▼ American foods

Foods first eaten in ancient Central and South America include tomatoes, avocado pears, chillies, squashes, potatoes and cocoa. Today they are enjoyed everywhere in the world.

avocado pear

▼ Keeping it sweet

In ancient Egypt, Greece and Rome there was no sugar made from cane. Instead, cakes and puddings were sweetened with honey. Honey bees were kept on farms.

▲ Roman take-away

Street stalls and bars sold food and snacks in Roman towns and cities. People ate pies and sausages on their way to the Colosseum, the circular theatre where they watched fights between gladiators.

▶ A castle banquet

During the Middle Ages in Europe, poor people went hungry while splendid banquets were held by lords and ladies. They dined off boar's head or swan meat, ate the finest white bread and drank wine.

Wow!

When Vesuvius blew its top in AD79, it buried the whole town of Herculaneum in ash and mud. It preserved the food laid out for lunch for hundreds of years.

Forces

Forces are the natural properties of the world around us. Engines produce forces that make machines work. Without the force of gravity, we would fly off the world's surface, as the Earth spins. Friction is a force that stops us from slipping over. Inertia stops us from being pushed over by a gust of wind.

◀ Wind force

Wind provides the force that pushes a sailing boat along. As the wind flows over the sail, it creates high pressure on the inner curved surface. This pushes against the lower pressure on the other outer side of the sail. The difference in pressure makes a force that moves the boat.

Slip and slide!

Place a stone on a sheet of wood, then tilt the wood until the stone begins to slide. Now spread washing-up liquid on the wood and try again. See how the stone slides much more easily. Like oil, the washing-up liquid is a lubricant, reducing friction.

▲ Pulling power

Gravity pulls a heavy object down. However, the object can be lifted by using a stronger force, pulling on a rope passing over a pulley.

◀ Under pressure

The force of gravity on our bodies produces pressure where we stand on the ground. This is why footprints show up on snow or mud.

▼ Keep moving!

There is a natural law (rule) which says that, once something is set in motion, it will carry on in the same direction and at the same speed until some other forces act on it. Air resistance or friction will slow this ball down. Gravity will pull it towards the ground.

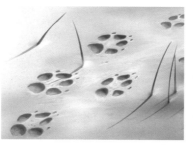

path of the ball without gravity or air resistance

air resistance

path of ball when gravity and air resistance are at work

the ball is kicked

air resistance

gravity pushes down on the ball

gravity pushes down on the ball

Forests

Find out more:
Conservation • Plants • Rainforests • Trees

Forests cover about one-fifth of the Earth's land. Every forest is filled with millions of living things, from tiny creatures that bury themselves under the leaves on the forest floor to the birds that nest high up in the branches and the trees.

the red squirrel makes its home in forest branches

Wow!
Scientists found 10,500 different kinds of living thing in a deciduous forest in Switzerland.

▼ Forest animals

Many animals find food and shelter in the forest. Small creatures such as squirrels and mice feed on leaves, fruits and seeds. They are eaten by larger animals such as stoats, weasels and wild cats.

▼ Oxygen-givers

All forests have an important job to do. Their trees take in carbon dioxide gas from the air and give off oxygen, the gas that animals and plants need to stay alive.

wild cat
deer
stoat
tortoise
shrew
mouse   toad   snail   snake

◄ Cold forests

In cool parts of the world, and in mountain areas, grow conifers — trees such as pines, firs and spruces. These trees are evergreens — they keep their leaves all year round.

▼ Changing colour

In places with warm summers and cool winters, many forests are deciduous. This means their trees have leaves that change colour and fall off in autumn.

Forests: animals

Find out more:
Birds • Forests • Squirrels

Some woods go brown in winter, others stay green.
In deciduous woodlands the trees lose their leaves in autumn, while in conifer woods they remain on the trees. These two main kinds of woods have different types of animals. Most obvious are birds and active mammals such as deer, wild pigs and squirrels. Less familiar are hosts of smaller mice, voles, lizards, snakes, insects, spiders and worms.

green woodpecker

▲ Badger sett

Badgers and their young live in tunnels and chambers called a sett, lined with soft materials. At dusk badgers look for worms, eggs, bugs, grubs, berries, fruits and shoots.

▶ Woodpeckers

Woodpeckers peck wood to find their favourite food of grubs and insects under the bark. At breeding time they chip at the wood to hollow out a hole for a nest. The noise they make hammering at the wood tells other woodpeckers to stay away!

▼ Kiwi

Shy and secretive, kiwis live in thick woodlands in New Zealand. At night they feed on worms, grubs and beetles, soft berries and fruits. If a predator appears they cannot fly away – their wings are too small, so they run.

▲ Wild boar

This wild pig (boar) is widespread in woods across Europe, Asia and Southeast Asia. Wild boar dig into the ground with their snouts for roots, bulbs, nuts, fruits and small soil animals. Male wild boar live close to herds of females. At breeding time they fight rival males with their tusks.

Find out more:
Animal Kingdom

Word box

canopy
the 'roof' of a forest, formed where tree branches, twigs and leaves form a continuous layer

timber
pieces of wood cut from trees

Tropical rainforests have the richest wildlife on Earth. There are members of nearly every kind of animal group, from worms and grubs to elephants, crocodiles and gorillas. They also face great threats, as people cut down trees to sell for timber, then clear the ground for farmland.

spider monkey

▶ Insects

Millions of kinds of insect teem in tropical rainforests. This morpho butterfly of South America glitters blue to attract a mate and warn off predators as it flutters through the rainforest.

▼ On the ground

At ground level, the tropical rainforest can be quiet, dim and still. In South America, piglike peccaries snuffle for roots, shoots and grubs. One of their treats is fruit, dropped by birds and monkeys from high above.

▲ Tree mammals

Tree mammals include squirrels, tree rats and small types of wild cats. There are also monkeys such as the spider monkey of South America, which can grasp equally well with its hands, feet and tail.

◀ Birds

Most tropical rainforest life is 30 metres or more above the ground in its canopy of branches. In Africa and Asia, hornbills, such as this yellow hornbill, flap and squawk as they delicately pick small berries and fruits with their huge bills. Other rainforest birds include parrots, colourful sunbirds and birds of paradise.

Fossils

A fossil is the remains of a plant or animal that lived a very long time ago. It can be the shell, the skeleton or just the outline shape of a dead animal. It can also be the marks left by an animal as it moved across the land. By studying fossils, scientists have learned much about the plants and animals that lived on the Earth thousands and millions of years ago.

▲ Trapped!

The whole body of this insect has turned into a fossil. Millions of years ago, it was trapped inside the sticky substance that oozed from pine trees. The sticky stuff hardened to form amber, which we make into jewellery and ornaments.

▼ Making fossils

Fossils are usually found inside rocks that were once covered by seawater.

I

2

3

4

1. when a sea creature died, its body fell to the sea-bed

2. it was then covered by mud and sand

3. seawater dissolved the bones, and the mud and sand slowly turned into rock

4. the hollow shape of the animal was left in the rock

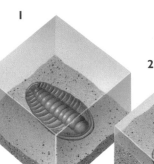

Solve the riddle

Solve this riddle to find a five-letter word.
My first is in RAIN but not in REIGN.
My second is in MOLE but not in POLES.
My third is in ABLE but not in TALE.
My fourth is in TEA but not in TAR.
My last is in ROSE but not in TOES.

answer: AMBER

► Discovered!

In far northern parts of the world, scientists have found the bodies of woolly mammoths which lived thousands of years ago. The skin, hair and body parts of the mammoths, such as those shown here, had been preserved in the frozen ground.

Foxes, wolves and dogs

Foxes, wolves, wild dogs and jackals form a group known as canids. Most are predators but they can also survive on fruits, berries and scraps. Wolves and wild dogs form groups called packs. Foxes and jackals usually live as female and male parents with their young.

Word scramble

Unscramble these words to find the names of five types of canid:

a. DILW OGD
b. KLACAJ
c. OXF
d. GINOD
e. REYG FLOW

answers
a. wild dog b. jackal
c. fox d. dingo
e. grey wolf

▲ Small cub, big ears

The African bat-eared fox is one of the smallest foxes. It uses its huge ears to detect insects. The cubs (young) like this one grow up with their parents and then leave to set up a family in their own area.

▶ No escape

Once African wild (hunting) dogs start to chase a victim, there is little escape. They speed along at 40 kilometres an hour, bringing back meat for females with cubs, and for sick or injured pack members.

▶ Leader of the pack

Grey wolves live in packs of about ten members in most northern lands. Only one pair breed – the rest help by bringing food such as smaller mammals for the cubs in their den (home).

▶ Maned wolf

The maned wolf lives in South American grasslands. In some areas it is kept as a tame pet, but in other places it is killed as a night-time attacker of farm animals.

France before the Revolution

Find out more:
France after the Revolution

After the Romans left Gaul (France), it was invaded by the Franks, who came from Germany. So the country became known as France. During the Middle Ages, France became one of the most powerful countries in Europe, famous for its arts and learning and the fine manners of its knights and ladies.

▲ Charlemagne

He was a great king of the Franks from AD768 to AD814. He ruled over an empire that stretched all the way from the borders of Spain to central Europe. Charlemagne means 'Charles the Great'.

▲ Joan of Arc

During the Middle Ages, France was often at war with England. In the 1420s, a girl called Joan of Arc claimed that she heard voices from God, saying that the English soldiers must be thrown out of France. She fought at the head of the French army but was captured and burnt alive by the English.

▲ The Sun King

Louis XIV (Louis the Fourteenth) was king of France from 1643 to 1715. He ruled over a glittering court and was very powerful. He was nicknamed the 'Sun King'.

◀ Notre Dame

In 1163, workers began to build an impressive cathedral beside the river Seine, in Paris. It was called Notre Dame, which means 'Our Lady'.

Word box

cathedral
an important church building, where a bishop or an archbishop is based and has his throne

court
the lords, ladies and officials at a royal palace

In 1789, the whole of Europe was shocked by what was going on in France. The French kings had become more and more powerful and unpopular. They made people pay unfair taxes, so the French people seized control of their country in a violent revolution. In 1793, they even beheaded the king and queen, Louis XVI (Louis the Sixteenth) and Marie-Antoinette.

◀ 'Long live the emperor!'

Napoleon Bonaparte lived from 1761 to 1821. He was a brilliant soldier who fought in the Revolution, and later made himself emperor of France. He won great battles all over Europe and made new laws.

▲ Days of terror

This dreadful machine was called the guillotine. It was designed for cutting off people's heads. During the Revolution, rich lords and ladies were sent to the guillotine. Then the rebels began to quarrel amongst themselves and sent each other to be killed instead.

Word scramble

In the 1800s, Napoleon's armies fought against the following countries. Can you unscramble their names?

a. ISURATA
b. ASSURI
c. PASSIRU
d. REGAT NIBITAR

answers
a. Austria b. Russia c. Prussia d. Great Britain

▲ Waterloo

The cannons crash, soldiers yell and horses neigh. In 1815, the French and their emperor, Napoleon, were finally defeated at Waterloo, in Belgium, by the British and Prussian armies.

◀ Naughty nineties

In the 1890s, Paris was famous for the wild lives led by its artists, poets, dancers and performers. A high-kicking dance called the cancan was all the rage.

Freshwater animals

We see only shadowy shapes near the surface.
Yet rivers, lakes, streams, ponds and other freshwater
habitats teem with animal life. In small puddles there are
tiny worms and water-fleas that would easily fit into this
'o'. Then there are aquatic insects, snails, thousands of
kinds of fish, frogs and snakes, waterbirds and otters.
The largest water animals are giant hippos and crocodiles.

▲ Deadly teeth

Piranhas eat all kinds of foods,
from seeds to worms. If a large
animal in the water struggles or
bleeds, dozens of piranhas gather
in a 'feeding frenzy' and bite lumps
off it. In a minute or two they strip
its flesh, leaving just the bones.

Word scramble

Unscramble these words to find
the names of five types of river
and pond animals:

a. SHIFERGINK (bird)
b. RATEW WERSH (mammal)
c. ERGEN GROF (amphibian)
d. GIVNID ELEBET (insect)
e. SHERFRATEW SELSUM
   (shellfish)

answers
a. kingfisher b. water shrew
c. green frog d. diving beetle
e. freshwater mussel

Word box

freshwater
non-salty water

graze
to eat grasses and other
low-growing plants

rodent
gnawing mammal, like a rat

▼ Lightweight trotter

Jacanas or lilytrotters have very
long toes, angled out wide to
spread their weight, so they really
can walk on lily pads. Like many
waterbirds they swim well. They eat
a mix of small animals and plants.

◄ Grazing giant

Hippos wallow in African rivers
and lakes by day, then graze on
nearby grasslands at night. Males
fight in water with their huge, tusk-
like teeth to claim their territory,
so they can mate with females.

► Huge gnawer

The capybara of South America
is the largest rodent. It weighs
60 kilograms — as much as an adult
person. It lives in family groups around
swamps and lakes. To escape its main enemy
on land, the jaguar, it dives into the
water. But it may be snapped up by
a crocodile-like caiman.

Frogs and toads

There are more than 4,200 types of tail-less amphibians around the world. These are frogs and toads. Frogs have smooth, moist skin, slim bodies and long legs and tend to leap, while toads have drier, lumpy skin, tubby bodies and shorter legs and usually waddle.

▼ Frog face

The American bullfrog has large, bulging eyes to see prey and a wide, toothless mouth to grab it. It also has a round eardrum to hear well – especially the croaks of other frogs at mating time. Usually only males call out, to attract females and frighten off rival males.

eardrum

▼ Horns like thorns

The strange points over the Malaysian horned frog's eyes resemble plant thorns. Like many frogs it has long rear legs for jumping, and a long, sticky-tipped tongue that it flicks out to grab prey.

Word scramble

Unscramble these words to find the names of four types of frogs and toads:

a. RETE GROF
b. PEDASTOOF ADOT
c. ENERG OGRF
d. NEDROH OTDA

answers
a. tree frog b. spadefoot toad c. green frog d. horned toad

► African bullfrog

Big and strong, this bullfrog eats many creatures, including snakes, lizards and other frogs. The male guards the eggs (spawn) that the female lays, and he also protects the tadpoles when they hatch.

▲ Giant toad

The giant, marine or cane toad has a head and body 25 centimetres long. Like most frogs and toads, it puffs itself up and hisses when in danger. Its skin makes a poison that can kill predators.

We use gas and oil to power our cars, planes and trains, to heat our homes, and to make electricity. Oil supplies about half of all the energy we use in the world. We find gas and oil in rocks deep under the ground or below the sea-bed.

▲ Out at sea

This oil rig is floating in the middle of the sea off the coast of Scotland. Special anchor ropes hold the rig in place. Oil workers sleep, eat and work on the rig or on a separate rig nearby. They travel to and from the rig by helicopter.

▶ Transporting oil

The oil taken from under the ground or under the sea is called crude oil. It is transported along a pipeline or by a tanker. The tanker may be a ship, lorry or part of a train. The oil is taken to a refinery where it is turned into petrol for cars, diesel fuel for lorries and buses, and lots of other useful substances.

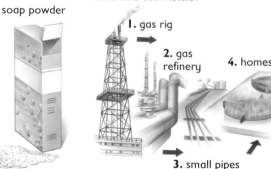

▼ Burning gas

We burn gas to heat our homes and for cooking. Gas comes into our homes through pipes under the ground. Many factories use gas to heat and cut metals.

▶ Useful products

Plastic items, lipstick, detergents, fertilizer, nylon and paint — these are just some of the many things we make from oil.

plastic cutlery set

soap powder

paint

lipstick

1. gas rig
2. gas refinery
3. small pipes
4. homes

◀ Running out

Almost half of the world's crude oil is used to make fuel for cars and small planes. But one day this oil will run out. Scientists think that there is possibly only enough oil to last for another 50 or 60 years.

Wow!

The Trans-Alaska Pipeline in North America crosses three mountain ranges, hundreds of kilometres of frozen ground and 300 rivers and streams.

Most substances exist in different forms.

Temperature and pressure play a major role. For example, most metals are solid at normal temperatures. However, they become liquid if they are heated strongly. The gas carbon dioxide becomes solid, like snow, if it is cold enough. Nitrogen gas turns into liquid when very cold.

Wow!
'Dry ice' is used for keeping things cold. But it isn't real ice – it is made from a gas called carbon dioxide.

solid – atoms or molecules cannot move

gas – atoms or molecules can move fast, and also come nearer or move farther apart from each other

heated liquid changes into vapour, or gas

warm air rises and cools

clouds form when air containing water vapour cools and forms droplets

liquid water cools and freezes and becomes solid ice

liquid – atoms or molecules can move or flow but they stay the same distance apart

▲ Our world

Everything around us is either a solid, liquid or gas, made up of units called atoms. Solid matter, like a volcano's rocks, is made up of tightly packed molecules that cannot move about. Liquids, such as water, contain molecules that are more widely spaced, and can move about more easily. Gases, such as air, are made up of molecules that can move about freely.

Gazelles and antelopes

Gazelles are long-legged, fast-running, grazing animals that live in Africa and Asia. Antelopes are similar but slightly bigger and broader, and not quite so speedy. Both are hoofed mammals, cousins of cows and goats. Most have long, curving horns, which are always growing slowly.

▼ Wild beast?

The wildebeest or gnu is a large antelope of African grasslands. Like most antelopes and gazelles, the females live in large herds. Males stay around the edge of the herd and form their own groups.

▼ At the waterhole

Kudus live in woods and grassland. At waterholes around dawn and dusk, they use keen senses of sight, hearing and smell to detect danger. A calf can run from enemies less than one hour after birth.

▲ Ready to go

The springbok of southern Africa is a very fast gazelle, bounding at more than 50 kilometres an hour. Like many antelopes and gazelles, herds migrate with the seasons to find fresh grass and water.

Wow!

An impala can jump more than 10 metres in one bound.

▼ Diving duiker

Duikers are small antelopes from central and southern Africa. Their name means 'divers' because they are very shy and dive into thick undergrowth to escape. Unusually for antelopes, they live alone or in pairs. They eat plants, termites, ants and even snakes!

Word scramble

Unscramble these words to find the names of four antelopes and gazelles:

a. SOMTHON'S LEZAGEL
b. ALAPIM
c. DELNA
d. OXYR

answers
a. thomson's gazelle b. impala
c. eland d. oryx

Word box

inherit
you inherit something passed on from your parents in their genes, such as your eye or hair colour

Genes are the tiny sets of instructions inside our cells that control how we develop and how we look. These have been passed on from our parents' cells. So, you might get your eye colour from your father and your hair colour from your mother. All living things have genes that control the way they grow and look.

DNA has a spiral shape like a twisted rope ladder

each 'rung' contains two special chemicals

▲ Pass it on!

Several generations (ages) of a family share similar genes. New genes may come into a family when its members marry. But because each of us has so many genes, some of the original ones stay in a family for centuries.

father has both blue and brown eye genes

mother has both blue and brown eye genes

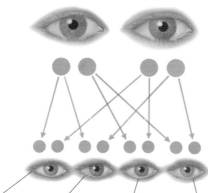

two brown eye genes will give brown eyes

one brown gene and one blue will give brown eyes

one blue gene and one brown will give brown eyes

two blue eye genes will give blue eyes

the four possible combinations

◄ Which gene?

You inherit genes from both parents. The way these genes were mixed when you were conceived controls how you look. In this example, both parents had genes for blue and brown eyes. Brown eye genes are stronger ('dominant') than those for blue eyes.

▲ Thread of life

Coiled up inside each cell of your body are molecules called DNA. Genes are small areas along threads of DNA. Each gene controls some tiny part of the way the cell and your body works. They store information about your body like the hard disk in a computer. The whole body needs about 40,000 genes and all of these are in each cell.

Germany

GERMANY UNITES
1815til1871
SWEDEN
DENMARK
UNITED
KINGDOM
RUSSIA
GERMANY
AUSTRIA
FRANCE
HUNGARY
ITALY

- German
  Confederation 1815
- German Empire
  1871
- Prussia 1866

For centuries, Germany was made up of hundreds of different states. Some of them were part of the Holy Roman Empire. During the 1800s, after the defeat of Napoleon, they began to group together and, by 1871, a united German Empire had been formed.

▼ Music-makers

In the 1700s and 1800s, Germany became a centre of the arts. Some of the world's greatest musicians lived here at this time, including Ludwig van Beethoven. Amongst his many masterpieces, he wrote nine symphonies, an opera, *Fidelio*, and a religious work called a Mass.

▲ Prussian power

The German kingdom of Prussia was founded in 1701. In 1756, it fought against Austria, starting the Seven Years War. By the 1800s, Prussia was the most powerful German nation.

◄ Fairy-tale palace

This fantastic castle was built for King Ludwig II. He ruled the southern German kingdom of Bavaria from 1864 until 1886, when he was declared mad.

Wow!
The world's tallest cathedral spire is to be seen in Ulm, Germany. It soars to a height of over 160 metres.

▼ One country

King Wilhelm I of Prussia was made emperor of all Germany in 1871. Berlin became the capital city of the united country. At this time many new factories, steelworks and mines were being built in Germany.

Why are giraffes like our fingerprints? Because no two have exactly the same pattern. The brown patches and creamy lines vary from one giraffe to another. They help the giraffe to blend in with the patchy shade of leafy branches in the grassy woods of Africa. Each giraffe roams around a home area, usually with others of its kind.

Wow!

The giraffe is the world's tallest animal. Males measure nearly 6 metres to their horn-tips.

▼ Giraffe herd

Male giraffes breed after winning 'necking' contests with rivals, bashing their necks together. A female leaves the group to give birth to the world's tallest baby, at 2 metres high. Most giraffes visit a waterhole at dawn or dusk, splay their front legs and lower their long necks to drink. They are rarely attacked – an adult giraffe can kill a lion with one kick of its dinner-plate-sized hoof.

▼ Okapi

The only close relative of the giraffe is the okapi, a rare and shy creature of central African forests. It looks like a combination of giraffe and zebra, lives alone, and eats leaves and fruits. Its horns are like the giraffe's, but only the male has them.

▼ Curly tongue

The giraffe's very long, powerful tongue grasps a twigful of leaves and pulls this into the mouth. Then the head jerks away so the teeth take the leaves off the twigs.

Grasslands

Find out more:
Africa • Grasslands: animals

Wide, flat areas of grassland are found in most of the world's continents. Grasslands have different names in different places of the world. The hot, dry grasslands of East Africa are savannahs, while those in South America are known as pampas. The grassy plains in central Asia are called steppes.

◄ From place to place

Mongolian nomads live on the grassland steppes of central Asia, where they raise herds of goats, cattle and yaks. These nomads live in tents called yurts, which are traditionally covered with felt.

Word box

felt
cloth made from pieces of wool that are pressed together

hide
the skin of an animal

nomad
someone who moves from place to place in search of grazing land

▼ The prairies

The grasslands of North America are called prairies. The soil here is fertile, and most of the grasslands have been ploughed up and turned into farmland for growing crops and rearing beef cattle.

Animal antics

Which of these animals lives on the grasslands of Africa?

a. lion
b. crocodile
c. gorilla
d. ostrich

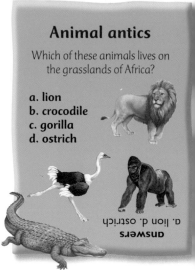

answers
a. lion d. ostrich

▲ Buffaloes

Millions of American bison, or buffalo, used to graze on the North American Prairies. Between 1850 and 1890, European settlers killed around 20 million of them, for their meat and hides. By 1900, only 1000 bison were left alive.

► In Africa

Large herds of zebra, antelope, wildebeest and other grazing animals wander across the savannah of East Africa. The animals are always on the look-out for danger from hunters such as lions and leopards.

Grasslands: animals

Find out more:
Cats • Cattle • Horses and zebras

Grasslands form where there is not enough rain for trees, but too much for a desert. Tall, waving plants are food for a huge variety of animals, from tiny termites and lizards, to huge grazers like bison on the North American prairies, and zebras and elephants on African savannas.

▶ Champion digger

The African aardvark is active at night. It uses its big ears and long snout to find ants and termites, then digs them out with its massive front claws, and licks them up with its sticky, long tongue.

▲ Striding birds

Many tall, flightless birds live on grasslands. The 1.2-metre-tall secretary bird of Africa can fly but prefers to stride along, covering 30 kilometres daily. It eats small animals such as insects, mice, birds and snakes, which it kills by stamping and pecking.

▶ Spotted serval

Africa has several grassland cats, including the cheetah, the fastest runner of all animals. The serval is like a small cheetah, with long legs and spotted fur to blend in with its surroundings. It catches and eats many creatures, including baby antelopes and low-flying birds.

serval

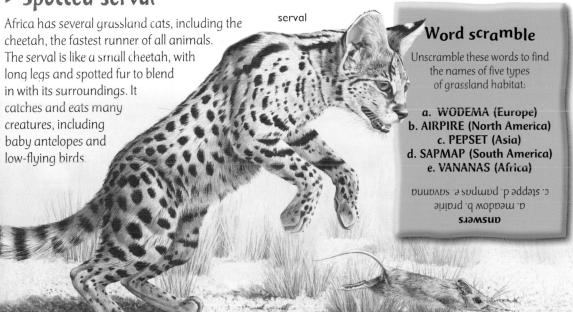

Word scramble

Unscramble these words to find the names of five types of grassland habitat:

a. WODEMA (Europe)
b. AIRPIRE (North America)
c. PEPSET (Asia)
d. SAPMAP (South America)
e. VANANAS (Africa)

answers
a. meadow b. prairie
c. steppe d. pampas e. savanna

Gravity

Gravity is a natural force that tries to pull us down towards the centre of the Earth. It is gravity that stops you from jumping very high. Astronauts need immense rockets to break away from the Earth's gravity when they travel into space.

◄ Floating in space

The further away an object is from the centre of the Earth, the lower the pull of gravity on it. In space, astronauts experience gravity at 95 percent of what it is at the Earth's surface. This means astronauts float around in space as if they were weightless.

▲ Weightless

The only easy way for you to feel weightless is by floating or swimming. The water supports your weight so you do not feel gravity pulling you down.

Wow!
When astronauts go to sleep in space, they have to strap themselves to their beds so that they don't float around!

▼ Using friction

On a rollercoaster ride, the force of gravity acts on the car. Gravity pulls the car faster downhill but also slows the car down as it climbs the uphill parts of the ride. Air friction slows the car, too, until it coasts gently to a halt once all of its stored energy has been used.

Greece: beginnings

Find out more:
Greek cities

Dolphins leap through sparkling blue seas.
Women shake their black, curly hair. Servants carry jugs of wine. All these scenes appear in wall paintings found in ancient palaces on the Greek island of Crete. They show us what it was like for kings and courtiers to live in Greece between about 3000BC and 1100BC.

▼ Stone cities

Kings in the south of Greece built stone forts called citadels. This one was at a place called Mycenae. It contained a royal palace, as well as houses for soldiers and craftsmen. It was surrounded by a stone wall.

store rooms for food

royal palace

city walls

grave circle (burial ground)

houses

the Lion Gate was the main gateway, decorated with two stone lions

▲ Monster in the maze

Greek myths tell how a terrifying monster lived on Crete in an underground maze called the labyrinth. He was believed to be half-man, half-bull and was called the Minotaur.

▼ The Wooden Horse

For years the Greeks tried to capture the city of Troy, in what is now Turkey. Finally, they came up with a plan. Legend says that in c. 1210BC they built a big wooden horse, and left it outside the city walls. Some Greek soldiers hid inside, while the rest sailed away. Puzzled, the people of Troy hauled the horse into the city. Little did they know what was hidden inside! The Greek soldiers burst out and attacked everyone.

▲ Thrills and spills

The king of Crete was called the Minos. The nobles at his palace liked to watch acrobats. These young people would somersault over the backs of fierce bulls and leap between their sharp horns.

Greek cities

After about 800BC, cities began to grow up all over Greece. Each city had its own ruler. In 508BC, the people of Athens decided to choose their own rulers from locals, or citizens. This new idea was called democracy, meaning 'rule by the people'.

Wow!

Alexander the Great used soldiers on elephants to charge at the enemy.

◄ Tough one:

In Sparta, both men and women were trained to be really tough. When a huge Persian army invaded Greece, Spartan soldiers like this one fought to the last ma

▲ City of the goddess

Athens was named after the goddess of wisdom, Athena. Her temple, the Parthenon, stood on a high rock above the city. The Athenians were great thinkers, poets, artists and craftsmen.

▼ To the east

In 334BC, Alexander led a Greek army to capture lands to the east. His soldiers we extremely well-trained. The Greeks conquered Egypt, naming a city 'Alexandria' after their leader. Then they took control of Persia before marching to India.

▼ A great leader

Alexander the Great, a brilliant soldier, came from Macedonia, to the north of Greece. All of Greece came under his rule.

Black Sea
Macedonia
GREECE
Caspian Sea
Mediterranean Sea
Alexandria
Babylon
PERSIAN EMPIRE
EGYPT
Red Sea
INDIA

Greek people

The people of ancient Greece had many important ideas about science, buildings, art, drama, poetry, athletics and government. Today we still feel the influence of these clever people, who lived more than 2,000 years ago. One of the most famous practices handed down from that time is the Olympic Games. In ancient Greece, this sporting contest was held every four years to honour the ruler of the gods, Zeus.

Athena   Aphrodite

Ares

Word box

geometry
the study of lines, angles and shapes

myth
a story with a moral or religious message

worship
to give praise to someone

▶ Greek gods

The Greeks worshipped gods and goddesses, who they believed looked after them in daily life. Zeus was ruler of all the gods. Shown here are Aphrodite, goddess of love, Athena, goddess of wisdom and Ares, god of war.

▶ Painted pots

Greek pottery was usually painted with scenes from daily life, or popular myths about gods and goddesses.

▼ Temples and theatres

The Greeks built magnificent temples, such as the Parthenon built on the Acropolis, a hill in the centre of Athens. The temple was dedicated to Athena, the goddess of wisdom. The Greeks also built huge, open-air theatres with seating for thousands of spectators.

▼ Greek maths

The Greeks were clever scientists and mathematicians. One famous mathematician, called Euclid, wrote several books on geometry. His ideas about this subject are still taught in schools today.

Wow!

In ancient Greece the Olympic Games were for male athletes only – and only male spectators were allowed to watch.

Hares and rabbits

Find out more:
Camouflage • Rodents

Hares and rabbits have long back legs, long ears, a 'bob' tail, a quivering nose and big eyes alert for danger. They are all plant eaters, and most dig underground homes called warrens. Although they look similar to rodents (gnawing animals), hares and rabbits have their own mammal group with 80 kinds worldwide.

▼ Common hare

A hare is like a large rabbit, with very long ears and legs. Hares live in open fields and hide from danger among the grasses. They are often active at night, when they nibble plants. Young hares are born with fur and their eyes wide open.

Word box

'bob' tail
a short, rounded or fluffy tail

moult
when an animal's fur, feathers or skin loosens and comes off, as a new layer grows beneath

warren
a rabbit family's home of burrows and chambers

◄▲ New coat

The snowshoe hare moults twice a year. In summer it is brown, to blend in with soil and dry grass. In winter it is white, to merge with the snow. Its camouflage makes it hard for predators, such as wolves and lynx, to spot it.

► Rabbit cousin

The rabbit group includes short-eared, short-legged members called pikas. Like rabbits, they eat grass and seeds. They live in family groups in burrows, in Asia and North America. Pikas store food in their burrows to eat in winter.

Wow!

Hares are some of the fastest runners, leaping along at more than 70 kilometres an hour.

◄ Whistling rabbit

Found only in a few mountainous places in Mexico, the small volcano rabbit has short ears and legs. It is noisy too! Most rabbits and hares thump the ground to warn of danger. The volcano rabbit whistles loudly to its family group.

Health

Good health is the result of eating the right foods, taking exercising, and getting enough rest and sleep. These all help to keep your body working properly. Looking after your health in this way makes it less likely that you will become ill.

◀ Sleeping soundly

We know that too little sleep can affect our health. Young babies sleep for most of the time. Many elderly people need less sleep than when they were younger because they are less active.

▲ Long life

Some of the oldest people in the world live in countries like Japan. There, the diet is very different from a Western one. In areas where people are long-lived, they usually eat simple diets, such as raw fish. This is full of vitamins and protein, but low in fat.

▼ Keeping fit

Exercise such as running, cycling or walking is vital for developing strong muscles, and keeping your heart healthy. It is just as important for adults, to prevent diseases and illness as the body gets older.

▼ Health checks

Even when you feel perfectly healthy, you should have regular check-ups at the doctor's. Many health problems can be spotted early on and treated before they get worse. Checks on the teeth and eyes are very important.

▲ Healthy food

Many of us eat too much ready-prepared, processed food. Eating fresh food is very important. For example, we should all eat plenty of fresh fruit and vegetables. However, if we store them for too long or over-cook them, we destroy their goodness.

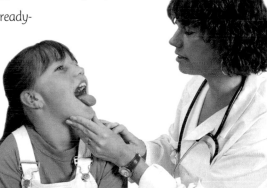

Heat

Heat is an important form of energy. It is produced in our own bodies as we break down and use the food we eat. We can release stored heat energy by burning fuels such as wood or coal. Heat can move from one substance to another in three different ways: by convection, by radiation and by conduction.

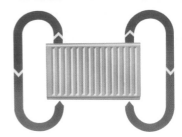

▲ Heat: convection

Above a radiator, warmed air gets lighter and rises. Cold air moves in to replace it, and is heated up. This is called 'convection'. Convection also takes place in liquids.

▲ Heat: radiation

Radiation is rays of energy. The Sun's rays travel through space and reach us as heat and light energy.

▲ Releasing energy

When we burn wood or coal on a fire, we start a chemical reaction that releases energy stored in the fuel. Flames are the area where substances in the fuel combine with oxygen in the air to release energy as heat and light.

Heat-carriers

Ask an adult to help. Take a metal spoon, a wooden ruler and a plastic spatula. Fix a frozen pea to one end of each with butter. Put the other ends in a jug of hot water. Heat is conducted from the water up each object, melting the butter. One of the objects is the best conductor — which one is it?

Word box

conductor
a substance that heat or electricity passes through easily

insulator
a substance that does not conduct heat or electricity well

▲ Heat: conduction

Conduction is the way heat spreads through a solid or liquid object. Metal is a faster conductor than glass.

Heat and temperature

Find out more:
Energy sources • Heat • Sun

While heat is a form of energy, temperature is a measure of heat. Temperature tells us how hot or cold something is, or how much heat it contains. It is measured in degrees Celsius (°C) or Fahrenheit (°F) or the absolute temperature scale, measured in kelvins (K).

solar panel

pipes of hot water

Temperature		
15,000,000°C		Centre of Sun
30,000°C		Inside lightning bolt
5,000°C		Centre of Earth
1,000°C		Lava from volcano
200°C		Oil in frying pan
100°C		Boiling water
37°C		Body temperature
0°C		Water freezes
−78.5°C		Solid carbon dioxide ('dry ice')
Absolute zero −273.16°C		

▲ Using the Sun

In some countries, houses are centrally heated using solar (sun) energy. A solar panel filled with liquid is placed on the roof of the house. The Sun's warmth heats up the liquid, which passes into the house to heat up radiators and hot water.

▼ How warm are you?

A thermometer is used for measuring heat. Digital thermometers contain an electronic part that is sensitive to heat. Your normal body temperature is about 37 degrees Celsius (°C), or 98.6 degrees Fahrenheit (°F)

◄ Heat extremes

There is no limit to how hot things can become. The hottest ever temperature achieved in a laboratory is 2 billion degrees absolute! But cold things do have a limit – scientists have come close to reaching absolute zero, at −273.16°C (−459.69°F), or 0 kelvins (K) on the absolute temperature scale.

Hedgehogs and moles

Hedgehogs, moles, desmans and shrews are all insectivores. They are a group of about 370 kinds of mammals – mostly small, sharp-toothed animals who eat insects as well as other bugs, grubs, worms and creepy-crawlies.

▼ Digging machine

A mole's front paws are massive, with wide claws like a spade to burrow through soil. Each mole digs a long network of tunnels. It lives in a chamber called a fortress with an extra-large molehill above.

▲ Hog in the hedge

The European hedgehog is named after its piglike snorts as it noses for small creatures in hedgerows, woods and meadows. It can roll into a prickly ball, protected by its 5,000 sharp spines. Like most insectivores, it usually lives alone.

desman

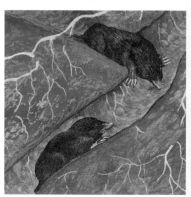

Wow!

The smallest land mammal is the pygmy white-toothed shrew, whose head and body is just 4 centimetres long – its tail is half this length.

▲ Diving desman

The insectivore group includes moonrats in Asia, solenodons in the West Indies and tenrecs in Africa. They are all shrewlike, with long whiskers, quivering noses and quick movements. The desmans of West Europe and Asia have part-webbed feet. They catch fish, grubs and worms in fast streams.

◄ Shrews

There are 250 types of shrew all around the world. They range in size from smaller than your thumb, to the size of a rat. They all hunt creatures – sometimes bigger than themselves. The smallest shrews have to eat a big meal every few hours or they starve.

Word box

insectivore
insect eater, although insectivores often eat many other types of small animal

quivering
shaking

Hibernating animals

Before the start of a long, cold winter, some animals fall into a deep sleep, called hibernation. This helps them get through a long, cold and harsh winter when there is very little food. An animal that hibernates cannot wake up, even if it tries, until its hibernation ends.

◄ A special day

The groundhog is a large North American ground squirrel. Tradition tells how it peers from its burrow on Groundhog Day, 2 February, to see if it is warm enough to stop hibernating. In fact, it usually hibernates until March.

▼ Who hibernates?

Mammals that hibernate include bats, hedgehogs and various kinds of rodents, such as mice, rats, marmots and some squirrels. In autumn they feast and store energy as fat in their bodies, to survive for their months asleep.

squirrel

bats hibernate in hollow trees or caves, where it is cold but rarely freezing

the dormouse hibernates in a snug nest of leaves, moss and twigs, among tree roots

hedgehog

Word box

burrow
a hole in the ground, dug by a small animal for shelter or defence

Holland and Belgium

Find out more:
Atlas: Europe

Belgium and the Netherlands (meaning 'lowlands') border the North Sea. Part of the Netherlands is called Holland, and many people use the word 'Holland' when they mean the Netherlands. The people of this region fought many European wars, but their greatest enemy has always been the sea, which has flooded this coast for thousands of years.

◄ Tulip madness!

In the 1600s, the Netherlands became a rich nation by trading around the world. At this time, there was a huge craze amongst merchants for buying and selling tulip bulbs. Tulips and other flowers are still traded today.

◄ Why windmills?

The countryside in Holland is dotted with old windmills. For hundreds of years, wind power was used to pump water out of the soggy farmland.

▲ Old Antwerp

Antwerp is an old Belgian port on the river Scheldt. In the Middle Ages it was an important centre for the cloth trade. This statue is of the painter Peter Paul Rubens, who made the city his home in 1608.

What did they do?

Can you find out? Match these famous Lowlanders with the part they played in history:

1. Jan van Eyck
2. Abel Janszoon Tasman
3. Erasmus of Rotterdam
4. Leopold I
5. William of Orange

a. The first king of independent Belgium
b. A great scholar
c. A Dutch ruler who became king of England
d. A famous painter of the Middle Ages
e. An explorer of the 1600s

1d 2e 3b 4a 5c
answers

Wow!

More than 40 percent of Dutch land used to be under the waves! Over the years it has been sealed off by sea walls and then drained.

▲ The lacemaker

Many great Dutch painters lived in the 1600s. This picture by Jan Vermeer shows a lacemaker. Holland and Belgium were famous for their fine lace.

Holy Roman Empire

Find out more:
Italy • Atlas: Europe

The Holy Roman Empire was an alliance of many small European states and nations. It followed on from the empire of Charlemagne. The states had their own rulers, but recognized the Holy Roman emperor as their leader. The Empire lasted from AD800 to 1806 and was at its height during the Middle Ages.

LAND OF THE EMPERORS IN THE MIDDLE AGES

Lowlands Saxony
GERMANY
Franconia BOHEMIA
Austria
BURGUNDY Bavaria
LOMBARDY
SICILY

▶ The Empire

The Holy Roman Empire was a group of lands that at various times included the Netherlands, Austria, much of Germany, central Europe and Italy.

▲ Red Beard

Frederick I, who became emperor in 1152, belonged to a powerful German family called Hohenstaufen. He was nicknamed Barbarossa, which means 'red beard'. He was drowned while on a Crusade in 1190.

▶ A two-headed eagle

The badge of the Holy Roman Empire was a two-headed eagle. After 1452, the Empire was ruled by a Swiss family called the Habsburgs. They also became rulers of Spain.

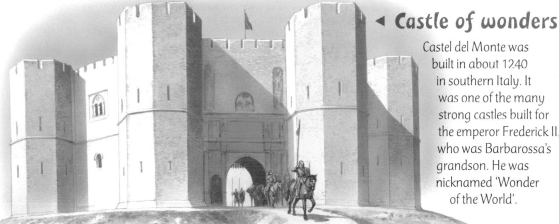

◀ Castle of wonders

Castel del Monte was built in about 1240 in southern Italy. It was one of the many strong castles built for the emperor Frederick II, who was Barbarossa's grandson. He was nicknamed 'Wonder of the World'.

Homes around the world

Find out more:
Buildings and bridges

Your home protects you from the heat and the cold, and from rain and snow. It is the place where you usually sleep, eat your meals and relax with family and friends. Around the world, people build many different styles of home to suit their way of life, the local climate and the building materials that are available.

▲ Keeping cool

These houses in Africa are made from wood and straw. The thick roofs help to keep the inside of the house cool when temperatures outside are very hot.

▼ Up on stilts

These homes in southeast Asia are built on stilts as swampy ground surrounds the villages. The land sometimes floods, so the stilts keep the houses above the water level.

▶ Tall homes

A multi-storey block of apartments is one way of saving space in a crowded city centre. Large numbers of families can make their home inside a single building.

▲ Houses in rows

A row of homes joined together like this is typical of many European cities and towns. These houses are built from baked clay bricks.

▲ A tented home

Bedouins live in large tents in the hot deserts of the Middle East and North Africa. Bedouins raise herds of sheep, goats and camels. They move their tents from place to place in search of water and fresh grazing for their animals.

Homes through the ages

Find out more:
Cities of ancient times

Human beings have always needed shelter and shade, and they have learned to make homes from whatever materials are available. Tents could be sewn from animal skins or cloth. Huts could be made from turf, branches, leaves or bamboo canes. Houses have been built from timber, clay or stone. Over time, people learned how to make bricks, concrete, iron girders and glass windows.

◀ Cave-dwellers

During the Stone Age, caves offered families shelter and protection from wild animals. However, they were often damp, dark and draughty.

▲ Brick and slate

Big cities were built in Britain in the 1800s, with inexpensive housing for factory workers. Bricks and slates for the roofs could be carried from far away by canals or railways.

▼ Timber frame

In the Middle Ages, most houses were built with timber frames. These made criss-cross patterns on the walls, as seen on this German house.

ornamental pool

courtyard

dining room

▲ A Roman home

Roman villas were built with tiled roofs and central courtyards. Many had beautiful gardens decorated with statues.

walled garden

kitchen

Horses and zebras

Find out more
Grasslands • Mammals • Pets

The horse's cousins include three kinds of zebras in Africa and two kinds of wild asses in Africa and Asia. Over 100 years ago, before cars and trucks were invented, horses were widely used for pulling loads and carrying people.

▶ Asses and donkeys

A few wild asses still roam dry areas in northeast Africa, the Middle East and central Asia. They survive great heat. Donkeys are domesticated versions of asses. They were tamed by people more than 5,000 years ago in the Middle East to be strong and carry heavy loads.

donkey

Wow!
Most wild horses no longer live wild. They are rare and are kept mainly in parks and nature reserves.

▼ Species of horses

All domesticated horses belong to the same group or species – from massive and powerful heavy horses such as shires to agile polo ponies, often used for playing polo, a ball game. Horses have been bred by people for different jobs for more than 4,000 years.

Word scramble

Unscramble these words to find the names of five breeds or types of horses:

a. HOCARERSE
b. SHRIE EROHS
c. RETHUN
d. STUMNAG
e. NIMOLOPA

answers
a. racehorse b. Shire horse c. hunter d. mustang e. palomino

heavy horse

polo pony

◀ Zebras

Like all horses and their relatives, zebras eat mainly grass. They have long legs, each with one large toe, capped by a hard hoof. Their keen senses detect distant danger and they can race away at more than 60 kilometres an hour. Each group or herd consists of mares (females) and foals (young), led by a stallion (adult male).

Human body

Your body is one of the most complicated living things. It runs itself almost automatically, provided you eat and drink when necessary. It contains several systems which look after different functions, such as breathing, digestion and movement. The most complicated of these is the nervous system, including the brain.

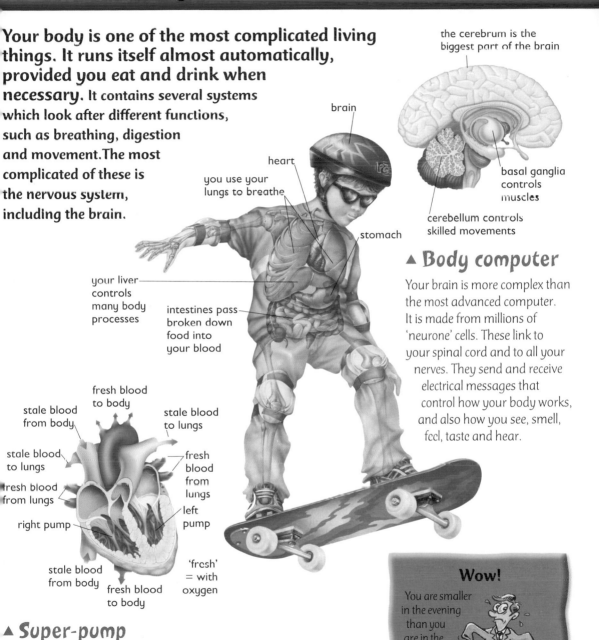

the cerebrum is the biggest part of the brain

brain

heart

you use your lungs to breathe

stomach

basal ganglia controls muscles

cerebellum controls skilled movements

your liver controls many body processes

intestines pass broken down food into your blood

fresh blood to body

stale blood from body

stale blood to lungs

stale blood to lungs

fresh blood from lungs

right pump

stale blood from body

fresh blood from lungs

left pump

stale blood from body

fresh blood to body

'fresh' = with oxygen

▲ Body computer

Your brain is more complex than the most advanced computer. It is made from millions of 'neurone' cells. These link to your spinal cord and to all your nerves. They send and receive electrical messages that control how your body works, and also how you see, smell, feel, taste and hear.

Wow!
You are smaller in the evening than you are in the morning!

▲ Super-pump

Your heart is a pair of pumps made mostly from muscle. It makes sure blood collects oxygen from the lungs and travels round the body. 'Valves' keep the flow in the right direction.

Human senses

Our senses make us aware of the outside world.
We use our sense organs to see, hear, touch, taste and smell
our surroundings. As well as these five senses, we also have
a sixth sense called balance. This enables us to stand and
move about on two legs.

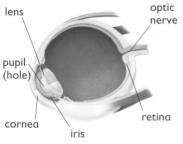

lens
optic nerve
pupil (hole)
cornea
iris
retina

▲ How we see

Light enters the eye through a clear layer at the front. It passes through a lens that focuses light on the retina, at the back. This causes 'receptors' to send nerve signals to the brain. The brain 'sees' these as pictures.

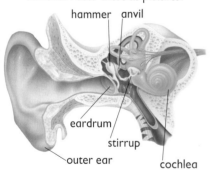

hammer anvil
eardrum
stirrup
outer ear
cochlea

▲ Pass it along

Sound waves vibrate the ear drum and pass on to tiny bony levers inside the skull. Hairs inside the coiled cochlea then pass messages to the brain so that we can 'hear' the sounds.

▼ Very tasty!

Your sense of taste is based on your tongue. Patches of receptors in certain areas on your tongue can taste things such as sweet, sour, salty and bitter. They produce messages that are passed to the brain. Taste works closely with smell.

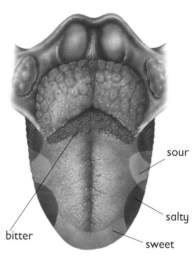

sour
salty
sweet
bitter

Sweet or salty?

Get someone to put a few grains of salt or sugar on your tongue. First on the tip, then the sides, then the back. See where you can taste the sweetness or saltiness.

▲ Touch and feel

Your fingertips contain lots of touch receptors. They are so sensitive that blind people can use their sense of touch to read Braille writing (tiny bumps on paper). You also have lots of touch receptors on your lips and around your eyes.

▲ Smelly signals

Tiny scent particles in the air pass to receptors in passages at the front of the skull. The receptors produce nerve signals that send 'smell' messages to the brain. Our sense of smell is poor compared to many animals.

Human skeleton

Without a skeleton you would be like a floppy bean bag. Your skeleton holds you together and gives your body its shape. It protects soft parts such as your heart and lungs. Joined to the bones of your skeleton are muscles. You use muscles to move every part of your body. There are even muscles in your face which help you to smile or frown.

▶ Broken bones

If you break a bone in your arm or leg it is usually set in a plaster cast. Sometimes metal plates like this one are used to help bones mend.

▶ On the move

Muscles pull on your bones to make them move. You use muscles to walk, run, jump – even to breathe. Your body has more than 650 muscles.

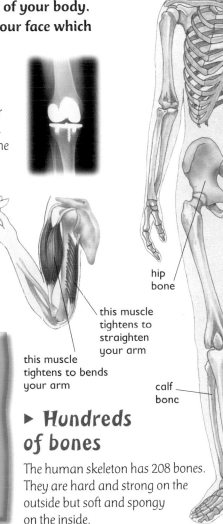

this muscle tightens to straighten your arm

this muscle tightens to bends your arm

Word scramble

Unscramble these words to find the names of four important body parts:

a. thare
b. kleonest
c. sculem
d. inbar

answers a. heart
b. skeleton c. muscle d. brain

▶ Hundreds of bones

The human skeleton has 208 bones. They are hard and strong on the outside but soft and spongy on the inside.

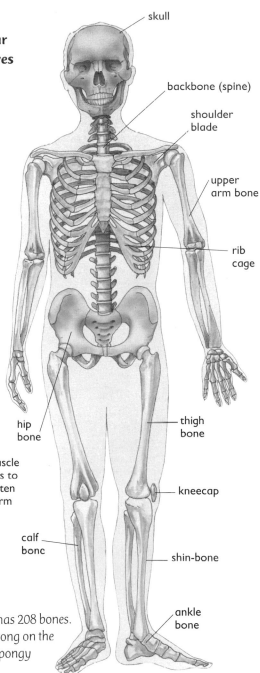

skull

backbone (spine)

shoulder blade

upper arm bone

rib cage

hip bone

thigh bone

kneecap

calf bone

shin-bone

ankle bone

Ice ages

Between about a million and ten thousand years ago, the Earth went through several periods when it was bitterly cold. Huge sheets of ice spread out from the Poles. During these ice ages, lands that now have a mild climate were deep in snow and their rivers were frozen solid.

upright man, about 1.6 million years ago

Neanderthal man, about 200,000 to 30,000 years ago

modern man, about 40,000 years ago to present day

Word box

climate
the kind of weather experienced in one place over a long period of time

Poles
the most northerly and southerly points on Earth

▲ Ice age people

Various types of human being lived through the ice ages and learned how to survive the cold. By the end of the ice ages, only modern man, our direct ancestor (relative from a long time ago), lived on Earth.

▲ Mammoth hunters

Big hairy elephants called woolly mammoths and woolly rhinoceroses roamed the land during the ice ages. People hunted them with weapons made of wood and stone.

When Spanish explorers reached South America in the 1500s they heard rumours of a fabulous land rich in gold. In fact, there had been splendid civilizations in the Andes Mountains and along the Pacific coast for thousands of years. The latest great empire was that of the Incas. It lasted from about 1100 to 1532, when it was conquered by the Spanish.

Wow!

The Temple of the Sun in Cuzco had a garden in which everything, including model plants and animals, was made of solid silver and gold.

▲ Nazca puzzles

The Nazca civilization was one of many before the Incas. It lasted from about 200BC to AD750. Its people scraped patterns on the desert floor. These may have shown routes for religious processions. Some, like this hummingbird, were animal shaped.

▲ Road-runner

Messengers like this one carried the emperor's orders through the Inca Empire. He carries a *quipu*, or bunch of cords. These were knotted as a way of remembering numbers or other information.

▼ The Inca Empire

The Inca Empire was called Tawantisuyu, which means 'the Four Quarters'. It was centred on Peru and also took in large areas of Ecuador, Chile and Bolivia. It stretched 3,600 kilometres from north to south.

the Inca Empire is represented by the orange area

SOUTH AMERICA

Andes Mountains

PACIFIC OCEAN

◄ Machu Picchu

The Incas built the city of Machu Picchu high in the Andes Mountains of Peru. It was so well-hidden it became a forgotten marvel lost for 400 years, until an American explorer rediscovered it in 1911.

India

Rich cloth, beautiful stone carvings, paintings and wonderful poetry were produced in ancient India. Several great empires grew up there. The Maurya Empire was at its height around 250BC and Gupta rule in about AD350. Hinduism and Buddhism also grew and spread during this period.

◄ Mughal Empire

Northern India was under Muslim rule from 1211. In 1526, the Mughal Empire was founded. This is Mughal Emperor Shah Jahan, who lived from 1592 to 1666.

▼ Taj Mahal

Shah Jahan had this marble monument built by the river Yamuna in honour of his wife, Mumtaz Mahal, who died in 1631. It was decorated with precious stones.

▲ Holy caves

There is a cave temple on Elephanta Island near Mumbai (Bombay) that is more than 1,200 years old. The temple has wonderful carvings of Hindu gods, such as Shiva.

◄ Indian dance

Indian dance has a history dating back thousands of years. It is said that the Hindu god, Shiva, set the world spinning by his dancing.

Indus Valley

The Indus River flows through Pakistan to the Arabian Sea. Between about 2500BC and 1750BC, a great civilization grew up in the Indus Valley. The people living there grew cotton and grain. They worked in metal and produced pottery, cloth and jewellery, trading with the peoples of western Asia.

◀ Mystery man

This stone head was made in Mohenjo-daro in about 2100BC. Whose face is it? Nobody really knows for certain. It might belong to a god, a king or a priest.

▼ How they lived

Pottery models, such as this one showing a two-wheeled cart drawn by bullocks, show us how people used to live in Harappa.

▲ Mohenjo-daro

The two greatest cities of the Indus Valley were Harappa and Mohenjo-daro. They had streets and drains, and houses built of bricks.

▶ Trade marks

Stone seals were used by the merchants of Mohenjo-daro to mark bundles of trade goods. Many show animals or a name.

◀ The great river

Flooding from the Indus river left behind rich soil for farming. The civilization that grew up along the riverbanks stretched into India.

Indus River
• Harappa
• Mohenjo-daro
INDIA
ARABIAN SEA

Industrial Revolution

Find out more:
Cities of modern times

The age of factories and machines began in Europe and North America in the 1750s. It is called the Industrial Revolution, a term used to describe the changes brought about when people used steam to make goods quickly on a mass scale. At first, the people who worked in the new factories had to work long hours for little pay.

▼ Steam power

The factory age was possible because of the invention of the steam engine. This engine was made in the 1700s, by an inventor called Thomas Newcomen.

▼ Cities and smoke

During the Industrial Revolution, cities grew and spread across Europe. This is a typical British city scene. It had street after street of small red-brick houses and tall chimneys belching out smoke.

Word box

factory
a building where machines are used to make goods on a large scale

steam engine
any machine whose movement is powered by the force of steam (which is made when water boils)

Insects

Butterflies and bees, moths and mosquitoes, cockroaches and crickets are all types of insect. Altogether there are more than one million different kinds of insect – and scientists think there are millions more that have not yet been named. Most insects are very small creatures, less than one centimetre long. There are some large ones, however, such as the giant Hercules moth from Australia, whose open wings measure 30 centimetres from tip to tip.

Word box

hatch
to come out of an egg

pupa
inactive stage in the life of some insects, while inside a protective case

thorax
the part of an insect that bears its legs and wings

thorax

antenna

head

abdomen

stag beetle

leg

▶ Body parts

All adult insects have six legs arranged in pairs. An insect's body is divided into three main parts: the head, the thorax and the abdomen. Most insects have wings and antennae, too.

▼ All colours

Some insects, such as dragonflies, are very colourful but others are a dull brown or black colour. Some look like leaves, sticks or tree bark to hide themselves from enemies. Others have bold spots or stripes to scare enemies away.

dragonfly

◀ Butterfly life

Most insects begin life as an egg. Caterpillars hatch from the eggs of a butterfly. A young caterpillar looks nothing like the adult butterfly. When a caterpillar stops growing, it turns into a pupa. Finally, an adult butterfly crawls out of its protective case.

1. the female butterfly lays her eggs and dies

2. the caterpillar hatches from the egg. It spends most of its time eating

3. when the caterpillar is fully grown, it is ready to turn into a pupa. A hard shell begins to form around it, protecting the butterfly developing inside

4. finally the adult butterfly pushes its way out of the hard shell

5. the butterfly is ready to fly after about an hour

Most insects have a very busy life. They have to build a home, look for a partner, hunt and collect food, fight enemies, lay eggs and some even look after their young. Some insects bite, spread disease and damage crops. However, insects are very important for life because they pollinate plants which form food for humans and animals.

bees carry pollen grains from plant to plant

▼ Huge nests

Termites live in big family groups called colonies. Some build tall nests that are home to thousands of termites. All the termites in a colony are the children of one female termite, the queen.

'chimney' can be 6 metres tall

wall made of earth

▶ Hungry insects

Locusts are a kind of grasshopper. They can travel long distances in huge crowds called swarms. One swarm may contain millions and millions of locusts. They swoop down to eat crops and other plants, destroying huge areas of plant life in a very short time.

locust

▼ Insect lights

Some insects even use special effects to help them find a mate. This firefly is able to flash a yellowish light on and off to attract a partner.

Word scramble

Unscramble these words to find the names of four insects:

a. AGRIWE
b. EBLETE
c. BLIYDRAD
d. GRANDLYOF

answers
a. earwig b. beetle c. ladybird d. dragonfly

▶ Going underground

These tall termite nests continue for some distance underground. Inside is a maze of chambers (rooms) where young are looked after by 'worker' termites and food is stored. Air passages keep the nest cool.

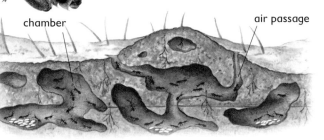

chamber

air passage

Across the world, millions of computers are able to 'talk' to one another. This system is called the Internet. Information is mostly passed from computer to computer by telephone wires. The Internet lets people get hold of all kinds of information, in just a few seconds.

Word box

modem
device which lets computers send or receive information using phone lines

server
computer that holds information used by other computers

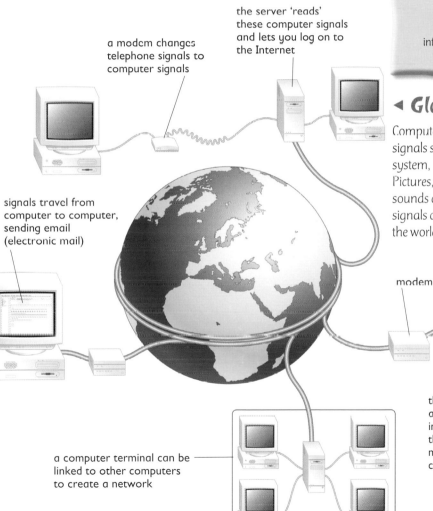

the server 'reads' these computer signals and lets you log on to the Internet

a modem changes telephone signals to computer signals

signals travel from computer to computer, sending email (electronic mail)

◀ Global network

Computer signals are changed into signals suitable for the phone system, by a device called a modem. Pictures, animations, words and sounds are all sent as signals. These signals can pass to the other side of the world in less than a second.

modem

the World Wide Web gives access to a huge amount of information. It is filled with thousands of web sites, each made up of documents called web pages

a computer terminal can be linked to other computers to create a network

Can you imagine a world without wheels, without petrol engines, without medicines? For thousands of years clever people have invented machines and gadgets. Many of these have made our lives easier, safer or healthier.

▲ The wheel

The wheel is one of the most important things ever invented. Flat wheels were probably first used by potters, to turn their clay into round pots. By about 3500BC, upright wheels were being used for transport on chariots or wagons in the Middle East.

▼ North, south, east, west

Compasses use magnetism to show which direction to travel in – north, south, east or west. The first compasses were made in China over 2,300 years ago. At first, they looked like metal spoons with handles that pointed south. Later, steel needles were floated in bowls of water.

Hooke's microscope

◄ Magnification

Microscopes make even the tiniest objects look big. The first ones were made in the Netherlands in about 1590. This one was made in England in 1665, by a scientist called Robert Hooke. It was the first one to look like a modern microscope. Hooke used it to study the structure of chemicals and plants.

► Thomas Edison

An American called Thomas Edison invented the electric light bulb in 1879. He had already invented the phonograph, which recorded sound and played it back again.

Learning how to smelt and then work iron was one of the most important discoveries ever made by human beings. Iron could now be used to make much stronger weapons and tools than had been possible before. It was being smelted by west Asian peoples, such as the Hittites, about 4,000 years ago. Iron-working skills soon spread to Europe, North Africa and other parts of Asia.

Word box

bellows
machines designed to puff air at glowing coals in a furnace, to make them hotter

ploughshare
the blade on a plough that turns over the soil

smelting
heating rock so that the metal it contains is melted and taken out

◀ Chinese plough

The ancient Chinese were very skilled iron workers. They made the first iron ploughshares in the world, over 2,500 years ago, to a design still in use today. They also invented cast iron, over 2,300 years ago.

◀ Iron swords

Iron was a deadly metal when used for making weapons. This short Roman sword was called a *gladius*. It was used by Roman armies to cut down their enemies.

the fire in the furnace needed to be extremely hot to melt the metal

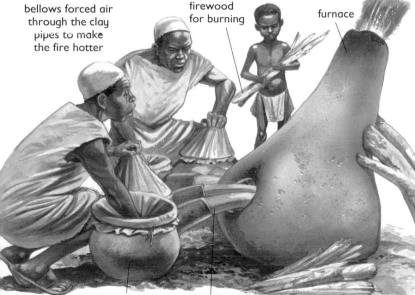

bellows forced air through the clay pipes to make the fire hotter

firewood for burning

furnace

bellows

clay pipes

◀ Iron in Africa

These men are using bellows to fan an iron-smelting furnace in Africa. Iron was being used south of the Sahara Desert by about 500BC, and had reached southern Africa by 200BC.

During the Middle Ages, Italy was split up into small states. Some of them were ruled by other nations, others were independent republics. The great city of Rome was the centre of the Catholic Church and the home of its leader, the Pope. It was not until the 1800s that the different regions of Italy began to join together as a single nation.

▲ Leaning tower

This bell tower in the city of Pisa was built in 1170. Standing on sandy soil it soon started to tilt – and is still leaning over at an angle today.

▼ Popes of Rome

During the Middle Ages, the pope was the most powerful man in Europe. He wore a special crown called a tiara.

▲ The Red Shirts

In the 1860s, Giuseppe Garibaldi and his followers, the 'Red Shirts', fought for a united Italy. By 1871, Italy had become one nation.

Make your own carnival mask

1. Ask an adult to help you. Cut a card mask to fit your face.

2. Paint it in gold or silver paint and decorate it with felt-tip pens.

3. Pierce two holes level with your ears. Tie string through the holes to attach the mask to your face.

▲ Venetian Carnival

The festival of Carnival has been held in Venice since the Middle Ages. People still wear masks and fancy costumes to the Carnival today.

Farmers have been growing rice on the lands around the Sea of Japan for over 2,000 years. Over the centuries, the islands of Japan were ruled by emperors and warriors, while powerful kings ruled over Korea. Beautiful buildings, pottery, paintings, prints, poetry and plays were all produced in this part of Asia.

◄ Knights of the East

The samurai were Japanese knights. They held great power between the 1100s and 1600s. The samurai fought for local lords, armed with sharp swords, bows and arrows, and later with guns.

▼ Tea time

In the 1400s, Buddhist monks in Japan made tea according to a long and complicated ritual. This became known as *chanoyu*, a tea-drinking ceremony which still takes place in Japan today. It aims to promote peace, respect, purity and tranquility, and takes several hours.

▲ Fine writing

In Korea, as in China, calligraphy (fine handwriting) is very much admired. Chinese, Western and Korean forms of writing may be seen in Korea. The Korean script is called *hangul* and it dates back as far as the 1400s.

▲ Japanese castles

During the 1500s, Japanese lords built towering castles. They were very strong, made of timber, earth and stone.

Wow!

Japan's royal family is the oldest in the world. It has ruled the country for over 2,000 years.

Jobs

Teacher, truck driver, dentist, sales assistant, builder and banker are kinds of job. A job is the work you do to earn money. Some people do outdoor jobs working on the land or at sea. Other jobs involve making things in factories and workshops, such as cars and computers. Some jobs provide help and information for others, for example in shops, hospitals, offices and banks.

Word box

assemble
to put together

natural resource
something useful from the land or the sea

▲ By hand

This potter is working with his hands. He uses machines as well in his job, such as a special oven called a kiln to bake the pots hard.

▲ Helping others

Jobs in offices, banks, hotels and shops are called service jobs. These jobs involve organizing and helping instead of working with natural resources or making goods.

◄ Healing power

People who work in the medical profession such as nurses, doctors and surgeons, have important jobs. Surgeons carry out complicated operations on their patients using the latest technology. This patient is having laser treatment to help correct his eyesight.

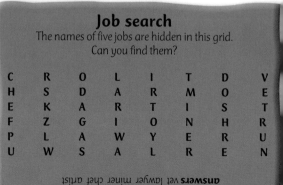

◄ Dangerous jobs

Fire-fighting can be a dangerous job. Fire-fighters have to be fit and strong and ready to risk their lives for other people. They also have to know about preventing fires, rescuing people and giving first aid in an emergency.

Job search
The names of five jobs are hidden in this grid. Can you find them?

C	R	O	L	I	T	D	V
H	S	D	A	R	M	O	E
E	K	A	R	T	I	S	T
F	Z	G	I	O	N	H	R
P	L	A	W	Y	E	R	U
U	W	S	A	L	R	E	N

answers vet lawyer miner chef artist

One of the world's speediest animals bounds along on its huge back feet at more than 50 kilometres an hour – the red kangaroo. At almost 2 metres tall, it is the largest of about 50 kinds of kangaroos and smaller wallabies. These marsupial mammals live in Australia, with a few in Papua New Guinea.

▲ Wallaby

There are many kinds of wallabies, with names such as wallaroos, pademelons, bettongs and prettyfaces. Some live in forests, while others prefer rocky scrub or grassy plains. Like kangaroos, they use their tail for balance when bounding and to lean on at rest.

Wow!

Some kangaroos live in trees! Tree kangaroos dwell in forests in Papua New Guinea and northeast Australia and have grasping hands and padded feet.

◄ Boomers and fliers

A big male red kangaroo, or 'boomer', can clear a fence 3 metres tall. Many red kangaroos vary in colour from cream to rusty brown. They live in groups in the outback and gather at waterholes during drought.

▼ Boxing kangaroos

Male kangaroos push, pull and wrestle with their arms, and may kick out with their great feet, using their strong tail for support. They are battling for females at breeding time.

▲ Mother and joey

A newborn kangaroo is smaller than your thumb. It stays in its mother's pouch for up to six months, feeding on milk and growing fast. Then the youngster, or joey, hops out for a short while, dashing back if frightened. It finally leaves at one year old.

Word box

drought
a long, dry period with little or no rain

marsupial
pouched mammal

One of the world's brightest-coloured birds is shy and quick to hide. It is the Eurasian kingfisher, with its brilliant blue-green and orange-red feathers. There are about 80 kinds of kingfishers around the world, and most are just as brightly coloured. They rarely form flocks and usually nest in holes in riverbanks or trees.

▼▶ Bee-eaters

Just as colourful as kingfishers are their close cousins, the bee-eaters. The 25 kinds live mainly in rainforests in Africa, southern Asia and Australia. They eat bees and wasps, after first knocking off the stings. Carmine bee-eaters breed in groups, in bank or cliff holes.

carmine bee-eater

Word box

migrate
to make a long journey, usually at the time of year when the weather starts to gets cold – many animals travel to warmer places to find food and raise their young.

▶ Rollers

Named after their acrobatic rolling, looping flight, 16 kinds of rollers are found in forests across Africa, southern Asia and Australia. They are close relatives of kingfishers and many have brilliant colouring. They catch flies and other small creatures, in the air and on the ground. Some, such as the lilac-breasted roller, migrate hundreds of kilometres in great flocks.

▼ Eurasian kingfisher

Most kingfishers perch near water and wait patiently for a fish, frog or perhaps a snake or baby bird. With a flash of colour the kingfisher dives in, spears the prey with its dagger-like beak, and flies away with the meal in its mouth, to its favourite feasting branch.

▼ Ha-ha-ha-ha-ha

One of the biggest, noisiest kingfishers is the kookaburra or 'laughing jackass' of Australia. Its call, to keep other kookaburras away from its territory, sounds like cackling human laughter.

Kings have ruled over people and kingdoms for thousands of years. Once, most kings had great power over their kingdoms. The majority of today's kings have much less control, and many have handed over their powers to a parliament elected by the people. There are still some powerful kings in Asia and Africa.

Wow!
Louis XIV's palace at Versailles, outside Paris, is almost half a kilometre long and has around 1,300 rooms.

▲ King Solomon

Solomon ruled over Israel about 1,000 years before the birth of Jesus Christ. He was a wise king and also a great builder. He ordered the building of the Temple in the city of Jerusalem.

▼ Beheaded!

Throughout history, people have sometimes turned against their king and tried to get rid of him. Charles I was king of England and Scotland in the 1600s. Although he lost a civil war in Britain, Charles still refused to give up his powers. He was finally beheaded in London on January 31, 1649.

▼ Macbeth

Macbeth (died 1057) was the Scottish king who became the basis for Shakespeare's tragedy *Macbeth*. He was general to Duncan I and siezed the Scottish throne in 1040. However, the real Macbeth killed Duncan in battle, not in his bed as in Shakespeare's famous play.

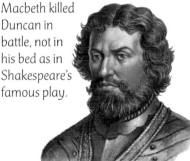

▼ Tudor king

Henry VIII (the Eighth) was king of England from 1509 to 1547. He married six times. His wives were Catherine of Aragon, Anne Boleyn, Jane Seymour, Anne of Cleves, Catherine Howard and Catherine Parr.

Knights

In Europe, between about 1000 and 1500, horseback fighters that were heavily armed became the most important soldiers on the battlefield. They were called knights. Many knights were well rewarded with land and money. They went on to become powerful lords.

chain mail

plate armour

◀ Take that!

Knights liked to take part in mock battles called jousts, to show off their fighting skills. They wore fancy armour and helmets.

▲ Shining armour

In the 1000s, knights wore armour made of small iron rings, called chain mail. Later, they wore plates of metal joined together to cover the whole body. This was plate armour.

sword

◀ Heavy weapons

Knights fought with long spears called lances, and with axes, swords and clubs called maces.

mace

Design your own coat-of-arms

1. Ask an adult to help you. Cut out the shape of a shield from cardboard.
2. Design and colour in your own coat-of-arms. You might want to show things you are interested in, or base the design on your name – a loaf for Baker, say, or a pot for Potter. If your name is Green or Brown, you might want to use that when choosing colours.

▼ Coats-of-arms

It was often hard to tell which knight was which when they were dressed in full armour. So the knights decorated their shields with their family badges, called coats-of-arms.

▲ Code of honour

Knights were expected to behave in an honourable way and to respect ladies. People loved to hear stories about chivalry, the noble manners of knights. In reality, many knights were brutal and selfish.

Lasers

Find out more:
Light • Light at work

Light from a torch spreads out quickly and does not travel very far. Light from a piece of equipment called a laser, however, can be very powerful. It can travel as far as the Moon, in a narrow beam. Lasers have many uses. They can be found in everyday household things such as CD and DVD players, or in factories, hospitals and even concerts.

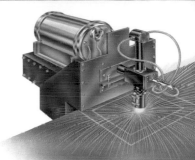

▶ DVD lasers

A DVD (digital versatile disc) uses a tiny laser. This produces a narrow light beam. The beam scans (passes over) the DVDs surface. It 'reads' data (information) such as pictures, music and movies.

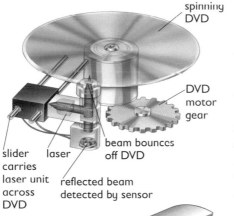

spinning DVD

DVD motor gear

beam bounces off DVD

slider carries laser unit across DVD

laser

reflected beam detected by sensor

▲ Lasers in industry

Laser light can contain enough energy to melt and cut through metal or almost any other substance. Factories that make clothes use computer-controlled lasers. They can cut out one shape in many thicknesses of fabric very quickly and accurately.

rays bounce off the mirrors at both ends, building up energy

mirror

half-mirror

laser light bursts from one end of the crystal

particles bounce around in ruby crystal

▼ Laser surgery

Lasers can be used to perform very delicate surgery, such as eye operations. Laser light does not spread out as normal light does. This means the beam can be very accurately directed and controlled.

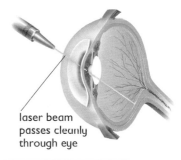

laser beam passes cleanly through eye

▲ How a laser works

Laser light is made by feeding energy, such as ordinary light or electricity, into a substance called the active medium. A rod of ruby crystal is the active medium in this laser. A powerful lamp causes the tiny particles inside the crystal to vibrate. The light builds up and is bounced between mirrors. The energy becomes so strong that it escapes from the laser as an intense beam.

Light is a type of energy that you can see. It is usually produced by a very hot object such as a light bulb or a fire, and heat is released. But there are also 'cold' types of light – for example, the light produced by deep-sea fish or by glow-worms.

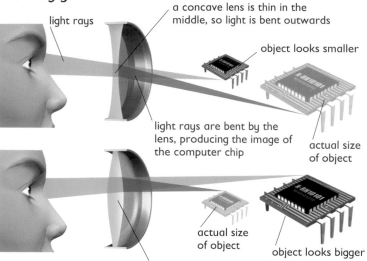

light rays

a concave lens is thin in the middle, so light is bent outwards

object looks smaller

light rays are bent by the lens, producing the image of the computer chip

actual size of object

actual size of object

object looks bigger

a convex lens is thicker in the middle, so light is bent inwards

▲ Using lenses

Lenses are found in many optical (seeing) instruments, such as glasses, cameras and microscopes. The lenses are curved, so when light hits them, the rays bend. This makes an object look bigger or smaller than it really is.

Mirror fun

Take a shiny metal spoon, and look at your reflection in its bowl. Notice how your reflection gets larger and smaller, and even turns upside down! This is because light is working in a similar way to the diagram above, bouncing off the curved surface into your eyes.

▲ Bending light

When a straw is placed in water, it looks as though it is slightly bent. This is because light rays bend when they pass through water. This bending of rays is called refraction.

▼ Mirror images

When light hits a very smooth surface such as a mirror, it reflects (bounces) off the surface. If it hits a mirror at an angle, it is reflected off at exactly the same angle.

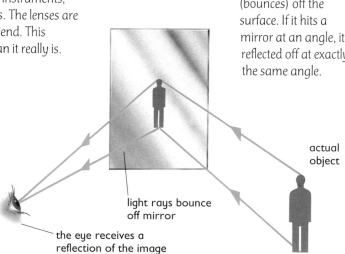

actual object

light rays bounce off mirror

the eye receives a reflection of the image

Light at work

Find out more:
Electricity • Energy • Lasers • Light

Light is essential for all kinds of things.
Plants need the Sun's light for energy. We need
light to grow food to eat and to be able to see
around us. We make our own light
with electricity or gas. In earlier
times, people used fires,
candles or oil for lighting.

◄ Cold light

Some animals produce an unusual kind
of light that gives off no heat. Fireflies and
glow-worms are insects that can make parts
of their bodies glow with light. They do this to
attract a mate. Some plants and
moulds also glow in the dark.

▲ Stop or go?

Train drivers obey signal lights, just
as drivers on the road obey traffic
lights. Train signals show just two
colours – red for stop and green for
go. Road traffic lights have one
extra colour – amber (yellow).

Wow!
Light travels through space at
300,000 kilometres a second. It is
the fastest thing in the Universe!

▼ Light shows

Light can be used to create exciting
displays. Laser light shows are often
used at pop concerts. The beam
from the laser is controlled by a
computer, allowing it to make
patterns in the air.

◄ Watch out!

For at least 2,000 years,
lighthouses have used their
flashing light to warn ships
of danger. Lighthouses are
tall, so that they can be seen
from far away. Each
lighthouse has its own
pattern of light flashes, so
that it can be easily
identified. People used to
work in lighthouses, but
modern ones are automatic.

Lions and tigers

Find out more:
Cats • Mammals

Lions and tigers are the largest big cats, strong and stealthy. Lions form groups called prides; tigers usually live alone. Lions like open grassland; tigers prefer thick forests and swamps. A lion is tawny or sandy brown all over; a tiger has black stripes on a yellow or gold background. Both are endangered – especially tigers.

▼ Pride life

A pride has up to six females with cubs, plus two or three males who form a friendship known as a coalition. The females care for and feed each other's cubs, and work together to chase and ambush prey as big as zebras.

Wow!
The Siberian tiger is the biggest big cat, 3.5 metres from nose to tail, and 300 kilograms in weight.

▼ Jungle king?

Lions rarely live in jungles, but the male lion is very kingly. He rarely hunts, but is first to feed. He defends the pride, patrols his region, roars loudly, and leaves signals such as dung to show the area is occupied.

▼ Troubled cats

Most lions live in central and southern Africa, with a few in northwest India. There are some very rare tigers, including the large Siberian tiger of east Asia, with just a few hundred remaining, and the smaller Sumatran tiger of Southeast Asia, with less than 600 left.

Siberian tiger

Word match

These lion words have got mixed up with their meanings. Can you sort them out?

a. pride
b. cub
c. coalition

1. baby lion or tiger
2. friendly males
3. group of lions

answers
a3 b1 c2

Lizards

Lizards range from tiny geckos to huge monitors as big as crocodiles. They form the largest group of reptiles and most of the 4,500 kinds live in tropical forests. There are also gila monsters in North American deserts, sand skinks in dunes, water-dragons in swamps and house geckos in people's homes. Most eat insects, worms and slugs but some feast on fruits.

Wow!

The slow-worm is not a worm and not always slow – it is a lizard without legs and it can wriggle quite quickly.

▼ Lots of lizards

Monitors are big and strong and catch larger animals such as rats, rabbits, fish, birds and eggs. Like most lizards they have scaly skin, four sprawling legs, four or five sharp-clawed toes on each foot, a long whippy tail, big eyes, and a tongue that flicks out to pick up smells in the air.

▲ Poke out that tongue

When in danger, many lizards hiss, puff themselves up, and perhaps rear up or strike with their claws. Australia's blue-tongued skink also pokes out its bright blue tongue!

the flying lizard of Southeast Asia can extend flaps of skin along its sides, to escape enemies by gliding down from a tree

the Nile monitor of Africa eats a range of food, from crabs to carrion, and is an expert swimmer

Gould's goanna from Australia is about 1.5 metres long and is also called the sand monitor

the Komodo dragon of Southeast Asia, the biggest lizard at 3 metres long, can catch wild pigs and deer

Machines

All machines do work for us. Door handles, can openers and wheelbarrows are simple kinds of machine. Computers, printing presses and motor cars are large complicated machines. All these machines help us each day by letting us do different jobs more quickly and easily.

▼ Heavy loads

We use a wheelbarrow to move a load that is too heavy or large to lift by hand. It is a simple example of a lever. Levers help you to lift heavy weights without using a lot of effort. You move one end of a lever in order to lift a heavy load at the other end.

▶ In the home

Everyday machines such as vacuum cleaners, electric kettles, food processors and dishwashers help us to clean, cook and wash up more quickly.

vacuum cleaner

▶ Cranes

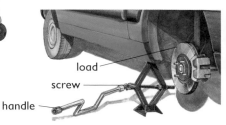

You can see cranes on building sites, in factories and in docks. We use cranes to lift and move heavy loads. A crane is a type of pulley, which is a simple machine made up of a wheel with a rope over it. You pull on one end of the rope to lift a heavy load attached to the other end.

▼ Jet power

A jet engine is a very powerful machine. Large passenger aircraft have three or four jet engines. A stream of gases shoots out of the back of the engine and pushes the aircraft forwards through the air.

air rushes in

hot gases leave the back of the engine

a mixture of air and fuel burn

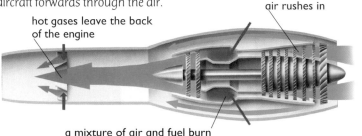

load

screw

handle

▲ Simple jack

A jack is made up of two kinds of simple machine: a lever and a screw. By moving the jack's handle, or lever, you turn the screw and lift up a heavy load such as a car. We use a jack when taking off an old car tyre or putting on a new one.

Machines in history

the *Gutenberg* Press

▲ Printing machine

This printing press was made in Germany about 550 years ago. The printer used it to make many copies of the same page of a book.

From the 1700s onwards, people started to use steam-powered machines to do their work. The first steam engine was made to pump water out of a tin mine in Cornwall, England. Later, steam engines were used to provide power for hundreds of machines, from weaving looms and spinning wheels to cars and ships.

▶ Archimedes' screw

This 'Archimedean screw' is named after the ancient Greek inventor, Archimedes (c. 287–212). Water fills the air pockets between the twists and travels upwards until it reaches the top. For thousands of years, it has been used to lift water from rivers to irrigate (bring water to) fields where crops grow.

Wow!

The pyramids in Egypt were built about 4,500 years ago from huge blocks of stone. But no one really knows what machines were used to haul them into place.

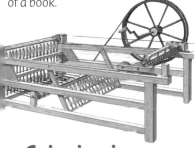

▲ Spinning jenny

This machine is called a spinning jenny. It is a kind of spinning wheel that spins lots of cotton threads at the same time. Before this machine was invented in 1764, each spinning wheel could only spin one thread at a time. In the cotton factories, spinning jennies allowed the spinners to produce enough cotton thread to keep the cotton weavers busy at work.

▼ Motor cars

The motor car is one of the world's most popular machines. One of the first proper motor cars was this three-wheeled vehicle. It was built in 1886 by a German named Karl Benz. Its engine was powered by gas.

Motorwagen, built by Karl Benz

Magnets

Some metals are magnetic. 'Magnetic' means a metal can be attracted by a magnet or made into a magnet. This is how the compass works – it uses a magnetic needle that always swings to point north. Magnetism can also be produced by an electric circuit. This is useful because it can be switched on and off as needed.

▲ Curved magnets

The most common magnets are shaped like a horseshoe. The magnetic field is strongest between the arms of the horseshoe. Because of this magnetic field, a piece of iron or steel placed across the arms will stick to them.

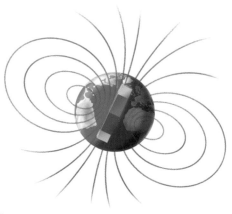

▲ Giant magnets

An 'electromagnet' is produced when electricity is passed through a coil of wire. It is only magnetic while the power is switched on. These magnets are used in industry to handle heavy steel objects.

Word box

electric circuit
a flow of electricity

magnetic field
area around a magnet where there is a magnetic force

Make a compass

You can easily make a simple compass. Take a small bar magnet (a straight magnet) and fix it to a piece of wood with sticky tape. Now float the wood in a dish of water and watch as the magnet slowly turns to point north and south. You can check that it is working properly with an ordinary magnetic compass.

▲ North and south

Deep down at the centre of the Earth is an enormous mass of iron. This acts as a huge magnet, which gives the Earth its magnetic field. The magnetic poles are not exactly at the North and South Poles. Also, they shift slightly every year.

◀ Pointing north

A compass is a tiny magnet, shaped like a needle and balanced so it can move easily. It turns to line itself up with the Earth's magnetic field, pointing to magnetic north. The invention of the compass was very important to early explorers.

Mammals

Bats and bears, monkeys and moles, wallabies and whales – all these animals are mammals.
Humans are mammals, so are many of the animals we see around us – our pet cats and dogs, and farm animals such as sheep and cows. Mammals are warm-blooded animals with a skeleton and most have fur or hair.

dolphin

▲ Odd mammals

The giant anteater of South America is a very strange-looking mammal. It eats only ants or termites, and its sharp claws are ideal for breaking into insect nests. The anteater's tongue extends to a length of 60 centimetres!

◄ Keeping warm

Whales, dolphins and porpoises are mammals that live in the water. Unlike most mammals, they do not have fur or hair. Instead, they have a layer of fat under the skin to keep their bodies warm.

▼ The smallest

One of the smallest mammals is a bat. It is called Kitti's hog-nosed bat and is less than 2 centimetres long – about the same size as a bumble bee.

◄ Brainy!

Mammals have better developed brains than most other animal groups. The most intelligent mammals, after humans, are apes and monkeys. Some chimpanzees use sticks as tools to catch termites!

▼ Comparing size

There are about 4,500 different types of mammal. The biggest living mammal, the blue whale, is shown to scale here with some other mammals. Even the biggest land mammal, the elephant, looks tiny next to the blue whale.

blue whale up to 30 metres long

giraffe 5.5 metres tall

human 1.7 metres tall

brown bear 2.4 metres tall

African elephant 3.3 metres tall

Mammals are the only animals that feed their young on milk. Many young mammals are born with hair or fur and they are cared for by their parents afterwards. A chimpanzee baby, for example, stays with its mother until it is about six years old.

▼ Living in a pouch

Kangaroos and koalas belong to a group of mammals called marsupials. They give birth to tiny, undeveloped babies. The babies crawl to a pouch on their mother's front. They stay there for about eight months, drinking their mother's milk until they are fully developed.

pouch entrance

1. newborn kangaroo crawls to its mother's pouch

2. in the pouch, the baby drinks its mother's milk

duck-billed platypus

▲ Biggest baby

The biggest mammal of all, the blue whale, also gives birth to the biggest baby. When it is born, the blue whale calf is already 6 to 8 metres long. Its mother's milk is rich, which helps the baby to grow quickly.

▲ Laying eggs

A few mammals lay eggs from which their young hatch. These mammals live in Australia and New Guinea. The duck-billed platypus is one of them. Its baby licks milk off its mother's belly.

the young kangaroo (joey) stays in the pouch until quite large, and covered in fur

▼ Caring for young

Most mammals care for their young for some time after they are born. Many young, like these cheetah cubs, rely on their mother for food and protection. They also learn how to hunt and look after themselves in the wild.

Word box

pouch
a pocket of skin

undeveloped
not fully-grown

Maps

We use maps to find our way from place to place. Maps also give us information about an area of land – a map can tell you where hills and rivers are, where roads and railways run, which countries make up a continent or where to find a certain street in a big city.

Wow!
One of the world's first maps was carved onto a clay tablet in the ancient city of Babylon 4,500 years ago.

▲ Maps for walkers

Hill-walkers use maps that show the physical features of the land, such as hills, valleys, rivers and lakes. Some physical maps also show the route of public footpaths, cycle tracks and nature trails.

▼ Matching maps

Here are two maps of Africa. The one on the right is a political map, it shows the different country boundaries. The one shown below is a physical map. It shows the natural features of the land, such as forests, mountains and rivers.

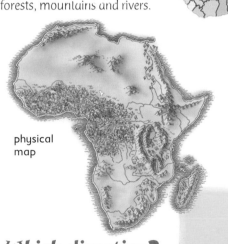

physical map

political map

▲ GPS maps

Drivers use Global Positioning System (GPS) maps to get directions to different locations. GPS is a navigation system based on satelites which transmit signals to recievers that create maps the driver can use for navigation.

▼ Which direction?

Walkers, climbers, sailors and pilots need to know which direction they are travelling in before they can use a map properly. They find out with the help of a magnetic compass. It has a small needle that always points in the direction of north.

Word box

boundary
a place where one country's land ends and the next country's land begins

magnetic
points to North at one end and South at the other

tablet
a flat piece of a material such as wood or stone

Marsupials

The koala bear is not a real bear, the banded anteater is not a real anteater and the Tasmanian devil is not a real devil. In fact, they are all marsupials. Most mother marsupials have a pouch or pocket of skin on the front of their body. Their tiny babies stay there for weeks, feeding on their mother's milk until they grow strong enough to look after themselves.

> ### Word box
>
> **carnivore**
> an animal that mainly eats the meat of other animals
>
> **scavenge**
> to search for bits and pieces of left-over food, such as the remains of other animals' meals

▲ Numbat

Many marsupials in Australia are similar to other mammals elsewhere. The numbat, or banded anteater, is a marsupial version of the anteater. There are also marsupial rats, mice and shrews, marsupial moles and marsupial cats, called quolls.

▼ Koala

Cuddly-looking koalas live in eucalyptus or gum trees and eat only their leaves. Their close marsupial cousins are wombats, which live in underground tunnels. Other marsupials include kangaroos, wallabies, possums, gliders, bandicoots and bilbies.

▼ Tasmanian devil

The largest marsupial carnivore, the 'devil', has very powerful jaws and teeth, which can even crush bones. It wails and screeches at night, to find a mate or warn other devils to stay away. The female's pouch is a flap of skin and opens 'backwards' towards her tail.

▼ Virginia opossum

Most marsupials live in Australia, some live in Southeast Asia, and a few live in South America. Only the Virginia opossum has spread to North America. It makes its den near people's homes and eats left-over foods.

babies in mother's pouch

Materials

Wool, paper, copper, steel, concrete and plastic – all of these are materials. We use materials to make things. We choose the right material for the right thing. For example, a ball is not made out of glass or paper because they are not suitable materials. Instead we choose a material, such as rubber, because it is stretchy and bouncy.

sunglasses

pegs

▲ Useful steel

Stainless steel is a very useful material because it does not rust easily. At a steelworks, the metal is heated to a high temperature and then formed into different shapes.

▼ Plants and animals

Many of the materials that we use every day come from plants or animals.

wood, paper and rubber come from trees

the wool for a warm sweater comes from sheep or goats

the cotton to make a t-shirt comes from cotton plants

▲ Useful plastic

Look around and count how many plastic things you can see. The answer is probably 'lots'. Plastic is one of our most useful materials because we can make it into many different shapes. Plastic can be something clear or coloured; it can bend and stretch and be hard or soft. Most plastic is made from petroleum.

Wow!

A strong but lightweight metal called magnesium is found in seawater – we use it to make parts for cars and planes.

Word box

petroleum
a thick oil found under the ground or under the sea-bed

space shuttle
a spacecraft that can be used again and again

▶ Protective materials

The space shuttle becomes very, very hot when it returns to the Earth from space. The underneath part is covered with special tiles made from ceramic, a mixture of baked clay and other materials. The tiles protect the shuttle from the extreme heat.

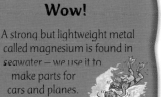

shuttle re-entering Earth's atmosphere

Materials in nature

Find out more:
Conservation • Recycling

Every substance is made from material, or a combination of materials. The first materials used were natural. People wove fibres, built houses from straw and wood, and shaped stones and metals. We still use these materials today, but we must conserve and recycle them as much as we can, so they do not run out.

▼ Silk spinners

Silk is a strong, shiny fibre that is used to make cloth. It is made from the cocoons of caterpillars called silkworms. To make the cocoon, the silkworm produces a liquid that hardens into silk threads. At the same time it gives off a gum which sticks the threads of silk together.

silkworm

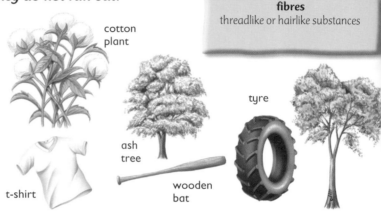

cotton plant

t-shirt

ash tree

wooden bat

tyre

rubber tree

▲ Using nature

A large number of everyday materials are made from plants, such as cotton, wood and rubber. Some everyday items are shown here, next to the plant that was used to make them.

▶ Simple straw

Natural materials such as straw have been used to build houses since ancient times. Straw consists of dried stems of grasses such as wheat, oats and barley. This Chinese hut has a thatched roof made of straw and is held up with poles and beams of wood.

thatched roof

Materials today

Many materials we use today are natural, but synthetic (chemically made) ones are also very common. Plastic, steel and glass are examples of synthetic materials. Sometimes materials can be a mixture of both natural and synthetic – these are often used to make clothing.

main body of the car made from carbon fibre

▶ Strong and light

The main body of a racing car is made from carbon fibre. Carbon fibres are silky threads of pure carbon that are used to reinforce (strengthen) plastics. This mixture creates a light but very strong material.

▼ Body-builder

Titanium is a metal stronger than steel but half its weight. Also, it doesn't wear away easily. It is used in aircraft and spacecraft. Titanium and plastic parts also replace human body parts, such as knees and hips, when they wear out.

▲ Mixing it up

Plastics can be mixed with natural fibres to make strong fabrics for sails, parachutes and hot-air balloons. Nylon, acrylic and polyester are types of plastic which are spun together with cotton or wool.

Wow!
Glass can be specially treated so that it becomes extra tough – strong enough to be made into bulletproof windows!

◀ Versatile plastic

Plastics are synthetic materials made mainly from the substances in petroleum, or crude oil. They can be made into different shapes by melting them or by changing them chemically. There are many kinds of plastics, all of which are usually strong, waterproof and long-lasting.

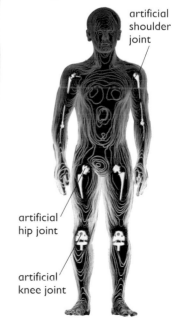

artificial shoulder joint

artificial hip joint

artificial knee joint

Measuring

Measuring helps you find the answer to questions such as 'How tall am I? How much do I weigh?' We use measurements all the time – in the kitchen, in shops, in the classroom, on a building site. We use many different tools to help us measure, such as scales and tape measures, clocks and thermometers, rulers and metre sticks.

▶ Hot and cold

A thermometer tells you how hot or cold something is – it measures temperature. A scale is marked along the side of the thermometer. Temperature is measured in degrees Celsius (°C) or Fahrenheit (°F).

Length and weight

This table explains units of length and weight. The units are sometimes shortened, or abbreviated, to save time and space. For example, mm is short for millimetre, and kg is short for kilogram.

Units of length
10 millimetres (mm) = 1 centimetre (cm)
100 cm = 1 metre (m)
1,000 m = 1 kilometre (km)

Units of weight
1,000 milligrams (mg) = 1 gram (g)
1,000 g = 1 kilogram (kg)
1,000 kg = 1 tonne (t)

▲ Telling the time

A clock tells you what time it is. We measure time in hours, minutes and seconds. The time of day is split into morning and afternoon – a.m. stands for morning and p.m. for afternoon.

Word box

scale
a row of steps or marks that are used for measuring something

▶ How long?

We use rulers or tape measures to find out how long something is. Every measurement consists of a number and a unit. If the side of a box measures 10 centimetres in length, then 10 is the number and centimetres (cm for short) is the unit of measurement.

tape measure

▲ How heavy?

Balances and scales help us to find out how heavy something is. The needle on the dial points to the correct weight.

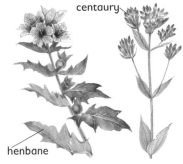

Our body can usually look after itself very well, but sometimes things go wrong. Some of the thousands of chemicals in the body may get out of balance. Perhaps a part wears out. Germs may attack and cause disease. Medicines are designed to put these things right and to make us feel better.

▲ Pills and capsules

Most medicines are swallowed as tablets or capsules. These are specially designed to dissolve properly in the stomach so they will be absorbed, or taken into your body. They are made in all kinds of colours, so people do not mix them up.

Word box

anaesthetic
a drug that takes away any feeling, so that no pain is felt during an operation

antibiotics
medicines used to treat illnesses caused by bacteria

vaccination
medicine given to a person to stop them getting a harmful disease

centaury

henbane

▲ Nature's cures

Plants have been used as medicines for thousands of years. Some, like henbane, can be very poisonous unless they are used in tiny amounts. Bitter-tasting centaury is still used as a tonic and to reduce fevers.

▼ Self-protection

People are vaccinated by being given doses of a dead or harmless germ. The body thinks that these are dangerous, so it produces lots of substances called antibodies. These prevent you from getting the real disease later on.

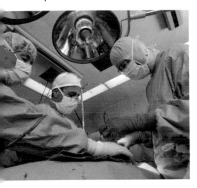

▲ Body repair

Doctors called surgeons repair damage and remove diseased parts during operations. The invention of substances called anaesthetics meant that people could have operations without pain. Heart and liver transplants are among the most complicated types of surgery.

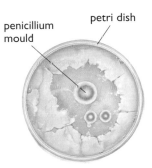
penicillium mould

petri dish

▲ Bacteria-killer

Penicillin is an antibiotic that has saved the lives of millions of people. It first came from a mould – like the blue mould seen on stale bread. This was accidentally found to be able to kill bacteria.

Medicine in history

Find out more:
Medicine • Science

Doctors have been treating ill people for thousands of years, but with much less knowledge than doctors today. Some of them discovered useful plants for medicines, but many of the potions they mixed up did not help their patients at all. Great advances in medical knowledge came in the 1600s, and by the 1800s and 1900s many lives were saved.

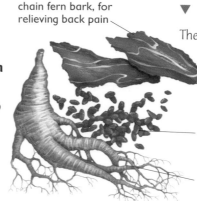

▼ Old remedies

chain fern bark, for relieving back pain

These Chinese medicines have been used for hundreds of years, and are still in use today.

wolfberry, for improving eyesight

ginseng, a root used to stimulate the body

▲ Florence Nightingale

In the 1850s, Florence Nightingale became famous for her care of wounded British soldiers. Horrified by poor standards in hospitals, she devoted her life to improving them and set up nurse training schools.

Lister's antiseptic spray

◄ Safe operations

In 1867, an English surgeon called Joseph Lister worked out how to kill germs during operations. He used a disinfectant spray to kill germs in the air and saved many lives.

▲ Understanding germs

A French scientist called Louis Pasteur, who lived from 1822 to 1895, discovered bacteria (germs) caused disease.

Metals

Find out more:
Iron Age • Materials • Recycling

Metals are mostly shiny, strong materials that are solid at room temperature. They can be hammered into different shapes. They can also be shaped by being melted and poured into a mould. Metals have been used since earliest times and have allowed modern civilization to develop.

▲ Save and reuse

It is mostly cheaper and less wasteful to reuse metal than to dig up more ore and process it. Metals such as old drinks cans, cars and other waste can be recycled (reused). They are crushed into blocks and sent off to be melted down again.

Word scramble

Unscramble these words to find the names of different kinds of metal or alloy:

a. NIRO

b. ZENORB

c. POPERC

d. NIT

answers
a. iron b. bronze c. copper
d. tin

Word box

alloy
a mixture of metals, or a metal and a non-metal

ore
a mixture of different substances, of which metal is one

▲ Metal money

Coins are stamped out of strips of metal such as copper, silver or mixtures of metals called alloys. Coins are heavy and difficult to handle, so paper notes are used for large amounts of money.

▼ Old iron bridge

The world's first cast-iron bridge was built in 1779. It spans the Severn Gorge at Ironbridge, Shropshire, England. Cast-iron is a hard and brittle form of iron. It is made by putting molten (melted) iron into moulds and allowing it to harden.

► The age of bronze

Bronze is an alloy (mix) of copper and tin. Copper is a very soft metal, but adding tin makes it much harder and stronger. This was discovered thousands of years ago, during the Bronze Age, when people made bronze axes that still survive today.

Mice are smaller than rats – otherwise there is little difference between them. All are rodents, with long incisor teeth for nibbling and nipping. Most eat plant foods such as seeds, fruits and roots. They have big eyes and ears, long whiskers and a long tail. They move quickly to escape enemies and breed quickly to keep up their numbers.

mouse

▲ Friendly or harmful?

Mice and rats can be bred and raised as friendly pets. Others are used in scientific research. Wild rats and mice can cause damage to buildings and spread diseases.

Word box

scientific research
experiments that are carried out to find out more about something

sewage
human waste that is carried away in drains

Make some whiskers!

Mice and rats use whiskers to feel in the dark – you can too!

1. Ask an adult to help. Cut a straight line from the edge of a paper plate to its centre. Roll the plate into a cone shape.
2. Stick a few straws onto either side of the cone.
3. Thread some elastic through two tiny holes at the wide end of your cone, to hold the whiskers on your nose.
Now you have your very own mouse whiskers!

▶ Desert-dweller

Like a tiny kangaroo, the jerboa hops at great speed across the sand of the Sahara Desert, using its long tail for balance. Like most rats and mice it hides by day in a burrow and comes out at night to feed.

▲ Country house

The tiny harvest mouse lives in the countryside. Its nest is the size and shape of a tennis ball. The female gives birth to more than ten babies.

Wow!

The house mouse is found in more places around the world than any other animal.

▶ Water rats

Many rats can swim well. A water rat is often just a brown rat searching for fish or crabs (or gobbling up sewage). The Australian water rat is a large rat, with a head and body 35 centimetres long. It dives well and eats frogs, fish, lizards, snakes, other rats and mice, waterbirds and even fish-catching bats.

Australian water rat

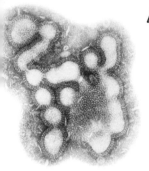

A microscope lets us see tiny things that we cannot see with our own eyes, such as bacteria. It works by using groups of lenses. Lenses are made from see-through materials and are shaped to make things larger or clearer for us. Electron microscopes allow us to see even smaller things, such as viruses. Studying their structure helps us produce treatments for the diseases they cause.

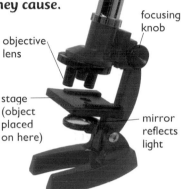

eyepiece

focusing knob

objective lens

stage (object placed on here)

mirror reflects light

▲ The flu virus

This is the flu virus, viewed under an electron microscope. Chemicals, called fixatives, preserve the viruses so that they are not smashed by the microscope's electron beam. This allows the virus to be examined.

Word box

virus
the simplest form of life; viruses live inside a cell, so the body finds it hard to attack them

▼ 3D pictures

This piece of hair is being viewed under a binocular microscope. A binocular microscope has two eyepieces and two objective lenses. It gives a 3D view with depth.

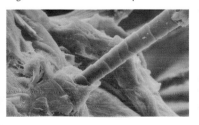

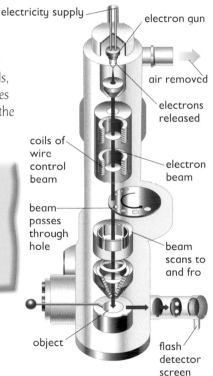

electricity supply

electron gun

air removed

electrons released

coils of wire control beam

electron beam

beam passes through hole

beam scans to and fro

object

flash detector screen

▲ Particle power

An electron microscope is very powerful. It can magnify an object (make it look larger) by up to a million times. It works by firing special particles called electrons at the object. The electrons bounce off the object onto a viewing screen.

▲ Using lenses

'Compound optical' microscopes use two or more lenses to make images up to 2,000 times bigger. An objective lens bends light rays to enlarge the object. An eyepiece lens then lets you see the final image.

Make a microscope

Use a magnifying glass to look at something small. Note how big the glass makes it look. Now use another magnifying glass, held under the first. The image looks even bigger. As you move the lenses up and down the size of the image changes. It will become sharp or blurred. This is what happens inside a microscope as the views are focused.

There are millions of creatures all around us that we cannot see – they are too small. We need a microscope to view this tiny world. Some of these micro-living things are true animals, but very small. Others are made of just one living unit or 'cell' each, and they often have both animal and plant features. These are not true animals. They are known as protists.

▼ Round animals

The rotifer has a circle of micro-hairs around its mouth end, like a crown. The hairs wave and filter any edible bits from the water and pass them into its vase-shaped body. This tiny creature is also called the 'wheel-animacule'.

▲ Water-bears

Big tardigrades or water-bears are just about large enough for us to see, with their tubby bodies and stubby limbs. They live in water and damp places like moss. These animals can survive being dried out, frozen or almost boiled.

▶ Amoeba

Like most protists, the amoeba lives in water. It is a single cell, flexible and baglike, and oozes along in pond mud. It catches even smaller living things, such as bacteria, by extending bloblike 'arms' around them or simply flowing over them.

Word box

cell
a self-contained unit of life –
a protist is just one cell

silica
a natural substance or
mineral that forms sand, glass,
and the shells of some
living things

tentacle
a long, slim, bendy body part

▲ Shrimp cousins

Copepods are tiny cousins of shrimps and crabs. They swim by waving their very long antennae (feelers), and swarm in their billions. Their bristly front limbs filter food particles from sea water. Copepods are food for bigger ocean animals such as baby fish.

▼ Swarming seas

A drop of sea water contains thousands of tiny living things. Heliozoans are protists with a central shell-like chamber made of silica. Their long, thin, starlike 'arms' catch even smaller prey. Foraminiferan protists look like micro-snails and also have a hard-shelled central part with flexible tentacles.

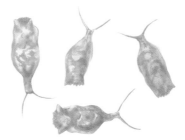

Middle Ages

The period known in Europe as the Middle Ages lasted about 1,000 years. It was given that name because it lay in-between the ancient world and the modern age. The ancient world ended with the fall of the Roman Empire in AD476. The modern world began with the great voyages of exploration and scientific discoveries of the late 1400s and 1500s.

▶ Holy journeys

Religious people who went on journeys to holy places were called pilgrims. Places of pilgrimage included Jerusalem, Rome and Canterbury in England. The pilgrims wore special badges to show which sites they had visited.

▲ A life of toil

In the Middle Ages farm workers, called serfs, were forced to work for the local lord in exchange for some of the food they grew. They were not free to move away from their village.

pilgrims

▲ In praise of God

By the 1100s, most Europeans were Christians. Many cathedrals were built at this time, including this one at Chartres in France, built between 1195 and 1220.

Make a quill

During the Middle Ages, people used feathers called quills as pens. Next time you find a big feather, cut the end like a nib, dip it in some ink and use it to write your name.

▶ Fine words

Europeans did not learn how to print until the end of the Middle Ages. Before that, books were carefully copied out by hand. Words in religious books were beautifully written and decorated with pictures and patterns.

Migrating animals

Find out more:
Bird life • Whales

Every spring in Europe, swallows and swifts appear like magic, and in North America, monarch butterflies do the same. These are migrants. They make long journeys, usually to the same place and back again each year. They go to the best place for finding food or raising their young, usually somewhere warmer.

grey whale migration route

Wow!

The Arctic tern travels further than any other bird. It has two summers each year, in the Arctic and Antarctic — a return trip of 30,000 kilometres.

▶ Birds

Birds migrate farther than any other animal. Many kinds, from geese to buntings, leave Europe, central Asia and North America in spring for the Arctic summer, then return south in autumn. Swallows spend the winter in Africa and come to Europe for the summer.

▼ Reptiles

Sea turtles, such as green turtles, are wandering migrants that roam the oceans. Every two or three years they may swim about 1,000 kilometres to the beaches where they hatched, to lay their own eggs.

▲ Mammals

Many great whales, such as greys, swim from warm tropical waters to the far north or south, for the brief summer when food is plentiful.

◀ Insects

Monarch butterflies spend the winter crowded in roosts in south-west North America. In spring they head north to Canada, breeding as they go. Their 'grandchild' butterflies come back in autumn.

Word box

roost
a resting or sleeping place, usually for flying animals such as birds, bats and insects

tundra
treeless land around the Arctic Ocean, with low bushes and mossy bogs, covered in snow in winter

Minerals

When metals and other useful materials are dug out of the ground, they are in the form of minerals.
Many minerals are formed and reformed when molten rock (magma) pushes up from below the Earth's crust. It then cools and becomes solid. Minerals are mined (taken from the Earth) by digging deep holes, or they are taken from riverbeds and seabeds.

◄ Crystal clear

Minerals often form as crystals. This is when minerals cool slowly. Quartz is a compound of silicon and oxygen. Quartz has many uses, such as measuring time in watches and clocks.

quartz
crystal

► Deep in the soil

Soil contains minerals which supply nutrients (goodness) to green plants, helping them grow. The plants take in, or absorb, these minerals through their roots.

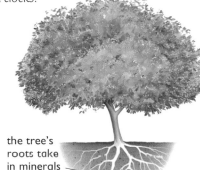

the tree's roots take in minerals from the soil

▲ Rainbow colours

Some minerals have bright colours and are sometimes used as pigments (coloured substances) to give paints, dyes and inks their colour. Iron oxide, for example, gives the colours red and yellow.

Word box

ceramics
objects shaped from clay that have been baked at a high temperature

compound
substance containing more than one type of element

◄ Clay for pots

Clay is used for making pots, bricks and other ceramics. It is found in most types of soil, and is made up of a group of minerals called silicates. Clay is also used in farming – it helps soil to keep in the minerals that plants need to grow (see 'Deep in the soil').

Money and trade

We use money to buy things – from chocolate bars to computers, from toys to train tickets. Money can be in the form of paper notes or metal coins. We can also pay for something by writing a cheque or using a credit card.

► The first coins

The world's first coins were made about 2,500 years ago in a country called Lydia (part of modern Turkey). The coins, which were a mixture of gold and silver, had a design stamped on the front and back.

Word box

cash
coins and paper money

cheque
a piece of paper on which someone writes to tell a bank to pay out money from their bank account

credit card
a card that lets you buy something now but pay for it at a later date

◄ Cash machines

You can collect money from a cashpoint machine. You insert a special card into the machine and key in your personal number. The machine, which is connected to your bank, gives you an amount of cash. The same amount is then taken out of your bank account.

▼ Making money

Money is made in a special factory called a mint. In the past, coins were made from gold, silver and other expensive metals. Modern coins are made from a mixture of metals such as zinc, nickel and copper.

► Long distance trade

In the ancient world, people traded over long distances. Egyptian ships carried goods from Crete, Arabia and East Africa to towns up and down the river Nile. The ships were propelled by sail and oar power.

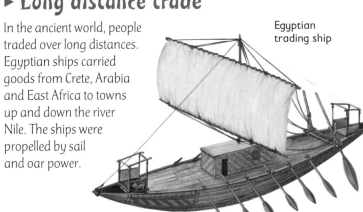

Egyptian trading ship

Mongol Empire

The rolling grasslands of eastern Europe and Asia are called steppes. In ancient times and during the Middle Ages, most of the people living there were nomads. They moved across the land with their herds and flocks, living in tents rather than towns. Some of the fiercest warriors came from the steppes of Mongolia.

▶ Riders of the steppes

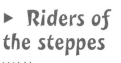

Wild horses were first tamed on the grasslands. The peoples of the steppes were all expert riders.

▲ Into China

In 1211, the Mongols crossed the Great Wall and invaded northern China. Kublai Khan, grandson of Temujin, became the Chinese emperor in 1271.

▼ Ak Sarai Palace

Timur the Lame (1336 to 1405) ruled over Samarkand, a city in Uzbekistan, and conquered lands stretching from Russia to India. The Ak Sarai Palace was built for him and its ruins still stand today.

▼ Genghis Khan

Temujin lived from about 1162 to 1227. He became the ruler of the Mongols when he was 44 and was soon leading his warriors into battle across Asia and eastern Europe. He became known as Genghis Khan, or 'mighty ruler'.

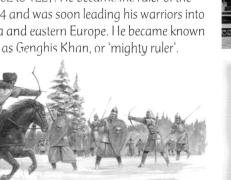

Word box

steppes
dry grasslands, usually without trees, found in Asia and Eastern Europe

Monkeys

Find out more:
Apes • Mammals

Most monkeys are bright-eyed, long-tailed, clever, day-active tree-dwellers with grasping hands and feet. They live in troops, communicate with noisy whoops and chattering, and eat plant foods such as flowers, fruits, berries and shoots. There are 240 different kinds of monkey.

▼ White-cheeked

Over 20 kinds of small monkeys live in Central and South America. Many have long, silky fur, and claws rather than fingernails and toenails. Mangabeys sleep and spend nearly all their time in the trees. Troops of about 10 to 30 live together and are extremely noisy, constantly chattering across the treetops.

white-cheeked
mangabey

Word scramble

Unscramble these words to find the names of five types of monkeys:

**a. EQUACAM
b. LIRDNALM
c. RELSQURI YEKNOM
d. REDISP YEKNOM
e. BUSCOLO**

answers
a. macaque b. mandrill
c. squirrel monkey
d. spider monkey e. colobus

▲ Hungry monkey

When the weather is hot and dry, and there is little else to eat, a baboon can survive on a diet of grass for many weeks. Hungry baboons will eat anything. This baboon finds a meal by picking out seeds and undigested plant matter from elephant dung.

▶ Vervets

Vervets range widely across Africa. They climb well, run fast and swim rapidly. They live in grassland, scrub and forest. Vervets eat plants, small animals and insects.

▶ Ring-tailed lemurs

Monkeys are in the primate group of mammals, along with apes and prosimians — 80 kinds of lemurs, bushbabies, pottos, lorises and tarsiers. These are mostly small tree-dwellers. Lemurs, such as this ring-tailed lemur, are found only on Madagascar, an island east of Africa.

Moon

The Moon is our closest neighbour – it is nearer to the Earth than any other object in space. The Moon travels around the Earth and takes about one month to make a complete journey. The Moon seems to be shining because it reflects light from the Sun.

◀ Close up

This is a close-up view of the Moon taken from space. The darker patches are plains, called maria. The word 'maria' means seas, but there is no water on the Moon. The lighter areas are highlands. There are also lots of craters on the surface of the Moon.

▲ In the shadows

When the Moon passes into the Earth's shadow, it is called a lunar (Moon) eclipse. The Moon grows darker and redder. A solar (Sun) eclipse is when the Moon passes between the Earth and the Sun, blocking the Sun's light (above).

▼ Changing shape

The Moon seems to change shape from day to day. It takes about 29 days to pass through all these changes, which we call phases. Sometimes we see just a tiny slice of the Moon – this is because the side of the Moon facing us is in darkness.

New Moon

Crescent Moon

First Quarter

Gibbous Moon

Full Moon

▶ Moon walk

The *Apollo 11* spacecraft landed on the Moon on July 20, 1969. Two astronauts stepped onto the Moon's surface. Several *Apollo* Missions have landed since then.

Word box

crater
a dent in the ground

plain
a wide, flat area

Mountains

Find out more:
Rocks • Rocks and minerals

Sharp peaks covered with ice and snow, long steep slopes, rivers that flow quickly, rocky valleys – these are just some of the sights you might see in the mountains. A mountain is usually much higher than the land around it. When several mountains are grouped together they form a mountain range. The Alps in Europe are an example of this.

▼ Mountain forms

There are three main ways in which mountains are formed.

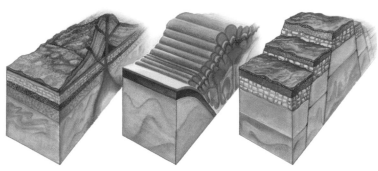

1. volcanoes form mountains when lava gushes out and hardens

2. layers of rocks are forced up into 'folds'

3. rocks may crack, causing faults, allowing large areas of rock to be pushed up

Word scramble

Unscramble these words to find the names of five large mountain ranges:

a. SPAL
b. SKICORE
c. NASED
d. ASLAMYAIH
e. SALTA

answers
a.Alps b. Rockies c.Andes
d.Himalayas e.Atlas

▲ Mountain range

A group of mountain ranges called the Alps stretches across parts of France, Italy, Switzerland and Austria. The Alps are very popular for winter sports, such as skiing.

▼ Mountain life

This mountain goat has a thick coat to keep it warm, and feet that are good for climbing in rocky places.

▼ The Rockies

The Rocky Mountains run for about 4,800 kilometres down the west coast of North America, Alaska and Canada. There are several national parks and ski resorts in the spectacular scenery.

▼ Top of the world

For hundreds of years people have enjoyed climbing mountains. In 1953 for the first time, two climbers reached the top of the world's highest mountain, Mount Everest, in Asia. They were Edmund Hillary from New Zealand, and Tenzing Norgay, his guide.

Mountains: animals

Mountains are harsh, dangerous places, as snowstorms howl across icy cliffs. Yet some animals are specialized to survive here. Mountain creatures need warm coverings of thick fur or feathers, and feet with strong grips for slippery rocks. Many larger animals migrate or journey higher in summer, as the ice melts and plants grow in alpine meadows. They travel back down to the sheltered lower forests for winter.

▼ Lammergeier

Great birds of prey seek old, sick or injured animals to eat. The lammergeier, a vulture of Europe, Africa and Asia, takes an animal bone up high. It drops it onto a rock, to break it open so it can eat the soft marrow inside.

▲ Mountain lion

The mountain lion, also called the puma or cougar, is not a real lion – but is a similar colour. It once thrived in many habitats throughout the Americas. But hunting by people drove it to remote mountains. This cat eats a variety of prey, from rabbits to mountain goats, sheep and deer.

▼ Chilly chinchilla

Many mountain animals have become rare, killed for the thick fur that keeps them warm on the cold heights. The chinchilla, a plant-eating rodent of the Andes Mountains, in South America, is still rare in the wild. But it is also bred for its fur, and as a soft, cuddly pet.

▲ Apollo butterfly

The apollo of Europe and Asia can flap strongly in the wind to fly at over 3,000 metres – higher than almost any butterfly. It feeds on nectar from alpine flowers. Most mountain insects survive winter as eggs, or hide in cracks in rocks.

Word box

alpine
to do with mountains – Alpine with a capital 'A' is to do with the Alps range of mountains in Europe

marrow
soft, jelly-like substance inside many types of bones

remote
distant

Music and dance

You can hear the sounds of music almost everywhere you go. Music can be a pop song on the radio, a choir singing in church or an orchestra performing. We listen to music to enjoy ourselves and to relax. People dance to music all over the world. Music can be used as part of a ceremony or celebration, to express emotions, to entertain others – or simply to have fun.

Wow!

The Austrian composer Wolfgang Amadeus Mozart composed his first piece of music at the age of five.

▼ Playing music

Music is played on instruments such as the piano, recorder or clarinet. Many children learn to play a musical instrument at school. Can you play any of these instruments?

trumpet

guitar

flute

violin

◄ Traditional dances

In many places around the world, such as this Gambian village, dance steps and music are never written down. They are part of oral and visual tradition. People learn them by following instructions and taking part.

▲ Electronic sounds

Many modern musicians use electronic instruments to create sounds in recording studios. Instruments called synthesizers can copy perfectly the sound of, say, a drum or a guitar.

Word box

float
a vehicle decorated to be in a street parade

orchestra
large group of musicians playing different instruments

► Carnival dances

In Brazil during carnival time. the streets are thronged with parades. People wear brightly coloured costumes and perform a dance called the samba. They compete for prizes for magnificent floats.

Music and dance in history

Stone Age people used to make pipes and whistles from bones and reeds. Drums too have been used for many thousands of years. People danced in honour of the gods or as a thanksgiving for spring or the harvest. Different kinds of music developed across the world at the same time.

▼ Flamenco!

Flamenco music is played in Spain. It includes strummed guitars, singing, shouting and clapping. Dancers strut, whirl and stamp. Flamenco probably began in the 1400s, when the Roma people (gypsies) first arrived in Europe. Over the years it has blended with Arab, Jewish and Spanish musical styles.

▲ Ancient Egypt

Ancient Egyptian musicians played harps, rattles, flutes and bells while dancers performed in temples and at royal feasts.

Wolfgang Amadeus Mozart

Johann Sebastian Bach

▶▲ Great composers

In Europe, a great tradition of music developed. Two of the greatest composers were the German Johann Sebastian Bach, who lived from 1685 to 1750, and the Austrian Wolfgang Amadeus Mozart, who lived from 1756 to 1791.

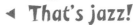

◀ That's jazz!

From the early 1900s, African American musicians played a new kind of music called jazz. Players improvised (created music as they went along), without being bound to a written score. Louis Armstrong (1901–71) was one of the greatest jazz stars.

Native Americans

Find out more:
New World • Wild West

Perhaps as much as 30,000 years ago, hunters from Asia crossed into North America. They were distant relatives of the Native Americans, the first people to live in North, South and Central America. Native American peoples lived by hunting and fishing, and many also became farmers.

birch bark canoe

▲ Travelling light

Around the Great Lakes and rivers of the Midwest, canoes made of birch bark were the best way of travelling.

▼ Plains hunters

Peoples of the Great Plains hunted buffalos which roamed the prairies. Buffalos provided meat and skins for making clothes. People lived in tents called tepees that were also sewn together from buffalo skins.

▲ Troubled times

In the 1800s, more and more settlers of European descent moved into the United States. Europeans called the Native Americans 'Indians'. They stole their land and killed the buffalo. From the 1860s to the 1890s, the Native Americans were defeated in a series of brutal wars.

▲ Ancient Ones

A farming people who built dwellings in the canyons of the southwest between about AD500 and 1200 are known as the Anasazi, or 'ancient ones'. By the 1100s, they were living in cliff dwellings, like these ones at Mesa Verde.

Nests

Our homes are, in a way, our nests. A nest is a place where a creature can safely rest and raise its young. It is usually comfortable, lined with grass, moss, hairs, leaves or feathers. Birds are well-known nesters. Some build nests from twigs. Others peck a hole in a tree or steal another animal's burrow. Many other animals make nests too, from ants to alligators.

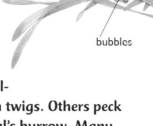

bubbles

cichlids

▶ Bubble-nesting fish

Some fish make nests of mud, twigs, pebbles – or bubbles. Certain gouramis and cichlids 'blow' long-lasting bubbles with a foamy liquid. The bubbles collect under a leaf or among stems. The female lays her eggs there and the male protects them until the baby fish develop.

▲ Wasp nest

Insects that make nests include bees, wasps, ants and termites. Wasps make a papery substance by chewing wood with their saliva (spit), and build their nest with it.

Wow!

The biggest mammal nests, made in bushes by wild pigs and hogs, are 3 metres across, with bent-over branches forming a roof.

▲ Food delivery

Many birds use natural holes rather than building a nest. The colourful hoopoe of Europe, Africa and Asia nests in a hole or opening in a bank, wall, tree or even a building. The female sits on her eggs to keep them warm and safe for about 15–18 days, and the male brings her food.

New World

In 1492, a European explorer called Christopher Columbus landed in the Americas. He was the first of many. Soon the Spanish and Portuguese were greedily claiming large areas of Central and South America, while the English, Dutch and French were settling in North America. They had discovered a 'New World' of land and natural riches.

▲ Conquistadors

Spanish soldiers called *conquistadors* (conquerors), invaded Mexico in 1519. Their leader was called Hernán Cortés. His forces defeated the Aztec people who lived there.

▲ Pocahontas

Pocahontas lived from 1595 to 1617. She was the daughter of a Native American chief called Powhatan. She tried to make peace between her people and the English, who were settling in Virginia. She married John Rolfe, one of the settlers, but died during a visit to England.

◄ African slaves

In the 1500s, Europeans and African traders started a cruel trade in slaves. People were taken by force from West Africa and shipped to the Americas. There, rich landowners made them work for no money on plantations of sugar or cotton.

Word box

plantation
a piece of land given over to the growing of a particular crop for money

slave
someone whose freedom is taken away and who is forced to work for no money

► The Pilgrims

These English people left Europe because of their strict religious beliefs and so became known as 'pilgrims'. In 1620, they sailed to North America in a ship called *The Mayflower*. They built a new settlement called Plymouth.

Little islands and coral reefs are scattered over a vast area of the South Pacific Ocean. Over thousands of years they were settled by seafarers. We call these peoples Melanesians, Micronesians and Polynesians. They grew coconuts and sweet potatoes, fished and raised pigs. In the 1800s, many of the islands were settled by Europeans.

The voyagers

he Polynesians originally came from outheast Asia, sailing in canoes. etween about 1500BC and AD1000 ey settled an area of the Pacific ean twice the size of the USA.

▲ The Maoris

A Polynesian people called the Maoris reached New Zealand over a thousand years ago. They farmed the land and hunted the big birds called moa that lived there. Some Maoris continue to live in New Zealand, keeping their traditions and ceremonies alive.

Big heads

about AD400, the Polynesians iiled from Tahiti to Easter Island. etween 1000 and 1600 they eated these huge heads of irved stone on the island.

◄ Wool wagons in New Zealand

In the 1800s, British settlers came to New Zealand for sheep-farming. Here they are using ox-carts to carry bales of wool to market.

Normans

In the AD800s, the Vikings made many attacks on northern France. The French king decided to buy peace and loyalty by giving them land. This region became known as Normandy ('land of the Northmen') and their descendants were known as Normans. The Viking leader, Hrolf, married a French princess called Giselle.

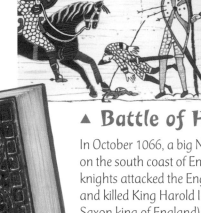

▲ Battle of Hastings

In October 1066, a big Norman fleet arrived on the south coast of England. Their knights attacked the English near Hastings, and killed King Harold II (the last Anglo-Saxon king of England). The Bayeux Tapestry (above) tells the story of the battle.

▼ William the Conqueror

Duke William of Normandy was crowned King of England in London, on Christmas Day 1066. Within two years, most of the country was under Norman rule.

▲ Domesday Book

The Normans wanted to make the English pay taxes. To do this, they wrote down details of nearly all the land in England. In 1086, this information was put together in the Domesday Book.

Wow!

Hrolf, the first Duke of Normandy, was said to be so tall that he could not ride a horse. He was nicknamed 'the ganger', which means 'walker'.

▼ Normans ashore

In 1060, the Normans invaded the island of Sicily, in Italy. They conquered England in 1066, and later went on to seize land in Wales and Ireland and to settle in parts of Scotland.

The continent of North America is made up of the three large countries of Canada, the United States of America and Mexico, as well as a number of smaller countries. These smaller countries include the island of Greenland, the countries of Central America and the islands dotted around the Caribbean Sea.

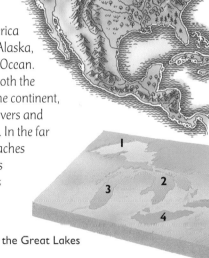

▼ Tallest trees

Thick forests of huge redwoods, cedars, firs and spruces can be found in California and Oregon.

These huge trees thrive on mountain-side slopes which face the Pacific Ocean. Redwoods are the tallest living things and can grow to heights of 80 metres.

▶ From north to south

In the far north of the continent of North America are the frozen lands of Alaska, which border the Arctic Ocean. Mountains run down both the east and west sides of the continent, with wide plains, long rivers and large lakes in the centre. In the far south are the sandy beaches of the Caribbean islands and the hot, wet jungles of Central America.

the Great Lakes

◀ Very deep

In the southwest of the continent is the amazing Grand Canyon, the deepest canyon in the world. This steep-sided valley was carved out by the Colorado river over millions of years.

▲ Great Lakes

On the border between Canada and the United States are the five Great Lakes: **1** Superior, **2** Huron, **3** Erie, **4** Ontario, **5** Michigan. Together these lakes make up the largest body of fresh water to be found anywhere in the world. Lake Superior has the biggest surface area of all fresh water lakes.

North America is a land of different peoples.
It includes some of the world's biggest and most famous cities, such as New York, Los Angeles and Mexico City.

Many North Americans are descended from Europeans, who began settling in North America in the 1500s. People already living there were called Native Americans.

▲ Skyscrapers

Many North American cities are very densely populated, and so they have a huge number of buildings. In Los Angeles skyscrapers have been so densely built that they crowd against the city's night skyline.

▼ Fast sport

Ice hockey is the national game of Canada, and thousands of people follow the progress of their favourite teams. Ice hockey is a very fast sport and the players wear protective clothing.

▼ Playing baseball

Baseball is one of the most popular sports in the United States. Millions of people watch games each week, either live at their local ballpark or on television.

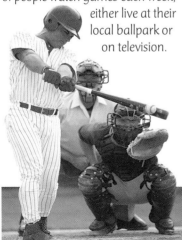

▲ Space centre

American spacecraft are launched into space from Cape Canaveral, on the coast of Florida, in the southeast of the United States. The first spacecraft to land on the Moon lifted off from here in 1969.

▼ Cities and temples

The ruins of ancient Aztec cities are scattered across Mexico. The Aztec people built several beautiful temples and a grand palace at Tenochtitlan. In the 1500s, Spanish invaders conquered the Aztecs and destroyed their empire.

Numbers are how we store information about amounts. They also let us calculate (do sums). In the simplest type of calculation, we use our fingers to help us count. Modern computers can make trillions of calculations in just one second.

▲ Fun with numbers

Numbers can be fun! Many games use numbers to count scores and to have fun with your skill and luck. Card and dice games are major number-users. They have been played for hundreds of years and are still popular.

▲ Computer bits

Computers use a code called the binary code to make calculations. This code uses only two numbers: 0 and 1. Each 0 or 1 is called a 'bit', short for binary digit. The 'bits' combine in different ways to make letters, symbols and numbers. Each combination of 'bits' is called a 'byte'.

Roman									
I	II	III	IV	V	VI	VII	VIII	IX	X
1	2	3	4	5	6	7	8	9	10

Mayan

•	••	•••	••••	—	•̄	••̄
1	2	3	4	5	6	7

•••̄	••••̄	=
8	9	10

Chinese

一	二	三	四	五	六	七
1	2	3	4	5	6	7

八	九	十	十五	五十
8	9	10	15	50

Hindi

٩	٩	३	४	५	६	७	८	९	१०
1	2	3	4	5	6	7	8	9	10

Wow!

Any number between 10 and 99, when written three times, can be divided by seven to give a whole number as a result. For example, 121212 divided by 7 = 17316.

▲ Round the world

Many civilizations invented systems of numbers. Most ancient systems did not use the number zero. This made counting hard. Arabic numbers are now the main system, because they are easy to use.

▲ Ancient adding

The abacus is a very ancient adding machine. It uses a series of sliding beads to count, and it is still used today in some countries. It looks very simple, but with practice people can add large sums really quickly.

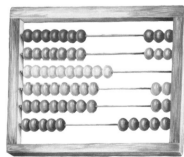

Australia is by far the largest country in the continent of Oceania. The two other sizeable countries are New Zealand and Papua New Guinea. The rest of Oceania is made up of hundreds of islands in the Pacific Ocean.

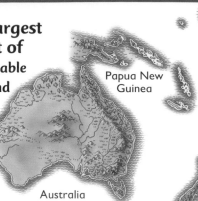

Papua New Guinea

New Zealand

Australia

▲ Traditional craft workers

Wood carving is a traditional craft of the Maoris of New Zealand. They decorate their meeting house with carvings.

▲ Island continent

The land of Australia is mostly flat. In the east, mountains separate the dry inland areas from a narrow strip of fertile land along the coast. New Zealand is made up of two islands: North Island and South Island. High mountain peaks, active volcanoes, hot, bubbling springs and green lowlands are to be found on the islands. Mountains and thick forests cover much of Papua New Guinea, Oceania's third largest country.

coral polyps

▲ The largest reef

The Great Barrier Reef lies off the northeastern coast of Australia. It is the world's largest coral reef and stretches for 2,000 kilometres. Coral is made up of the skeletons of tiny sea animals called polyps.

▶ Koalas

The koala is one of Australia's most famous animals. It eats only one kind of food – the young leaves and shoots of eucalyptus trees. Like a kangaroo, a koala mother keeps her baby in a pouch on her stomach.

▶ Active volcanoes

On the small islands around New Zealand active volcanoes exist. This means there is a chance they could erupt. This volcano is on White Island and it often gives off smoke.

▲ Sacred rock

Uluru is a sacred place for the Aborigines, the native people of Australia. Called Ayers Rock in English, it is one of the largest rock mounds in the world. Inside the rock are many caves. Their walls are covered with paintings made by Aboriginal artists thousands of years ago.

Oceania covers a large area of the world but only about 30 million people live there. Around 19 million people live in Australia – that's roughly the same as live in the tiny country of Nepal in Asia. Most Australians live along the coast, where there is plenty of rain. The two largest cities – Sydney and Melbourne – are in this coastal strip. There are few towns in the huge inland part of Australia.

Word box

Aboriginal
original inhabitant

harbour
a place of shelter for ships

landmark
a famous sight

Wow!

The first people from Europe to settle in Australia were prisoners and their guards from England – they sailed there in 11 ships in 1787.

▲ First to arrive

The Maoris were the first inhabitants (settlers) of New Zealand. They came by canoe around AD800 from islands far to the northeast. Europeans arrived in the late 1700s. Maoris are skilled woodcarvers and stone sculptors.

▼ Sydney harbour

The Opera House (completed in 1973) in Sydney's great harbour is Australia's most famous landmark. Sydney is Australia's biggest city – one-fifth of all Australians live here.

▼ Rugby fans

Australians and New Zealanders are very keen on sport and other outdoor activities. The game of rugby is very popular in both countries. The New Zealand team is known as the 'All-Blacks' because of the colour they wear.

Oceans and seas cover more than two-thirds of the Earth's surface. Amazingly, they contain 97 percent of all the water in the world. The oceans are about four kilometres deep on average, but in some places the ocean floor plunges down even deeper. The deepest place in the world is at the bottom of the Pacific Ocean – the Marianas Trench is more than 11 kilometres below the water's surface.

Wow!
In December 2004, there was a tsunami in the Indian Ocean which caused waves to grow up to 24 metres in height.

▶ Ocean waters

There are five great oceans, which are joined together by smaller seas and other stretches of water. From largest to smallest, the oceans are: the Pacific, the Atlantic, the Indian, the Arctic and the Southern.

ARCTIC OCEAN

ATLANTIC OCEAN

PACIFIC OCEAN

INDIAN OCEAN

SOUTHERN OCEAN

▶ Moving water

The water in our oceans and seas is always moving. As wind blows across the water's surface, it creates waves. Waves move around the world in swirling, circular patterns called currents.

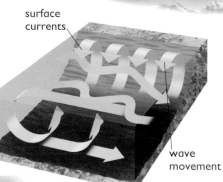

surface currents

wave movement

▼ Giant waves

Earthquakes under the sea-bed can produce giant waves that race towards land at speeds as fast as 970 kilometres an hour. These waves may be 30 metres high near the shore. They are called *tsunamis*.

◀ Seaweed harvest

Some farmers grow seaweed. In shallow, tropical waters, people grow their own on plots on the seabed. The harvested seaweed is a useful ingredient in products such as plant fertilizer and ice cream.

▼

Ocean life

Find out more:
Oceans and seas • Sea animals • Water

The oceans are filled with living things. These range from the tiny shrimp-like creatures that float on the surface to strange-looking fish that crawl across the sea-bed. Most ocean creatures live in the warmer, sunlit waters near the surface, where most of their food supply is found.

▼ Floating life

Tiny plants and animals called plankton drift through the surface of the water in huge numbers. They become food for larger ocean creatures.

▼ Ocean creatures

Sharks, dolphins and turtles live near the water's surface. Large mammals such as the sei whale dive to lower levels. The waters at the bottom of the ocean receive no sunlight. Only a few kinds of sea creatures such as deep-sea fish and starfish can survive in this cold, dark world.

1 Dusky dolphin	8 Ocean sunfish	14 Banded sea snake
2 Kittiwake	9 Ridley's turtle	15 Yellowfin tuna
3 Northern right whale	10 Cuttlefish	16 Common squid
4 Man 'o' warjellyfish	11 Tiger shark	17 Mako shark
5 Great skuas	12 Yellow-bellied	18 Nautilus
6 Pacific white-sided dolphin	sea snake	19 Commerson's dolphin
7 Broad-billed prion	13 Tarpon	20 Sei whale

Squid belong to the animal group called molluscs or 'shellfish'. The squid has a shell, but it is small and flat, inside the body. Its close cousins are octopuses, cuttlefish and nautiluses. They all have big eyes, squishy bodies and long, flexible tentacles with suckers for grabbing their prey. These animals are all fierce predators.

▼ Twilight hunter

The nautilus's curly shell is mostly filled with gas, to help it float in mid-water. The animal itself takes up only the wide opening. It hunts fish and other prey, using its huge eyes to see in the dim depths.

▲ Hidden arms

The cuttlefish's two long 'arms' are usually hidden under its eight tentacles. They shoot out to grab crabs, small fish, shellfish and worms. Cuttlefish can change their colour more, and faster, than any other animal – from almost white to nearly black in a second.

▲ Lurking in a lair

The octopus's eight tentacles join its body around its beaklike mouth. By day it lurks in a sea-bed cave or among rocks. At night it catches crabs, fish and other victims. In captivity, an octopus can recognize shapes and colours and learn tricks.

Wow!

The giant squid is the largest invertebrate (animal without a backbone) – it has a total length of more than 20 metres.

Word box

captivity
when an animal is kept and looked after by humans

siphon
in molluscs, a bendy tube on the side of the body, through which water can be sucked in or squirted out

▶ Squid

The giant squid is a huge deep-sea predator, with eight tentacles and two longer sucker-tipped 'arms'. Like octopuses, squid swim by taking in water and squirting it out as a powerful jet through their siphon.

No other bird looks quite like an owl. There are about 200 kinds. These birds hunt prey in darkness using their huge eyes and amazingly good hearing. They catch it with their large, strong toes tipped with sharp talons. By day, most owls rest on a branch or in a hollow tree, cave or quiet building.

◀ Tawny owl

Most medium-sized owls, such as the tawny, hunt mice, rats, baby rabbits, insects such as large beetles and grasshoppers, and perhaps small birds and bats. As it rests on a tree branch by day, its patterned brown plumage makes it very difficult to see.

◀ Spotted eagle owl

Eagle owls are among the biggest owls, with wings spanning 150 centimetres. They mainly catch other birds as they sleep, including pigeons, blackbirds and thrushes. Bats and other owls, such as tawnies, are also their prey, and they even snatch baby eagles or hawks from their nests.

Wow!
The barn owl lives almost everywhere except icy Antarctica — no other land bird is so widespread.

Word scramble
Unscramble these words to find the names of five types of owls:

a. NOWYS
b. NYWAT
c. NOGL-REDEA
d. SHROT-RAEDE
e. RINGOWRUB

answers
a. snowy b. tawny
c. long-eared d. short-eared
e. burrowing

▶ Barn owl

The ghostly-white barn owl once roosted and nested in hollow trees or caves, but barns, churches and outbuildings do just as well. Like other owls it has a wide, round, bowl-shaped face. Its feathers have very soft edges so they make almost no sound as the owl flies and swoops.

Parrots

Noisy, colourful and clever – parrots are popular as pets. But capturing them from the wild means some of the 350 kinds are now very rare. The parrot group includes parakeets, lorikeets (lories), cockatoos, rosellas and macaws. Most live in tropical forests and eat fruits, seeds, nuts and other plant parts. Smaller types such as budgerigars and lovebirds thrive in captivity.

▶ Rainbow lorikeet

Like most parrots in flocks, rainbow lories are noisy, with endless flapping and squawking. Nicknamed 'painting-by-numbers' birds, from their bright patches of plumage, lories are bold. In Australia and the West Pacific islands they can be seen in parks and gardens.

Wow!
Budgies (budgerigars) are bred in all colours, from red and blue to yellow, white and grey. All wild budgies that live in Australia are green.

▲ Scarlet macaw

This huge macaw cracks nuts with its powerful beak. Female and male stay together, even flying with wings almost touching. They may form larger family flocks of about 20, in woods and on farms across Central and South America.

▶ White cockatoo

This is one of several parrots that can learn tricks such as counting. Many parrots also 'talk' by copying human voices – but they don't understand what they are saying!

▲ Parrot

Parrots are brilliantly coloured birds that chatter loudly as they fly around the rainforest. Their bills are specially shaped for eating nuts.

Word box

diseases
illnesses caused by germs that are caught and can be quite serious

swarm
a huge gathering of insects or similar small animals

It is a picnic on a sunny day. A wasp hovers near the jam, a fly lands on the food, the apple has a huge maggot in it, and the bread has been nibbled by a mouse! Animal pests are everywhere. Some eat or spoil our foods, either as crops growing in fields, or stored in warehouses or cupboards. Other pests spread germs and diseases. There are even pests, such as woodworms and termites, which eat through furniture and wooden houses.

▲ Locusts

In some years, locusts breed to form gigantic swarms. They darken the sky like storm clouds, and destroy whole farms. 'Locust-watcher' workers report their build-up, so they can be sprayed with poison before the swarm grows too big.

▲ Red-billed quelea

This African seed eater, a type of weaverbird, is sometimes called the 'feathered locust'. It forms huge flocks that land on farms and eat wheat, rice and similar crops. Guns, nets, traps and poisons have been tried against the quelea, but it is still a major pest.

▼ Pesky rats!

Brown, black and rice rats, and house mice, can be great pests. They ruin stores of food by leaving urine and droppings in them. They also gnaw electrical wires. The fleas that live on black rats can spread diseases.

black rat

◀ Tiny but deadly

Flies are perhaps the most deadly animals in the world, because they spread the germs that cause diseases. Houseflies enter homes and infect food. Mosquitoes like this one carry malaria and yellow fever, blackflies carry river-blindness and testse flies spread sleeping-sickness.

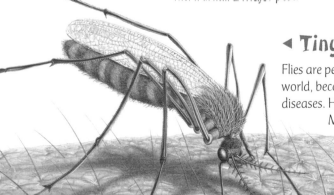

Pets

Some of our best friends are animals – dogs, cats, gerbils, hamsters and budgies. Pets are animals we look after, and they provide interest and fun. Some people keep unusual pets such as snakes or lizards, or even tarantulas! Various kinds of pets are popular in different parts of the world, such as monkeys in Asia, parrots in South America, possums in Australia, raccoons in North America and mongooses in Africa.

Word scramble

Unscramble these words to find the names of five types of dogs and cats:

a. PANSILE
b. BATYB
c. BOLARRAD
d. SEEMAIS
e. REXBO

answers
a. spaniel b. tabby
c. labrador d. siamese e. boxer

◄ Lots of space

A pony needs lots of space, time, food and care. It can give rides or pull a cart. Like many pets, it can be taken to shows and maybe win prizes!

zebra fish

◄ Fish

Fish in an aquarium or tank depend completely on their owner. They need to be fed daily. The tank must be regularly topped up with water – and cleaned out.

◄ Best friend

Dogs can be marvellous pets, but sometimes they have a hard time. They may not be taken for enough walks. They try to behave well, but their owners may teach them badly, and then shout at them. With time and thought from a caring owner, a dog's life can be very happy.

▼ Suitable pet

Hamsters are small, quiet, and happy in a large cage with plenty of toys, tunnels and rooms. They suit people who have little space.

► Pet needs

Cats can look after themselves and be left alone more than dogs. But like any pet, they have needs – fresh water, healthy food and cleaning out when necessary. Cats need a quiet place to rest and sleep, and, like other cuddly pets, a friendly stroke.

bulldog

Photography

Photography is the process of making pictures by using light. Photographs are made using cameras. Like the human eye, some cameras take in light from an object, and record this image on film. Images can also be produced in digital cameras, which, instead of using film, are processed in computers.

▲ Digital photos

Older cameras record pictures on film, but the modern digital camera records them in electronic form. The pictures can be loaded into a computer, printed or viewed on screen. The digital image can be changed in any way you want.

Wow!

Some cameras can see in the dark. They make a black and white picture by picking up the faintest traces of light from the stars or the Moon.

▼ Old times

The first photographs were made in the 1840s. Early photography used a different method for printing. Instead of being printed in black and white, the pictures came out in a brownish colour called sepia.

▼ Get snappy!

Modern automatic cameras do most of the work for you! They control the amount of light falling onto the film or electronic detector, the size of the image, and how long the light falls on the film (the shutter speed). With the older manual camera, you would have to make all these calculations and adjustments yourself.

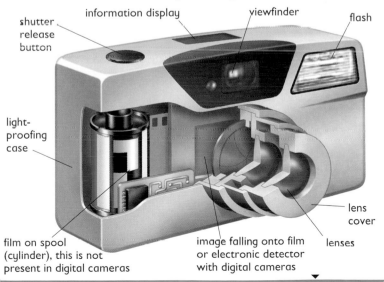

shutter release button

information display

viewfinder

flash

light-proofing case

▶ Watch out!

Digital cameras are now made so small that they can be fitted into a mobile phone. Mobiles can record images and even short videos, which can then be transferred to a computer.

lens cover

film on spool (cylinder), this is not present in digital cameras

image falling onto film or electronic detector with digital cameras

lenses

Pirates

The sight every sailor feared was a pirate ship on the horizon.
For thousands of years, pirates robbed ships and attacked or killed their crews. Some pirates were adventurers seeking treasure and thrills. Others were murderers and madmen.

▲ Buccaneers

All sorts of outlaws and criminals settled on the Caribbean islands in the 1600s. These 'buccaneers' lived by hunting wild pigs and by attacking Spanish ships that were laden with treasure from the New World.

▲ Women pirates

Mary Read and Anne Bonny dressed as men and sailed with pirates in the Bahamas. They were captured with the rest of the crew in 1720 but the women were not executed.

▶ Blackbeard

Edward Teach, or 'Blackbeard', terrorized the North American coast, in his ship the *Queen Anne's Revenge*. He was killed in 1718 and his head was cut off. People believe he buried treasure somewhere before he died. They have been searching for it ever since!

Wow!

When Blackbeard went into battle, he lit the fuses used to fire guns and tied them in his hair. They smoked and fizzled and made him look like the devil!

▶ Scary flags

Pirate captains flew their own flags, called blackjacks, to strike terror into the enemy.

Planets

Find out more:
Earth • Space travel • Universe

Planets are large bodies of
rock, metal and gas that travel
round a star. Eight planets, including
Earth, orbit our own star, the Sun. The
Earth is a small planet, while planets such
as Jupiter and Saturn are far bigger. The Earth
is at just the right distance from the Sun for life
to exist here.

Word box

orbit
travel round

star
a ball of very hot gas

► Saturn's rings

Saturn is often called the Ringed Planet. It is the
second largest planet in our Solar System, almost ten
times the size of Earth. It is surrounded by flat rings that can
be clearly seen through a telescope. They are only about 100 metres
thick – the planet's width is 60,000 kilometres. Although the rings look
smooth, they are made up of millions of pieces of ice and rock. These orbit
the planet and stretch thousands of kilometres out into space.

▼ Our Solar System

Together with the Sun, various moons and lumps of rock, the planets make up
the Solar System. Mercury, Venus, Earth and Mars are known as the 'inner
planets' because they are closest to the Sun. Jupiter, Saturn, Uranus
and Neptune lie farther away, so are known as the 'outer
planets'. Outer planets take much longer for
each orbit – Neptune takes nearly
164 of our years.

Sun
Venus Mercury
Earth
Moon
Jupiter
Mars
Saturn
Uranus
Neptune

Plants

Like the animal kingdom, the plant kingdom includes a huge range of living things. Unlike animals, plants can make their own food, from light, water and air. Using photosynthesis, they change sunlight into sugar. This gives them energy for life and growth.

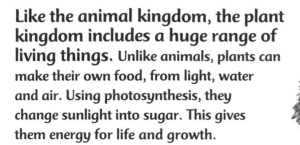

broadleave trees and bushes, flowers an herbs

grasses, lilies and palms

gingkos

conifers

cycads

ferns

club mosses

horsetails

mosses

liverworts

fungi

lichens

Word box

classify
divide living things into groups to make them easier to study

photosynthesis
a process plants use to turn energy from sunlight into food

▶ Plants galore!

Scientists 'classify' the many types of plants, shown here. They are usually grouped by comparing the structure of their stems and leaves, how they take in food and water and how they reproduce.

larger algae (seaweeds)

tiny floating algae

Grow an orange tree!

Grow your own tropical plant from fruit!
Seeds or pips from oranges will grow if you plant them in soil and keep them on a sunny windowsill. Water them regularly, but don't make the soil soggy. In just a couple of weeks, a tiny orange tree will begin to grow.

Plants: habitats

Find out more:
Plants around the world • Forests

Plants grow all around you – in the garden and in the park, on the window-sill, in the farmer's fields, in woods and forests, on rocks and cliffs – even on the beach. The biggest plants are giant sequoia trees that tower more than 80 metres above the ground. Among the smallest ones are hairy mosses that spread like a carpet over rocks and stones.

Word box

germination
the stages of seed growth

carbon dioxide
a gas in the air that plants need for photosynthesis

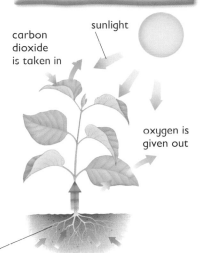

carbon dioxide is taken in

sunlight

oxygen is given out

water taken up by the roots

▲ Mossy rocks

These rocks have turned green with moss, a tiny plant that grows in large numbers. Most mosses live in moist, shady places, and form soft 'mats' over rocks and around the bases of trees.

▶ Making food

Green plants make their own food by using light from the Sun. This process is called photosynthesis. It happens inside the plant's leaves. A special substance in the leaves uses water from the soil, carbon dioxide gas from the air and sunlight to make food. The food travels through the stems to reach all parts of the plant.

▼ Life underground

Once a seed has found a suitable place, it begins to grow. This process is called germination.

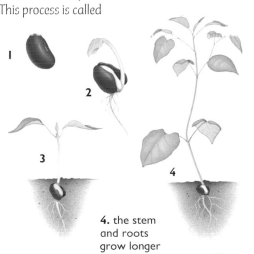

1

2

3

4

1. the seed lies in the ground until conditions are right

2. the seed sends a shoot up and a root down

3. the shoot pushes its way above ground

4. the stem and roots grow longer

Green hair

You will need
knife pumpkin spoon cotton wool
water cress seeds black marker pen

1. Cut the top off a pumpkin and scoop out some of the flesh.
2. Fill the pumpkin with cotton wool.
3. Moisten the cotton wool with water and sow the cress seeds on top.
4. Draw a happy face on your pumpkin with black marker pen.
5. Keep the seeds watered and watch your pumpkin's green hair grow over the next few days.

Plants: life

The way a plant lives depends on many things, such as climate and soil. The simplest plants, such as algae ('algee'), do not even need soil. They grow in ponds, lakes and oceans. Other plants, such as cacti ('cacteye'), grow in dry deserts. They can live without water for long periods of time.

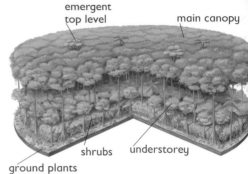

emergent top level   main canopy

shrubs   understorey

ground plants

◀ Desert plants

Cacti are specially adapted to stop them from losing too much water in the hot sun. They are often covered with spikes, to prevent animals from eating them.

▲ Layers and layers

In tropical rainforests, different plants grow at different heights, depending on the amount of light available. Sunlight passes through the highest trees to a more even layer – the main canopy. This thick layer blocks out most of the light, so that only a few plants, creepers or bushes can grow underneath.

Word box

canopy
layer of plants in the rainforest 'roof'

understorey
layer of plants in the rainforest found below the main canopy

▲ Going up...

Weather conditions get colder and windier high up in the mountains. On lower slopes, conifer trees such as pines and firs grow. Higher up, above what is called the tree-line, it is too cold for trees. Instead, shrubs, grasses and tiny flowers grow.

▶ Venus fly-trap

Insects are lured into the jaw-like leaf trap of the venus fly-trap with nectar. Once the insect lands, the jaws clamp shut on the victim. The plant then makes juices that drown and dissolve the insect. The trap will only shut if touched at least twice in 20 seconds.

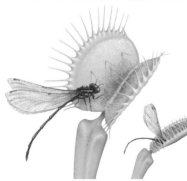

Poisonous animals

Find out more:
Insects • Snakes • Spiders

Several kinds of animals are poisonous to people. Some are truly deadly. But their venoms are not designed to kill us. The animal uses its poisonous bite or sting to catch its prey, or to defend itself against enemies. There are various kinds of poisonous snakes, fish, scorpions and insects, as well as the blue-ringed octopus, snail-like animals called cone shells, and stinging jellyfish.

Wow!

Australia has more poisonous animals, for its size, than any other country – including eight of the world's ten deadliest snakes.

▼ Ready to strike

Cobras have large fangs that inject strong poison. Like most other creatures, they bite only if cornered, trapped or surprised. The poison is really meant for prey. The king cobra is the biggest poisonous snake, at 5 metres long, and its victims are other snakes.

arrow-poison frogs

cobra

lionfish

▲▶ Warning!

The bright colours of arrow-poison frogs and lionfish (dragonfish) are a warning: leave me alone! The poison is in the frog's skin and the fish's fin spines. Any animal that tries to eat them becomes very ill, and learns to avoid warning colours.

Word box

warning colours
bright colours and patterns that warn other creatures to stay away

venom
another name for poison

▼ Similar colours

Several very different kinds of animals are yellow and black or red and black in colour, to warn others about their stings, poisonous flesh or skin. They include bees, wasps like this hornet, beetles such as ladybirds, butterflies, frogs, toads, snakes and salamanders.

▼ Desert scorpion

The scorpion's tail-tip is poisonous. When the scorpion feels threatened, it arches its tail over its head. It might use the sting to quieten a struggling victim like a mouse. Otherwise, it is used for self-defence.

Pollution

Humans do all kinds of things that produce waste materials, and these pollute our world. Smoke from factories damages the air. Waste from factories, homes and similar places pours into rivers and is carried out to sea. Cars and other vehicles produce huge amounts of pollution in many of the world's cities, even making it hard to breathe.

▼ Self-destruction

We are beginning to see the damage we are doing to the world around us. New filters and chemicals called catalysts can reduce dangerous fumes. Many organizations are now working to stop us doing further harm. But we still have a long way to go.

Wow!

If pollution continues at the current rate, 30 to 50 percent of all living species may be extinct by the middle of the 21st century.

▲ Water pollution

Factory and human waste are the usual causes of river pollution. These waste materials take oxygen from the water. This kills fish and other water life.

factories pump out chemicals that escape into the atmosphere, making rainwater acidic. This can kill trees and damage soil

cutting down trees destroys forests and wildlife

factories make huge piles of waste

rubbish is dumped in rivers or landfill sites

exhaust fumes from traffic can make it hard to breathe

Prehistoric life

Find out more:
Art • Dinosaur ages • Dinosaurs

The first human beings lived on Earth a long time ago – around two million years ago.
At this time most of the world was cold and icy, but Africa, South America and parts of Asia were warmer. These early people learned how to make fire, hunted animals and made simple tools from wood, stone and animal bones.

▲ Making fire

The earliest use of fire-making was for warmth. But people eventually discovered the uses of fire – for cooking, to shape weapons and tools, and to give light.

▲ Early humans

Very early humans were called *Homo erectus*, which means 'upright human', and they were as tall as us. These first humans spread from Africa, across Asia, and into Europe.

▼ A long time ago

The word 'prehistoric' means the time before people could write. It is the time before about 5,000 years ago. This period of prehistory is called the Stone Age. People made their own tools and weapons out of stone.

this stone tool was used for scraping flesh from the skin of wild animals

Word box

bison
huge prehistoric cattle

Stone Age
a period of early history when tools and weapons were made of stone

woolly mammoth

▲ Mammoth hunts

Early people hunted birds, small reptiles and larger animals such as deer, bison, bears and huge elephant-like animals called woolly mammoths.

Animal match

These prehistoric animals are either mammals, reptiles or amphibians. See if you can tell what they are.

a. Pteranodon

b. Smilodon

c. Ichthyosaur

d. Diplocaulus

answers
a. reptile b. mammal
c. reptile d. amphibian

Queens

A queen is either the ruler of a country or the wife of a king. In history, several powerful queens have reigned for many years. Elizabeth I ruled England for 45 years. She beat off an invasion by a fleet of ships from Spain, and kept tight control over her country.

◄ Queen Anne

Anne was the younger sister of Mary II. Her reign (1702 to 1714) saw major changes in Britain. Parliament passed laws uniting England and Scotland and banning anyone but a Protestant from being the British king or queen.

◄ Queen Elizabeth II

As head of the Commonwealth – an organization of former British lands – Elizabeth II has travelled farther than any other British monarch. She celebrated her Golden Jubilee (50 years as queen) in 2002 with parties, free concerts and a huge firework display.

Wow!

People tried to kill Queen Victoria on six different occasions.

▼ Queen Victoria

Queen Victoria was such an important queen that her name is used to describe a whole period in Britain's history – the Victorian Age. She reigned for 63 years, from 1837 to 1901, and had nine children. While she was queen, Britain became one of the world's richest and most powerful countries.

► Queen Elizabeth I

In certain countries, only men were allowed to rule. But some of the world's strongest rulers have been women. Queen Elizabeth I ruled England from 1558 to 1603. Very few people dared to argue with her!

Queen Elizabeth I

◄ Queen Beatrix

Several European countries are ruled by queens, but their power to make decisions is limited. A queen has ruled the Netherlands since 1890. The present one, Queen Beatrix, became queen in 1980.

Rainforests

Find out more:
Conservation • Forests • Plant life • Trees

Rainforests are thick forests of tall trees that grow in hot, rainy parts of the world. These forests stay green all year round. The largest rainforest of all, the Amazon, once took up one-third of the continent of South America. Many thousands of different kinds of animals and plants live in rainforests.

Wow!
Every second, humans cut down an area of tropical rainforest that is bigger than a football pitch.

▼ Top to bottom

A rainforest is packed with life. The treetops form a covering, called the canopy. Eagles (1), monkeys (2), butterflies (3) and macaws (4) live in the canopy. Sloths (5) hang from the middle branches, and jaguars (6) climb into lower branches. On the forest floor, millipedes (7) and beetles (8) move through the leaves.

▶ Bright colours

Many rainforest animals are very colourful, like this orange birdwing butterfly. Its colours warn other animals that it is not good to eat.

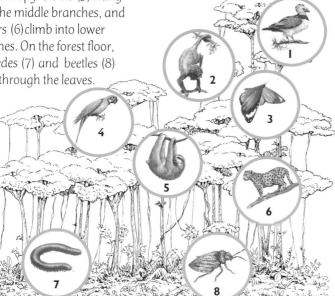

▼ Destruction

Farmers clear land in rainforests by cutting down trees and burning them. The soil in many rainforests is poor, and after a few years the farmers' crops no longer grow well. This means they have to clear another patch of rainforest. In this way people are destroying large areas of the world's rainforests.

◀ Rainy forest

In a tropical rainforest, you need your umbrella every day! Rainforests have rainy weather all year round – but there is still a wet and a dry season. It is just that the wet season is even wetter!

Recycling

Find out more:
Conservation • Materials • Pollution

Pollution is less of a problem when waste materials are reused instead of being thrown away. Glass is easily melted down for recycling. Paper can also be recycled, saving millions of trees. Today there are all kinds of schemes that help people to recycle things.

▼ How we recycle

Waste material from homes and factories is taken to recycling centres. In the recycling process, useful materials are picked out and stored, ready to be changed back into many of the things we use every day.

Recycle it!

Keep an eye on the things that your family throws away each day – but don't start sorting through yucky rubbish! Try to think of things that could be taken to your local recycling centre, such as paper, plastic, cans and bottles. As much as half of your family's waste can be recycled.

▲ Farming trees

Instead of destroying forest trees for wood and paper, it is better to grow trees specially, on big plantations like this one. Fast-growing trees are used. They are cut down as soon as they reach a useful size and are quickly replaced with new trees.

1. used glass or plastic bottles, aluminium cans and newspapers are collected from recycling centres

2. the objects are recycled to make raw materials

3. the raw materials are reused to make new bottles, cans and paper

▲ Sorting it out

Useful rubbish from ordinary homes needs to be sorted out first by hand, before it goes to the recycling centre.

Religion

A religion is a set of ideas and beliefs, which usually centre around one god or several gods. There are more than 1,000 different religions in the world. They have their own ceremonies and festivals, where followers often come together to worship the god of their religion. In most religions, people come to a special place, such as a church, a temple or a synagogue, to pray and worship.

▼ Jesus

Christians believe that a Jew called Jesus, who lived 2,000 years ago, was the Son of God. He was killed by the Romans, but Christians think he came back to life and then went to heaven. This picture of Christ was made in Roman Britain, when Christianity was starting to spread across Europe.

the Pope is based at the Vatican, the smallest state in the world, in the city of Rome, Italy

▲ In nature

Shinto is a religion of Japan. Its followers believe that good spirits live in the natural world – in rocks and mountains, in forests and rivers, in animals and trees.

▲ Religious leaders

Religious leaders can have many different names, according to the religion they represent – monk, priest, imam and rabbi are some of the most common ones. The Pope is the head of the Roman Catholic Church, which is a branch of the Christian religion.

▼ Holy place

In India, Sikhs are a group of people who believe in one God. They follow religious teachings and are taught to lead pure lives. The Golden Temple at Amritsar is their most Important holy place.

▲ Finding peace

This Buddhist temple is in Bangkok, Thailand. Buddhists follow the ideas of Buddha, an Indian prince who lived about 2,500 years ago. He believed that people could find peace and happiness if they followed a certain way of life.

Word box

holy
very religious

synagogue
a building where Jews worship

Religion and people

There are many religions and each has its own followers. The most well known are Christianity, Hinduism, Buddhism, Islam and Judaism. Many believers follow the rules of their religion very strictly. For example Muslims, who follow the religion of Islam, must pray five times each day: at sunrise, at midday, in the afternoon, in the evening and at sunset.

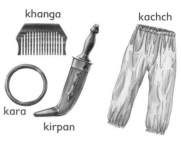

khanga

kachch

kara

kirpan

▶ Muslims at Mecca

The holiest place for Muslims is the city of Mecca in Saudi Arabia. Inside the Great Mosque is a black stone, which Muslims believe was given to Abraham by the Angel Gabriel. All Muslims try to visit Mecca at least once in their life. Around one million people crowd into the city each year during the six days set aside for this visit.

▲ Religious symbols

The Sikh religion was founded in the Punjab area of India in the 1500s. Spiritual teachers set guidelines on how Sikhs should lead their lives. Followers of the religion wear the five 'Ks'– kesh (uncut hair), khanga (comb), kirpan (sword), kara (steel bangle) and kachch (knee-length trousers).

▼ Place of worship

Here, Jewish people are praying at the Western Wall in Jerusalem. This wall is the only remaining part of The Temple, a very holy place of worship founded by King Solomon almost 3,000 years ago. Jewish people travel from all over the world to pray here.

▲ Holy waters

The ancient religion of Hinduism is at least 4,000 years old. More than three-quarters of the people in India are Hindus. The Ganges river in India is a very holy place for them. Pilgrims come from all over India to bathe in its waters. By doing this they believe they wash away their sins, and become pure.

Religious buildings

Find out more:
Religion • Religion and people

Ancient peoples often believed that parts of the landscape, such as mountains or springs, were holy. They soon began to build sacred places, too. These included shrines, places of worship such as temples or churches, and monasteries, where monks could live in peace.

▶ Lalibela

This Christian church is in the African country of Ethiopia. It was cut from solid rock nearly 800 years ago. It is in the shape of a Christian cross. In this picture, part of the rock has been cut away, to let you see the whole church.

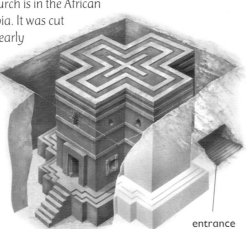

entrance

▲ Way of the spirits

Traditional Japanese people believe Mount Fuji is a holy mountain. It rises behind this Shinto shrine. Shinto means the 'way of the spirits' and is based on belief in the powers of nature. It is the most ancient religion in Japan.

Religious symbols

Religions have used special symbols for thousands of years. Can you find out which symbol belongs to which religion?

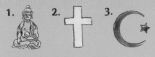

1.　2.　3.

a. Christianity **b.** Islam **c.** Buddhism

answers
1c, 2a, 3b

▶ All-seeing eyes

Holy mounds called *stupas* have been built by Buddhists in Nepal for over 2,000 years. This one near Kathmandu is decorated with eyes looking north, south, east and west.

Renaissance

Between 1350 and 1600 there were many changes in Europe. This period has come to be called the Renaissance, meaning the rebirth of knowledge. The Renaissance saw a growing interest in science, architecture, poetry, music and art, as well as ancient Greek and Roman culture. Students went to new universities in most European countries.

a model of Leonardo da Vinci's helicopter design

▲ 'Look up!'

Michelangelo, an Italian genius, painted the ceiling of the Sistine Chapel in Rome between 1508 and 1512. Although he had to work on high scaffolding, often lying on his back, many people agree that these pictures are some of the best ever painted.

▲ Renaissance man

Leonardo da Vinci lived in Italy from 1452 to 1519. He was a brilliant artist, sculptor, inventor, engineer, architect and musician. This picture is based on a drawing he made of a helicopter. The first modern version of a helicopter built in 1939, was inspired by his design.

◄ The city of Florence

The Renaissance began in Italy. The wealthy city of Florence became a centre of painting, architecture and sculpture. This is the Duomo, a cathedral that dates from 1296.

▲ New discoveries

The new interest in finding out how things worked led to great scientific discoveries. The Italian scientist Galileo Galilei, who lived from 1564 to 1642, studied the Sun, Moon and planets.

Reptiles

Alligators and crocodiles, lizards and snakes, tortoises and turtles are different kinds of reptile. Most reptiles have a dry skin covered with tough scales. Reptiles are cold-blooded, which means they lie in the sun to warm up before they can move around. There are about 8,000 different kinds of reptile.

grass snake

◀ Egg layers

Most reptiles lay their eggs in a warm, dry place. The heat of the sunshine makes the eggs hatch. A mother grass snake may lay her eggs in compost or manure heaps. The heat given off by these heaps helps to speed up the development of the eggs.

▲ Fire salamanders

Fire salamanders look like a cross between a lizard and a frog. They have bright patterns on their skin to warn predators that they are poisonous. The poison on their skin irritates and harms their predators.

▼ Fierce hunters

Alligators and crocodiles are fierce hunters with huge, sharp teeth. They use these teeth to hold onto prey in the water and to tear flesh. Their tails are long and powerful, helping them to swim swiftly. An alligator has a shorter, squarer snout than a crocodile.

agama lizard

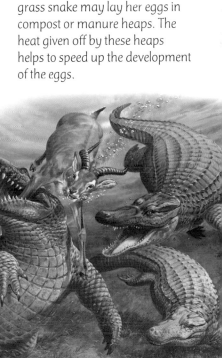

▲ Warming up

At night the male rainbow agama lizard of Africa is dull brown and grey. As it warms up in the morning sun its colours change to bright blues and reds.

Reptiles: habitat

Reptiles live in most places, except in the very cold areas in the far north and far south of the world. Many snakes and lizards live in hot deserts. Some kinds of reptile, such as sea turtles and sea snakes, spend most of their life in the water.

tree gecko

▲ Dragon lizards

The Komodo dragon is the largest lizard and can grow up to 3 metres in length. It lives on small islands in Indonesia. These lizards are very fierce, and will eat almost anything. That may be how they got their dragon name!

▲ Like a dinosaur

The tuatara lives on the islands of New Zealand. It belongs to a group of reptiles called 'beak heads' that first lived around the time of the dinosaurs – reptiles that roamed the Earth millions of years ago.

▲ Beautiful shell

The hawksbill turtle lives in warm seas all around the world. Its beautiful shell means it has been hunted so much that it has nearly died out. It is now protected in many countries.

▲ Sticky feet

The gecko is a lizard found in most warm countries. The biggest gecko lives in Southeast Asia and can be 30 centimetres in length. The tree gecko has hairs on its feet, which have a sticking effect. This enables it to walk on any surface, and even hang on by just one toe!

Wow!

A lizard that lives in the forests of Asia can glide from tree to tree through the air – it is known as a 'flying dragon'.

◄ Geckos

Web-footed geckos live in the Namib Desert in southwest Africa. It hardly ever rains, so geckos take in liquid wherever they can – and even lick their own eyes for moisture! Geckos eyes are very large, and licking them also helps to keep them clean.

Rhinos and tapirs

Find out more:
Endangered animals

Rhinos are the most threatened big animals in the world. There are only five kinds left. The African white (square-lipped) rhino numbers several thousand. But the black (hook-lipped) rhino, also of Africa, and the Indian, Sumatran and Javan rhinos of Asia are in desperate trouble. These massive plant eaters have lost their natural habitats and are killed for their horns.

Word box

horn
a long, sharp-pointed animal part, and also the substance from which scales and claws are made

◄▼ African rhinos

Most rhinos live alone, except for a mother with her calf (baby), or a male and female at mating time. In Africa the black rhino (seen below), which is really grey, eats leaves from bushes and herbs. The white one (left), which is also grey, or sometimes yellow-brown, prefers grasses.

▼ Rhino cousin

Tapirs are piglike animals from the forests of Southeast Asia, and Central and South America. Like rhinos, most have three hoofed toes on each foot. Tapirs love water and swim well. They sniff out plant food using their trunklike noses.

Wow!

The white rhino is the largest land animal after elephants – it is almost 5 metres long including its tail, and weighs more than 2 tonnes.

▼ Indian rhino

The rhino's horn is horn-shaped, but not made of the animal substance horn. It is made of hairs squeezed and stuck together in a hard mass, which grows in a horn shape.

Rivers and lakes

A river makes a long journey from its beginning, to the place where it empties into the sea, a lake or another river. Rivers give us water for drinking, washing and watering our crops. They also supply us with fish to eat. Rivers are important travel routes, and many towns and cities have grown up beside a river.

source
delta
river mouth

▲ Start to finish

The place where a river starts is called its source. It is often high up in the mountains, where melting snows begin to trickle downhill. Near the source, the land is often steep and the river is quite narrow, so its waters flow quickly. Lower down, the river becomes wider and flows more slowly and smoothly.

Word box

artificial
made by people

rapids
part of a river where water moves quickly and dangerously

► Amazon

The huge Amazon river in South America carries more water than any other river in the world. It is 6448 km in length and crosses the entire width of Brazil. A wide variety of wildlife lives in the river, including the Amazon river dolphin.

▼ Water sport

Fast-flowing rivers are exciting places for canoeists. Paddling through fast water is often called 'shooting the rapids'.

◄ Shopping by boat

In parts of Asia, people use waterways to buy and sell food. These Chinese people have come by boat to shop at a floating market.

◄ Making a lake

A lake is an area of water with land all around it. Some very large lakes are actually called seas, for example the Dead Sea and the Caspian Sea. This is Lake Kariba in southern Africa. It is an artificial lake, which was made by blocking the waters of the Zambezi river.

Word scramble

Can you unscramble these words to find the names of five large rivers?

a. SMATHE
b. NIHER
c. ZANAMO
d. ISPISIMISPS
e. SGEGNA

a. Thames b. Rhine
c. Amazon d. Mississippi
e. Ganges
answers

Roads

Millions of motor cars, buses and lorries travel along roads each day. Fast, straight roads called motorways link cities and large towns together. In the countryside, small narrow roads run between villages. About 2,000 years ago, the Romans built paved roads across parts of Europe and North Africa.

▲ Roman roads

The Romans built long, straight roads covered with flat stones, such as this one in Algeria, North Africa. They used these roads to move soldiers quickly from place to place.

Wow!
The world's longest truck, the Arctic Snow Train, is over 170 metres long, has 54 wheels and needs a team of six drivers.

▼ Building a road

To make a new road, huge earth-moving machines are used to cut away earth, flatten surfaces and smooth asphalt.

1. a bulldozer pushes away earth

2. a scraper levels the ground and smooths a path

3. a dumptruck brings crushed rock

4. a grader smooths rocks to make a flat base

5. a paving machine spreads on a mixture of sand, stones and tar (asphalt), which is then rolled by a rolling machine

◄ So many roads

We are building more roads to cope with the increasing amounts of traffic. Motorways can help to take the strain of all this traffic away from smaller roads, where traffic jams may begin.

▼ Heavy loads

You see many huge lorries like this one on motorways and other fast roads. They transport large loads, often from one country to another. These very large lorries are called 'juggernauts'.

Rocks on Earth

The hard surface of the Earth is made of rock. Many of these rocks were made deep inside the Earth, where it is very hot. Other rocks formed from mud and sand, under enormous pressure (force) and heat.

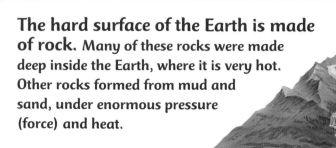

rock may be forced upwards to form mountains

the rocks dip down from the coast to make the deep ocean

some hot rock travels up through volcanoes

layers of rock beneath the sea

squashed rock can become folded

hot rock trapped in the crust can change the rock around it

▲ Above and below

Layers of rock form underground, in the Earth's crust. Some of the rock may be changed by great heat found deep inside the Earth. Rock can also be crushed and folded to form features such as mountain ranges.

chalk forms at the bottom of the seabed

limestone is made from seashells

▼ Rock types

There are many different types of rock. Their appearance, colour and structure depend on how they were formed. Some form as a result of volcanic activity. Others are produced from material that is carried by rivers and deposited (dropped) in the sea.

mudstone is made from squashed mud

▶ Wearing away

Strong desert winds carry grains of sand that erode (wear away) the rocks. Soft rocks may be worn into strange shapes like this arch. The sea and freezing weather can both wear away soft cliffs and rocks.

Rocks and minerals

Find out more:
Earth • Mountains • Volcanoes

Rocks are seen on hillsides and in mountains and river valleys. The tall cliffs at the seaside are made of rock. In other places you cannot see rocks because they are covered by soil and trees, grass and other plants. Every kind of rock is made up of smaller pieces called minerals.

▶ Buried treasure

Gold is a precious mineral that is found inside rocks, deep under the ground. Silver and quartz are other common minerals.

quartz

gold

silver

Wow!

About three-quarters of all the gold produced in the world each year comes from South Africa.

▼ Giant's rocks

The Giant's Causeway in Northern Ireland is made up of thousands of pillars of a black rock called basalt. It formed when hot, liquid rocks from deep inside the Earth gushed out onto the surface and then cooled and gradually hardened.

Word box

mineral
the building blocks of rock

monument
something built in memory of a special person or event

▼ Diamonds

Diamond is the hardest substance in nature. This mineral is used in industry for cutting. Cut diamonds sparkle so brightly that they make valuable gemstones.

▼ Beautiful marble

A rock called marble comes in different colours and patterns. The ancient Greeks carved statues out of marble. Today, we use it for buildings, floor and wall tiles, as well as for monuments. The Taj Mahal in India (right) has beautiful marble detail.

▼ Rare minerals

Some minerals are very rare and beautiful – and expensive too! We call them gemstones, or gems for short. Rubies, emeralds and sapphires are well-known gems that we make into jewellery and ornaments.

rubies

Match the names

Do you know the most common colour of these gemstones? Match the name of each gem with the correct colour.

1. emerald
2. sapphire
3. ruby
4. pearl
5. topaz

a. blue
b. yellow
c. white
d. green
e. red

1d 2a 3e 4c 5b
answers

Rodents

Find out more:
Beavers • Mice and rats • Squirrels

Gnaw, gnash, nibble, nip – rodents are all mammals with long incisor teeth. They use their teeth for many purposes – cracking open nuts and seeds, scraping bark, cutting through wood, digging in soil and biting in self-defence. With 1,700 types of rodents worldwide, they form the largest mammal group. Rodents include rats, mice, voles, lemmings, hamsters, gerbils, squirrels, gophers, beavers, porcupines and guinea pigs.

Word box

cavies
rodent group from
South America, which includes
guinea pigs, chinchillas, and
the huge capybaras

▶ Cute chipmunk

The familiar North American chipmunk is a type of squirrel. It visits picnic areas, parks and gardens for leftover foods, and is sometimes kept as a pet. It stores seeds, nuts and berries in its burrow to eat during the winter.

▼ Coypu cavy

At 1 metre from its nose to its tail, the coypu is like a huge rat. It belongs to the rodent group called cavies. Coypus swim well with their webbed feet, dig burrows in banks and eat water plants.

Wow!

A porcupine cannot shoot out its spines like arrows, but it can jab them into an enemy – and they are very painful to pull out!

▲ Gobbling gopher

Gophers are squirrels that live mostly underground and alone, like moles. They dig tunnels with their paws and teeth, and feed on roots, bulbs and other underground plant parts. Sometimes their burrows and eating habits damage farm crops.

◀ Prickly porcupine

Porcupines are plant eaters. There are about 20 different kinds, which are all active at night. They have long, sharp spines that are really extra-thick hairs.

Roman Empire

ASIA
BRITAIN
GAUL
SPAIN ITALY
• Rome • Constantinople
Carthage • GREECE
Mediterranean Sea •Jerusalem
NORTH
AFRICA Alexandria
EGYPT

Rome was the centre of the world.
Or that is how it seemed to people in Europe 2,000 years ago. From small beginnings, this Italian city grew and grew. It became the centre of a huge empire. Roman power lasted until AD476, when the city was captured by German warriors.

▶ Julius Caesar

Julius Caesar was the most famous Roman soldier of all time. He conquered Gaul (France) and attacked Britain. He became the leader of the Romans, but some people were unhappy that he held so much power and they murdered him, in 44BC.

▲ The power of Rome

The Romans conquered Greece and Egypt. Soon they ruled all the lands from sunny Spain to the deserts of Syria, from rainy Britain to the mountains of North Africa.

▲ High arches

Roman cities had paved streets with gutters and drains. Pipes and channels called aqueducts carried fresh water into the cities.

◀ On the march

The Roman army was divided into legions. The soldiers wore iron armour and helmets and fought with spears and short swords.

▼ Straight roads

Roman engineers built the best roads. They were made of stone and followed a straight line from one city to the next.

large stone slabs

drainage ditch

Word box

empire
many different lands that are ruled by one country

legion
a unit of the Roman army, made up of about 5,500 mounted troops and foot soldiers

Roman life

The city of Rome had bustling streets, crowded blocks of flats, markets, theatres, public baths and stadiums for horse-racing. Out in the country, rich people lived in fancy houses called villas. Some of these even had central heating! Roman farmers grew crops such as wheat, olives and grapes.

◀ At the baths

Many towns in the Roman Empire had public baths. These ones in Bath, England, can still be seen. People came here to meet their friends, to have a hot or a cold dip, or perhaps a clean with oil.

▶ Gods and thunderbolts

The Romans worshipped many different gods. Jupiter was the father of them all. He could send thunderbolts whizzing across the sky. Juno, his wife, was goddess of marriage. Their son was Mars, god of war.

Jupiter   Juno

▼ Dinner time

The Romans' main meal was usually in the late afternoon. Diners lay on couches around a low table. Pork, veal or goose might be on the menu – or, for a special treat, fat little dormice or flamingo tongues!

▲ Cruel combat

The Colosseum was a big arena in Rome. Up to 50,000 people could pack into the stands. They loved to watch trained fighters called gladiators battle to the death.

Make a mosaic

The Romans made floor pictures called mosaics from many little coloured tiles.

1. Cut out small squares of brightly coloured paper.

2. Arrange them to make a picture and stick them on to a large piece of card.

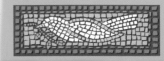

Russia

Russia is the biggest country in the world. Its western part was settled by a people called the Slavs after about AD400. By the 1400s Moscow was becoming the centre of the vast Russian empire, which survived until the revolution in 1917.

▼ St Basil's

In the AD800s, monks from the Byzantine Empire brought Christianity to the Slavs. This cathedral, with its colourful onion-shaped domes, is St Basil's, in the centre of Moscow. Building on it began in 1555.

▶ Catherine the Great

Catherine the Great was empress of Russia from 1762 to 1796. Under her reign, Russia gained many new lands in Europe and Asia.

▲ Revolution, 1917

The tsar (emperor) and nobles in Russia had great power and wealth, while ordinary people had little freedom. Many of them starved. During the 1800s more and more Russians tried to change the way in which their country was ruled. After a revolution in 1917, the communists seized power. They wanted to give power to working people.

▶ Soviet Union

In 1922, the leader of the Russian Revolution, Lenin (left), founded a new country called the Soviet Union. In 1924, Stalin (right) became leader. Communist rule lasted until 1991, when the Soviet Union started to break up.

Lenin   Stalin

Wow!

When Peter the Great came to the throne in 1682, he hated the long, bushy beards worn by the nobles, so he ordered them all to shave. He even cut some of their beards off himself!

Scandinavia

Find out more:
Atlas: Europe • Vikings

The far north of Europe is called Scandinavia. A snowy land of forests and farmlands, it includes the countries of Norway, Sweden and Denmark. Around AD800, Scandinavia was home to the Vikings. In AD1000, Viking kings set up Christian kingdoms. Sometimes one ruler united the kingdoms, sometimes they were separate countries, as they are today.

▼ Sky watch

Built in 1576 by the Danish astronomer Tycho Brahe, this building is an observatory for looking at the stars and planets. It was called *Uraniborg*, meaning 'Castle of the Heavens'.

▼ Wooden church

Wooden churches like this one were built in Norway during the Middle Ages. The Christian faith first reached Norway during the reign of King Olaf I, between AD995 and 1000.

▲ A battling king

In the 1600s, Sweden was one of the most powerful countries in Europe. It fought against the Holy Roman Empire during the Thirty Years War. The Swedes won the Battle of Lützen in 1632, but their king, Gustavus Adolphus, was killed in the fighting.

▼ The Little Mermaid

This statue in Copenhagen, Denmark, shows the Little Mermaid, from the famous story by Hans Christian Andersen. This author, who lived from 1805 to 1875, wrote many famous children's tales.

Word scramble

Can you unscramble these children's stories? They were all written by Hans Christian Andersen in the 1800s:

a. **EHT YGLU GLINKCUD**
b. **HET WONS NEQUE**
c. **TEH NIT RODLIES**
d. **HET SROMPREE WEN SETHCOL**

answers
a. The Ugly Duckling
b. The Snow Queen
c. The Tin Soldier
d. The Emperor's New Clothes

Schools

Find out more:
Books • Computers

Schools are an important part of our society.
They teach us skills which can help us in our daily lives
and prepare us for careers. These skills such as reading,
writing, and numeracy make it easier
to communicate with the world
around us. In the past
usually only boys from rich
families attended school,
but over time girls started
going to school too.

▲ Class of 1898

This class was photographed in
Canada in 1898. By then, education
was encouraged by governments.
Poor children, including girls,
started going to school.

▶ Learning to read

In the 1500s,
English school
children learned
to read letters and
standard sentences on
this hand-held panel,
called a 'hornbook'.

▲ In ancient Egypt

Egyptian boys went to school each
morning. They learned to do sums
and practised their writing on
broken bits of pottery. They were
expected to behave well and were
beaten if they misbehaved.

▶ Roman lessons

Roman children learned
arithmetic. They learned to
read and write in Greek, as
well as in their own language,
Latin. Older pupils were taught
history, poetry and how to
speak well in public.

Word box

arithmetic
a kind of mathematics that
involves doing sums

education
teaching and learning

Science is the study of everything about us, from the living world to the stars and planets. Sciences, such as astronomy and mathematics, are many centuries old. Other sciences, such as computer science, did not exist until 60 years ago. Science never stands still – new things are being discovered all the time.

▶ Which science?

There are many different kinds of science. Here are a few examples. All aim to examine a certain part of the world or Universe, and find an explanation. Many scientists work in more than one area, such as biochemistry (biology and chemistry).

Biology
How animals and plants live, grow, produce young and find food.
Why are leaves green?

Chemistry
What things are made from, and how they behave in different ways.
What is salt made of?

Physics
How the Universe works, how and why things happen to it.
How does an aircraft fly?

Geology
How the Earth was made, its structure, rocks and minerals.
How do mountains form?

Astronomy
The study of the Universe, its planets, stars and galaxies.
When did the Universe begin?

Archaeology
The study of ancient remains, such as skulls and bones.
How tall were the ancient Egyptians?

◀ Scientists at work

Some scientists work in laboratories. Here, they start with an idea, or theory, which asks how something will react in a certain situation. They then carry out experiments, or tests, to see what will happen. The results – what happens at the end – are written down and studied. Finally, the scientist thinks of reasons, or conclusions, for why certain things occurred during the experiment.

The first true scientists were people who would not accept traditional or everyday ideas about how things worked, but wanted to find out for themselves. Their new ideas were often disliked by other people, who were used to thinking in a certain way.

1500s **1600s**

1500   1550   1600   1650   1700

▼ **Leonardo da Vinci (1452–1519)**
An Italian artist who designed many devices, including a type of aircraft (see below). He also made detailed scientific drawings of the human anatomy.

design for simple flying machine

▲ **Galileo Galilei (1564–1642)**
An Italian astronomer who invented the first thermometer, and proved that the planets move around the Sun.

▼ **Isaac Newton (1642–1727)**
An English mathematician who devised the laws of motion and gravity. He also built the first reflecting telescope.

◀▼ Great minds

This chart shows just a few of the many scientists who have made ground-breaking discoveries in the last 500 years. Of course, many brilliant thinkers existed before this time. Around 235BC, for example, a Greek mathematician called Archimedes made several important scientific discoveries. These included how levers work and why an object floats.

1700s **1800s** **1900s**

1700   1750   1800   1850   1900   1950   2000

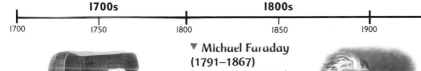

▼ **Michael Faraday (1791–1867)**
An English scientist who invented many electrical machines, like the motor and the dynamo.

◀ **Albert Einstein (1879–1955)**
German-born physicist who made discoveries about space and time, and about nuclear energy and the atom bomb.

$E=mc^2$

▲ **Antoine Lavoisier (1743–1794)**
French scientist who showed the importance of precision weighing in the laboratory, and is regarded as the founder of modern chemistry.

▶ **Alexander Fleming (1881–1955)**
A Scottish doctor who discovered penicillin, a substance important as an antibiotic (medicine used to treat illnesses).

Scorpions belong to a group of animals called arachnids.
This group also includes spiders, harvestmen and mites. Unlike insects, arachnids have no wings. They have four pairs of legs while insects have three. Scorpions and spiders are thought of as scary, but most do not harm humans. Mites burrow under skin, making it sore and itchy. Some pass on disease.

poisonous sting

leg

external skeleton

fangs

pincer (claw)

◄ Stinging tail

Scorpions live in warm places. They hide in the day and come out to hunt for food at night. A scorpion has a curved sting at the end of its long tail. It uses the poison in this sting to kill its prey. A scorpion sting is painful for humans but it does not usually cause death.

▼ Blood suckers

Ticks are small egg-shaped animals, and are cousins of mites. Some live on the bodies of other animals and feed by sucking their blood. Ticks are dangerous because they pass diseases into the blood of their victims.

this image has been magnified to show close-up detail of a tick

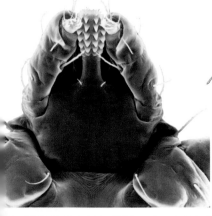

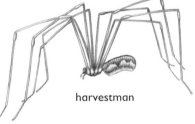

▲ Baby scorpions

Scorpions do not lay eggs — they give birth to live, fully formed young. The young hang onto their mother's back for the first two weeks after they are born.

harvestman

▲ Very long legs

The long-legged harvestman is a harmless creature. It eats small insects and fruit that it finds on the ground. .

Wow!

Female ticks can lay as many as 18,000 eggs at a time.

Sea animals

Find out more:
Dolphins • Fish • Sharks • Whales

The sea is the world's biggest habitat. It extends from rocky coasts, the shallows of coral reefs, and the icebergs of the polar regions. The vast open ocean stretches over most of the Earth and plumbs the darkest depths. All kinds of animals (apart from insects), live in the sea. Scientists are still discovering new kinds of creatures in bays, undersea caves and canyons.

▼ Snakes at sea?

Sea snakes are not just ordinary snakes out for a swim. They are fully suited to ocean life, with a flattened, paddle-like tail for swimming. Sea snakes are cousins of cobras and just as poisonous, killing fish for food.

▲ Millions of fish

Small fish move around in vast shoals of many millions. They are important links in the sea food chains. They feed on tiny plants and animals in the plankton, then they become meals for bigger fish and other sea predators.

Word box

canyon
a deep, narrow, steep sided valley

food chain
series of stages where a plant is eaten by an animal, and that animal is eaten by another, and so on

shoal
many fish swimming together

◄ 'Cow' of the sea

Manatees and dugongs live in tropical waters. They stay near the shore and eat sea-grasses and other plants, giving these animals the nickname of 'sea-cows'.

◄ Not what they seem

Sea creatures are often unfamiliar and puzzling. Jellyfish may look like floppy flowers, but they are proper animals – in fact they are deadly predators. Their trailing tentacles sting and capture prey, such as small fish.

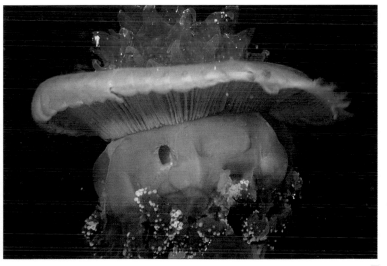

Sea birds

Sea birds depend on the sea for their food. Sea birds include huge albatrosses, smaller petrels and prions, tropic-birds, frigate-birds, gannets, boobies, gulls and auks. Most have long, slim wings for soaring, webbed feet for swimming, and catch fish and squid from near the water's surface.

Wow!

The wandering albatross has the longest wings of any bird – more than 3 metres from tip to tip.

▲ Dive of death

The gannet plunge-dives like an arrow from 30 metres up in the air and seizes its unsuspecting prey in its dagger-like bill.

▼ A place to breed

Most sea birds breed along cliffs and rocky shores. Puffins lay their eggs in burrows, which they dig themselves or take over from rabbits or other birds.

Word box

krill
small shrimplike creatures of the ocean

cliff
a high steep rock face

▲ Amazing albatross

An albatross glides for days, gaining height by heading into the wind. It swoops down to snatch food from the sea and touches land only occasionally to breed.

▲ Storm petrel

True to its name, the tiny storm petrel flies in the worst storms and gales. It skims over the sea, looking for food such as krill and baby fish. Some petrels form vast flocks of many millions of birds.

Seals and sea lions

Find out more:
Antarctic animals

Is the sea lion a 'lion-of-the-sea'? Yes, sort of. It is a fast, fierce and hungry hunter of fish, sea birds, shellfish and other creatures. In fact, a big sea lion is huge, weighing more than a tonne – four times as much as a real lion! All sea lions and seals are speedy hunters. They live mainly along coasts, coming onto land only to rest and breed.

◄ Seal or sea lion?

Seals have no ear flaps. They wriggle on land and swim with their back flippers. This Australian sea lion has tiny ear flaps. It props itself up on its front flippers, tucking the back flippers under to waddle on land. It swims mainly with its front flippers.

▲ On the rocks

Most seals and sea lions, like this northern fur seal, breed in groups on beaches or rocky shores. The pups (babies) soon have to learn to swim and survive on their own.

▲ Tusks

The Arctic walrus uses its tusks to pull shellfish from the sea bed – and to show off to other walruses at breeding time. Like many seals and sea lions, the walrus can dive deep under the water and stay there for over half an hour.

Make seal flippers

1. Swish your hand through a bowl of water with your fingers spread wide.

2. Now, put a plastic bag over your hand. Your hand is now like a seal flipper. Swish your hand through the water again – see how much more water a seal can push with its flipper.

A seal's flippers help it to swim faster!

Wow!
The male elephant seal can be more than six times heavier than the female.

► A cold baby?

No. Seals and sea lions have thick fur coats and also a layer of fat under their skin, called blubber. This keeps them warm, even when lying on ice! The young harp seal of the North Atlantic loses its snowy-white coat after a few weeks, and grows dark, waterproof fur.

Seashore life

Find out more:
Birds • Oceans and life

The seashore is the place where the water from an ocean or sea reaches the land. Some seashores are rocky places with colourful seaweeds and rockpools filled with crabs, shrimps and other sea creatures. Other seashores are covered with sand or mud, where crabs and small worms burrow beneath the soft, wet surface.

▼ Seashore life

The part of the seashore closest to the sea is wet for most of each day. Higher up the shore, it dries out when the tide goes out. The animals and plants that live on the seashore have to survive both wet and dry conditions.

oystercatcher

1. many seabirds build nests on high cliffs overlooking the shore. Some, such as the guillemot, never actually build a nest. Female guillemots lay eggs on narrow ledges.

2. seabirds such as curlews and oystercatchers have long, pointed beaks. They use these to stab shellfish, tear open shells or find worms that burrow in the sand.

curlew

Word box

anchor
to stop something from moving

burrow
to dig deeply

3. small sea creatures such as shrimps and crabs hide in rockpools to avoid being eaten by hungry birds.

starfish

shrimp

crab

▶ In a rockpool

Rockpool creatures such as mussels and limpets cling to the rocks so they are not washed away by waves. Their shells protect them from the sea and the Sun.

4. seaweeds grow along the seashore. They have a special part that anchors them to the rocks. This is called a holdfast.

limpet

mussel

Seasons

When each of the seasons arrives – spring, summer, autumn and winter – they bring changes with them. The weather and the temperature change, and days become longer or shorter. Some parts of the world have four seasons a year, others have only two – a wet and a dry season, or a dark and a light one.

▶ Moving Earth

The movement of the Earth around the Sun causes the seasons. As the Earth moves around the Sun, different places receive different amounts of sunshine because the Earth is tilted at an angle. For example, when the North Pole is tilted towards the Sun, places in the northern half (hemisphere) of the world have summer, while those in the southern half have winter.

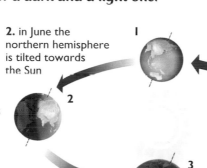

2. in June the northern hemisphere is tilted towards the Sun

3. in September the northern and southern hemispheres receive equal amounts of Sun

1. in March the northern and southern hemispheres receive equal amounts of Sun

4. in December the southern hemisphere is tilted towards the Sun

▼ Harvest time

Grapes are ready to pick at the end of the summer. The harvest is usually good after a long period of dry, sunny weather.

▼ Hot places

The Equator is an imaginary line around the middle of the Earth. Places here are hot all year because the Sun is nearly overhead all year. Rainfall in these places varies throughout the year – a dry season is followed by a wet, stormy one.

Wow!

In places near the North Pole, the Sun shines for 24 hours a day during the middle of summer. This part of the world is called the 'Land of the Midnight Sun'.

▲ Rainy season

In parts of Asia and Africa the rains are very heavy once a year. This is known as the monsoon season. It can cause floods, damage fields of crops and kill farm animals.

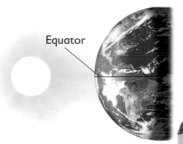

Equator

▼ Winter and summer

These mountains in Switzerland are covered with snow in winter. During summer, cattle graze on the grassy slopes.

Sharks

There are 330 kinds of shark and they are all meat eaters. Some sharks filter food from the water, or lie in wait for victims on the sea bed, rather than speeding through the open ocean after them. Although most fish are bony, the skeleton of a shark is made of cartilage. This is lighter and more elastic than bone.

◀ Hammerhead

Like all sharks, this 6-metre hunter has an amazing sense of smell and can detect blood in the water from many kilometres away. A shark's skin is like sandpaper, because its scales are shaped like tiny versions of the sharp teeth in its mouth. Most sharks live alone, but hammerheads will gather together in groups to breed.

▼ Stingray

Rays are close cousins of sharks. Most glide across the sea bed on their wide 'wings', searching for buried shellfish and worms, which they crush with their wide, flat-topped teeth. The stingray's poison sting is in a dagger blade halfway along its tail.

sting

Wow!

The whale shark is the world's biggest fish, 13 metres long and 15 tonnes in weight — yet it eats only tiny creatures such as krill and baby fish.

▼ Super-hunter

The great white shark is the biggest meat-eating fish, at 7 metres long. Its teeth are up to 8 centimetres — as long as a finger. This shark eats whatever it likes! Other fish, seals, sea birds, sea turtles, small dolphins and giant whales are all its victims. The smallest members of the shark group include dogfish, which are less than 60 centimetres long.

great white shark

Shellfish

Shellfish have shells, but they are not fish. Most belong to the animal group called molluscs, cousins of slugs and snails. Many live along the seashore, on rocks or in sand and mud. Their shells protect against the hot sun, drying wind, pounding waves and their enemies. Crabs, lobsters and shrimps are also sometimes called shellfish, although they are crustaceans, not molluscs.

mussels

Word scramble

Unscramble these words to find the names of five types of shellfish:

a. KHELW
b. SLACLOP
c. ZELLORARSH
d. LEKCOC
e. LEKWIN

answers
a. whelk b. scallop
c. razorshell d. cockle
e. winkle

▲ Strong mussels

Mussels, oysters, cockles, clams and similar shellfish take in sea water and filter tiny bits of food from it. Mussels attach themselves to rocks with strong threads, as though tied by string.

▲ Cone shell

Cone shells really do have cone-shaped shells. This is the West African garter cone, a typical example with its decorated shell. It can grow to 7 centimetres long.

▼ A lucky find

Some oysters contain beautiful shiny pearls, used for jewellery. The oyster makes the pearl around a bit of stone or grit that falls into its shell, which it cannot remove.

▲ Big blue lips

The giant clam is the biggest shellfish, and can be 1 metre across. Its fleshy, frilly 'lips' help it to breathe under the water and to see! Shellfish have no proper head and no ears or nose. But they have lots of tiny 'eyes' that can detect patches of light and dark and shadows.

Wow!

Cone shells have a very poisonous 'bite' that can even kill a person!

Ships and boats

Ships sail across open seas and lakes or travel along rivers and canals. They carry people and goods from place to place. Luxury ocean liners take thousands of passengers on holiday cruises. Giant oil tankers transport millions of tonnes of oil across rough seas. Cargo ships carry foods, cars and coal from one side of the world to the other.

◄ Small boats

A boat is a much smaller craft than a ship. Many boats have no engine and are propelled through the water by oars or sails. Most cannot travel across oceans or large bodies of water.

▲ Racing yachts

We sail yachts for pleasure and also for racing. Most yachts have one or more sails, but some have a motor engine only. Large racing yachts sail around the world with a crew of about 20 people on board.

▶ Sailing in style

The *Grand Princess*, built in 1998 is one of the largest passenger ships in service. It is a massive, luxurious, floating hotel, with numerous swimming pools and facilities. *The Grand Princess* has enough rooms for 2,600 passengers, and weighs 109,000 tonnes.

▼ Floating on air

A hovercraft is a ship that floats on a cushion of air. It can travel over land or water. Some hovercraft operate like car ferries and carry passengers and cars across water.

▼ Car ferries

Large ships called car ferries carry people and vehicles across small stretches of water. People drive their vehicles on and off through enormous doors at the bow (front) and stern (back) of the ferry.

Wow!

The largest tankers are over half a kilometre long. Sailors travel from one end of the tanker to the other by bicycle.

The first ships were either rafts made by tying logs together, or dugout canoes made from tree trunks. At first, boats were propelled by paddles, and then sails were added. Over 200 years ago steam-powered boats were developed. About this time, ship-builders began to build iron ships instead of wooden ones.

▲ Reed boats

More than 5,000 years ago the Egyptians built lightweight river boats out of bundles of reeds. They were propelled by a long pole and, later on, by oars.

Word box

propelled
pushed forwards

propeller
a set of spinning blades that drives a ship

Greek cargo ship

◄ Strong and fast

The ancient Greeks built cargo ships which carried goods for trading. On the side of the ship were painted 'eyes'. The sailors believed these scared away evil spirits and protected them from harm.

SS Great Britain

◄ Fighting ships

Ships called galleons sailed the seas and oceans during the 1500s. They were used as fighting ships and to carry cargo. Galleons and Galleasses from Spain and England fought against each other in the Armada battle off the south coast of England.

▲ Propeller power

The *SS Great Britain* was built in 1843. It was the first ship powered by a propeller to cross the Atlantic. The *SS Great Britain* was one of the first ships made of iron.

Wow!

Viking lords and ladies from northern Europe believed their warships had magical symbolism so they asked to be buried inside them. They believed the ships would take them safely to the 'land of the dead'.

Sloths and anteaters

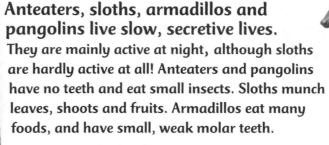

Anteaters, sloths, armadillos and pangolins live slow, secretive lives.
They are mainly active at night, although sloths are hardly active at all! Anteaters and pangolins have no teeth and eat small insects. Sloths munch leaves, shoots and fruits. Armadillos eat many foods, and have small, weak molar teeth.

three-toed sloth

▶ Scaly ball

Pangolins live in Africa and Asia, both on the ground and in trees. Like an armadillo, a pangolin can curl into a ball, completely protected by its hard plates of bone and horn. It licks up insect food with a long, sticky, flicking-out tongue.

▼ Insect-eater

The giant anteater of South America rips open an ant nest or termite mound and licks up a few hundred insects with its very long tongue.

▲ Grub-digger

The armadillo shuffles about at night and digs for grubs, worms, termites, shoots and fruits. Its daytime den is a long, deep burrow. When in danger it rolls into a hard-cased ball.

◀ Slow descent

A sloth usually hangs upside down from a branch, gripping with its long claws. It only comes down if it cannot reach another tree through the branches. The sloth drags itself along the ground on bent knuckles, watching for predators such as jaguars.

Juicy 'ants'

Pretend that some raisins are ants. Put some on a plate and try eating them like an anteater, with your tongue – no fingers! An anteater can lick up more than 300 ants each minute. How many can you eat?

Snails and slugs

Find out more:
Octopuses and squid • Shellfish

They move so slowly, it is amazing they survive at all. Slugs and snails thrive in woods, ponds, rivers, even dry grasslands and deserts. A snail has a curly shell for protection, but most slugs do not – except for shelled slugs! Slugs and snails are both molluscs, and there over 50,000 kinds worldwide.

flavescens slug

▲ Nudibranch

The name of this sea slug means 'naked gill'. Nudibranchs don't have a shell to protect their gills. They are poisonous and brightly coloured to warn predators to keep away.

Word box

mucus
a slimy, slippery, sticky substance made by animals (and by us in our noses)

predators
animals that hunt and eat other animals

Wow!

Some types of snail are male or female, some types change from one to the other as they grow, and some are male and female at the same time!

▼ Moving house

The snail's shell protects its body. The head has two or four tentacles, tipped with simple eyes that detect shadows and light areas. There is a mouth on the underside that they use to eat plant food like leaves.

giant snail

◄ Sliming along

Slugs and snails use plenty of mucus to slide along. The mucus puts off attackers who may want to eat them. Slugs and snails like damp places best and prefer to come out after rain or at night.

Snakes

It is hard to mistake a snake – it has no legs.
Because snakes are hunters they have long teeth for
grabbing prey. But these reptiles cannot chew – they must
swallow food whole. There are almost 3,000 kinds of
snakes, and apart from the icy polar regions, they live
all over the world – even in the open ocean. Less than
30 types of snakes are truly deadly to people.

Wow!
The longest snakes are royal
pythons, which grow up
to 10 metres long.
They could wrap
around you
12 times!

▼ Poisonous fangs

Poisonous snakes, such as this cobra, use their venom to kill or
quieten prey, so it cannot run away or struggle while being
swallowed. Cobras, kraits, mambas and coral-snakes have their
poison-jabbing fangs near the front of the mouth. The fangs of
vipers, sidewinders, adders
and rattlesnakes are hinged to
fold back when not being used.

Word box

pits
holes or bowl-like hollows

vibrations
shaking movements

▲ A big hug

Pythons and boas, like this
Madagascan tree boa, are mostly
big, heavy snakes. They can wrap
around prey so it cannot breathe.
Big pythons and boas can swallow
prey as large as wild pigs and small
antelopes – including the horns!

▶ See, hear, smell and taste

The Aruba rattlesnake shows how sensitive snakes
are. It sees quite well, especially movements. It hears
well too, and feels vibrations in the ground. The tongue flicks
out to smell and 'taste' the air. Rattlesnakes are pit-vipers and
have pits under the eyes. These detect heat, so the snake can catch
a warm-blooded victim like a mouse even in complete darkness.

Social animals

Find out more:
Insects • Wolves and dogs

Most animals spend much of their lives alone.
But some live with others of their kind, usually sharing jobs such as cleaning and finding food, warning of danger and even protecting each other. These groups are called animal societies. It is mainly insects, birds and mammals that form these societies. Usually there is just one leader.

▶ One for all, all for one

Bees form a society together, as do wasps, ants and termites. Worker bees clean the nest, gather food and tend grubs (young). They communicate by touches, smells and movements. They gather to attack and sting an enemy to protect their very close family.

▲ Sentry duty

Social living means there are many eyes and ears to detect danger. In southern African grasslands, some meerkats take turns to watch for danger while the others feed. When the lookout barks or growls, all the members race down into their burrows.

Word scramble

Unscramble these words to find the names of five animals that form societies:

a. TESTMERI
b. LASROGLI
c. NAST
d. WIERDBRAVES
e. SEVLOW

answers
a. termites b. gorillas c. ants d. weaverbirds e. wolves

▶ Bird 'skyscraper'

Sociable weaverbirds make a huge shared nest in an acacia tree. Each male and female has its own chamber, but the whole nest may contain over 200 birds. They are safe in numbers as they squawk, flap and peck enemies. They also feed together, always watching each other. If one finds food, the others gather to share it.

Sound

We hear sound all the time – from a ticking clock and a singing bird to a ringing doorbell or a car in the street. Every sound is made in the same way. An object shakes gently when it makes a noise. This shaking movement is called a vibration. The air around the object also starts to vibrate, and these vibrations travel through the air as waves of sound.

Concorde

◀ Bouncing waves

Bats produce high-pitched sounds that cannot be heard by humans or other animals. The sound waves bounce off the food they hunt, such as insects, then back to the bat, telling the bat where their food is.

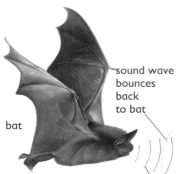

bat

sound wave bounces back to bat

moth

sound wave from bat

▲ At top speed

Sound travels through the air at about 340 metres a second. Sound waves travel more slowly than waves of light – light travels about one million times more quickly. Some jet aircraft travel faster than the speed of sound. When they do, they make a loud, booming noise.

clarinet

▶ Speak up!

Our voices make sounds by vibrating our vocal cords. These are the soft flaps of skin in the voice box, at the back of the throat. When air passes over the vocal cords, they vibrate and make a sound. We then use our tongue and lips to change the sounds and form words.

vocal cords are open and no sound is made

vocal cords close and air is forced out

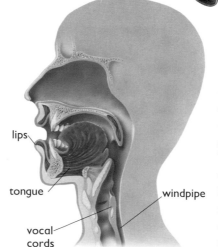

lips

tongue

windpipe

vocal cords

▲ Musical sounds

Musical sounds are made in many different ways. The sound from a guitar is made by plucking the strings, which start to vibrate. When a musician blows into a clarinet or a flute, the air inside the instrument vibrates, creating sound. The skin across the top of a drum vibrates when it is hit with a drumstick or a hand.

Sound and hearing

Find out more:
Human body • Music and dance • Sound

The sounds you hear have travelled through the air and into your ears. They travel as invisible sound waves. As they enter your ears, the sound waves make your eardrums vibrate. These vibrations pass to nerves in your ears, which carry messages about the sounds to the brain. Your brain helps you to understand the different sounds you hear.

Wow!

The smallest bone in your body is inside your ear – it is tinier than a grain of rice.

▶ Into the ear

Your ear is divided into three main parts: the outer ear, which is the part you can see and touch, the middle ear and the inner ear. Your eardrum (a piece of flexible skin) separates your outer ear from your middle ear.

ear drum

inner ear

nerves carry messages to and from the brain

middle ear

outer ear

▼ Levels of sound

Sound is measured in units called decibels (dB). For example, a whisper measures only 20 decibels, while an atomic explosion measures 200 decibels.

0   50   100   150   200

▼ On the move

You can listen to music on the move with the help of a small personal stereo. If you listen to very loud music too often, you may damage your ears.

▼ Without words

Deaf people hear either faint sounds or no sounds at all. Many deaf people communicate with each other with the help of sign language. They use their hands, face and the top half of their body to make signs. Each sign has a different meaning.

Word box

atomic
to do with atoms, the smallest parts of anything

nerve
a tiny thread that carries messages to the brain

South America

Find out more:
South America and its people • Atlas: South America

The continent of South America covers about 12 percent of the Earth's land area. You can find almost every kind of land feature there. South America has hot, steamy rainforests and dry deserts, towering, snow-capped mountain peaks and wide, grassy plains, active volcanoes and spectacular waterfalls. Brazil is by far the biggest country in South America.

▶ High and low

High up among the jagged peaks of the Andes Mountains rise the snow-covered tips of active volcanoes, such as Cotopaxi. This volcano, in Ecuador, has erupted over 25 times during the past 400 years.

▶ Copper mines

South America has huge amounts of valuable minerals such as gold, copper and lead. Some of the world's biggest copper mines are in Chile. Miners remove the copper ore from mines or open pits on the surface.

▼ Full of life

In the basin of the Amazon river lies the Amazon rainforest, the largest in the world. It contains more kinds of plants and animals than any other forest.

parrot   butterfly   toucan

jaguar   snakes   monkey

Word box

basin
the area where a river collects its water

jagged
sharp and pointed

mineral
a natural substance in rock or metal

South American people

About three-quarters of all South Americans live in cities and towns. **This is because many poor people leave the countryside to look for work in the city. There are groups of Native Americans living in many South American countries, such as the Aymara people of Bolivia. These peoples lived in South America before the settlers arrived from Europe. Many people have mixed ancestry and many languages are spoken there.**

Word box

native
someone born in a particular place

network
something that is linked,
like a series of roads

▲ Old traditions

The Aymara Indians of Bolivia speak their own language and follow a traditional way of life. Most are farmers, but they also weave textiles, build reed boats and make pottery to earn money.

▶ Big cities

Cities like Brazil's São Paulo (right) and Rio de Janeiro are growing quickly. São Paulo has towering skyscrapers and busy streets, but there are not enough houses, and many people live in poor areas called 'shanty towns'.

▼ Great builders

The Inca people ruled large areas of South America in the 1400s and 1500s. These great builders made a network of roads across the Andes Mountains. The walled city of Machu Picchu, now in ruins, was built by the Incas in Peru.

Where am I?

Solve this riddle to find the name of a South American country.
My first is in COUGH but not in BOUGH.
My second is in THEE but not in TEE.
My third is in PIG but not in PUG.
My fourth is in TALE but not in TEA.
My last is in SEW but not in SOW.

answer
CHILE

▲ Conquerors from Europe

In the 1500s, soldiers from Spain and Portugal came to South America to conquer the peoples living there. They took over their lands and riches. The Europeans were attracted by the gold they saw. They also wanted to teach the Christian religion to the people.

Machu Picchu

Southeast Asia is a region of tropical forests and islands. For thousands of years people grew rice and traded with India, China and Arabia. Some became Hindus, Buddhists or Muslims. Powerful kingdoms grew up in Southeast Asia between AD500 and 1300.

cinnamon

cloves

pepper

▲ Angkor Wat

The world's biggest religious site is in Cambodia and is called Angkor Wat. This temple was built in honour of the Hindu god Vishnu. It dates back to the 1100s, when the Khmer Empire ruled Cambodia.

▼ Ancient dances

Beautiful dances have been seen on the island of Java for hundreds of years. They were first performed at the royal court.

▼ Early entertainment

Puppets were being used on Java over 900 years ago. They were placed behind a cotton screen and lit from behind. When moved by sticks, they made shadows across the screen. Shadow puppets are still in use today.

▲ Spice islands

The islands of Southeast Asia produced precious spices. These included pepper, cinnamon bark and the dried flower buds of the clove tree. After the 1500s, merchants from Portugal, Britain and the Netherlands seized control of the trade in spices.

▶ Countries of Southeast Asia

A hundred years ago, most of Southeast Asia was ruled by European countries. At the end of the 19th Century, Southeast Asian countries began to fight for their freedom.

CHINA

MYANMAR

THAILAND VIETNAM

PHILIPPINES

CAMBODIA

BRUNEI PACIFIC

MALAYA OCEAN

Singapore

SUMATRA

BORNEO

JAVA Bali

Space travel

Find out more:
Moon • Planets • Spacecraft

The first person to travel in space was a Russian called Yuri Gagarin. In 1961 he circled the Earth for about 90 minutes in a tiny *Vostok* spacecraft. Eight years later, the first men walked on the surface of the Moon. Since then, astronauts have walked in space, repaired telescopes in space and lived for months at a time inside space stations.

Yuri Gagarin

▼ Space dog

A dog named Laika was the first living thing to go into space. In 1957 she travelled in a Russian spacecraft called *Sputnik 2*, and lived for about 4 days in space.

Wow!

A Russian cosmonaut spent 438 days in space inside the *Mir* space station.

▼ To the Moon

Three American astronauts flew to the Moon in the *Apollo 11* spacecraft. While one astronaut stayed in the main spacecraft, the others landed on the Moon in a smaller vehicle.

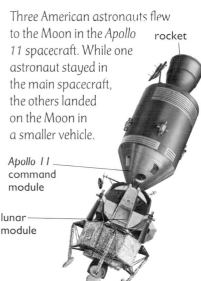

rocket

Apollo 11 command module

lunar module

▲ Protective suits

This astronaut is walking in space. His extra-thick suit protects him from any dangerous rays in space.

◄ Visiting crews

The American *Skylab* was launched in 1973. It was the second space station to be launched, beaten by the Russian *Salyut 1* in 1971. Despite a few problems, three 3-man crews visited *Skylab* and the longest mission lasted 84 days. The 75-tonne space station eventually burned up in the atmosphere in 1979.

Word box

astronaut
a space traveller

cosmonaut
a Russian space traveller

Spacecraft

Find out more:
Planets • Space travel • UFOs and aliens

Spacecraft have travelled enormous distances through space to visit all the planets. No human beings have landed on any of the planets yet. The first spacecraft were tiny capsules with no one on board. Astronauts now travel into space in a space shuttle or rocket. This spacecraft, which can be used again and again, lands back on Earth like an aircraft.

Wow!
The USA's two unmanned *Voyager* spacecraft carry recorded messages from people on Earth. This is in case they meet any other living things in space.

▼ Rocket power

The *Ariane* space rocket lifts off into space in a cloud of fire and hot gases. It launches satellites for many countries. The letters 'ESA' on the side of the rocket stand for European Space Agency.

◄ Space station

In the year 2000 the first crews arrived at the International Space Station, or ISS. This huge space station was built by sixteen different countries, and is a permanent research centre where scientists can conduct experiments and observe the Earth and outer space. Today it is even possible to go to the space station as a tourist.

▶ Back to Earth

The USA's space shuttle is launched into space by a huge rocket, but it lands back on the ground along a runway. A parachute at the back helps it to slow down after landing.

▶ Satellite in space

A satellite is an object that circles the Earth, up in space. Hundreds of satellites have been placed in space by scientists to send radio, TV and telephone signals around the world. *Sputnik 1*, the very first spacecraft, was a satellite. It was launched by the Russians in 1957.

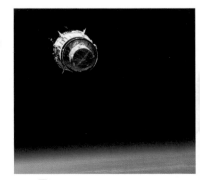

Spain and Portugal were the home of all sorts of peoples, including Basques, Goths, Iberians, Celts, Greeks, Romans, Germans, Moors, Jews and Roma (gypsies). In the 1500s, the kingdoms of Spain and Portugal conquered lands in the New World, making both countries rich and powerful. Spain ruled Portugal from 1580 to 1640.

▶ El Cid

The Spanish knight Ruy Diaz de Vivar was a hero of the Middle Ages. He fought against, and sometimes with, the Moors who lived in southern Spain. They called him *El Cid*, which means 'the lord'. In 1094, he captured the province of Valencia and became its ruler.

▲ The navigators

This statue in Lisbon, Portugal, recalls Portuguese explorers of the 1400s, such as Bartolomeu Díaz (Cape of Good Hope 1488) and Vasco da Gama (India 1498). They were some of the first Europeans to carry out long sea voyages, sailing around the coast of Africa and crossing the Indian Ocean.

Ferdinand of Aragon

Isabella of Castile

◀ Ferdinand and Isabella

In 1479 Spain became one country under the rule of Isabella of Castile and Ferdinand of Aragon. In 1492 Christian knights defeated the Muslim Moors.

◀ Spanish rebels

Between 1936 and 1939, Spain was shattered by a civil war. General Franco then ruled as a dictator until 1975, when Juan Carlos I became king and a democratic government was established.

Word box

Moor
a Muslim of Berber or Arab descent, who lived in Morocco or Spain in the Middle Ages

Spiders

A spider has eight legs, unlike insects, which have six legs. Nearly all spiders have a poisonous bite, using their fanglike mouthparts, but only a few are harmful to people. Most spin silk from their rear ends to make webs for catching small prey, such as flies.

tarantula

▲ Funnelweb

The funnelweb of Australia has strong fangs and powerful poison. It is dangerous because it lives in or near people's homes. It rears up and strikes quickly, unlike most spiders, which usually run away.

▼ On the prowl

Some spiders do not use webs for catching prey. They simply chase, overpower and bite their prey. The wolf spider is one of these. Like most spiders, it has eight eyes — and these are large, so it can follow its victim.

▲ Big and hairy

Tarantulas and bird-eating spiders are big, strong and hairy, and live in the tropics, mainly in the Americas. They hunt at night for small animals such as mice, shrews and baby birds.

Wow!

A web-spinning spider makes a new web almost every night — eating the old one to recycle (use again) the silk threads.

◄ House spider

The house spider spins an untidy web in a corner, and eats most small creatures that blunder into it. Spiders do not really like baths — they tend to slip in and cannot crawl out.

Sport

Sport provides entertainment for millions of people. Some sports are played individually, and others involve entire teams. Sport can also help to keep us fit. Many people play sport just for fun, but for others, it is their job. Great numbers of people watch athletes at stadiums (huge sports grounds), or follow them on TV or radio.

▼ In the basket

Basketball is played by two teams of five players each. It is the most popular indoor sport. A Canadian teacher invented the game in 1891 to keep his students busy and fit during the long, dark winters.

▼ Up in the sky

Skydiving involves jumping from an aircraft and performing special moves in the air. Skydivers wear parachutes that help them land safely on the ground. Teams of skydivers sometimes join hands in the air before their parachutes open up.

▲ Most popular

Soccer is probably the world's most popular sport. Top soccer teams play matches in stadiums in front of thousands of fans. The first rules for the game were drawn up in England in the 1848.

▼ Steering through the water

Windsurfing is a very popular water sport even though it only started about 40 years ago. The windsurfer must balance on a sailboard while steering it through the water at top speed.

Wow!

Each American football team has around 45 players but only 11 are allowed onto the pitch at one time.

a b c d e f g h i j k l m n o p q r **s** t u v w x y z **287**

Sport in history

People have always enjoyed playing and watching sports. In the ancient world, games were sometimes part of important religious festivals. Athletics helped to train warriors for war, too, and to keep them fit. Ancient Greek weapons, such as the javelin, are still thrown by athletes today.

▼ The Olympic Games

In 1906, the first of the modern series of the Olympic Games was held in Athens, Greece. The original games had been held between 771BC and AD393. Ancient events included discus-throwing, running, jumping and wrestling.

1906   771BC

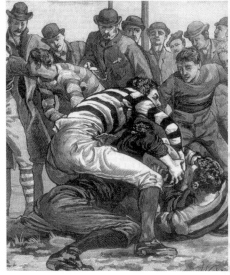

▲ Making up the rules

Rugby football was invented in 1823 by a schoolboy who picked up a football and ran with it. Many other sports became popular in the 1800s and were given standard rules. These included lawn tennis, netball, badminton and baseball.

Support your team!

What is your favourite team sport and which team do you follow?

See if you can find out the facts below. Then make a chart that you can stick up on the wall, and decorate it with club colours and badges.

1. When was your favourite sport first played?
2. Where was the sport first played?
3. When was your team founded?
4. Which year was the most successful in its history?
5. Who was its best player ever?

▼ Speed sports

New machines meant new and ever faster sports were taken up in the 1900s. Racing cycles, motorcycles, cars and aeroplanes now pulled in big crowds of spectators. These racing cars date from 1953.

Sporting events

A top sporting competition is a major event. For example, the Wimbledon tennis tournament is held each summer in London. The world's biggest sporting event is the Olympic Games, which features a huge variety of sports. This takes place every four years, as does soccer's World Cup. People come from all over the world to watch sport and represent their countries.

Word box

bobsleigh
a fast-moving sledge

circuit
a motor racing track

▲ World class

The best tennis players can earn millions of pounds. They receive prize money when they win a competition. Pete Sampras, shown above, has won Wimbledon a record seven times. World-class players also receive money from sports companies whose clothing and equipment they wear and use.

▶ Hard work

Gymnasts have to train very hard to be able to perform in national and international competitions. The very first gymnasts were soldiers in ancient Greece.

▲ Winter sports

The most important competition for winter sports is the Winter Olympic Games, which takes place every four years. The main sports held are skiing (above), ski jumping, skating and bobsleigh racing.

▼ Game of strategy

At the world chess championships millions of people follow every move of the champion players. Chess is a board game that is played by two players. It is a game of skill and patience. The winner is the one who traps the main piece, the king, of the other player.

▼ Motor racing

Large numbers of people watch motor racing, either at a circuit or on the television. The fastest cars are called Formula One cars. They take part in about 17 races around the world each year, to find the best driver and the best make of car.

Wow!

A bobsleigh can travel at over 130 kilometres an hour along a track made of of solid ice.

Squirrels

Squirrels have bright eyes, a bushy tail and sharp claws. A typical squirrel leaps through trees, nibbles seeds and buries nuts. Some squirrels prefer flowers or fruits to nuts. Some glide on flaps of furry skin that lie along the sides of the body. Others have small, stumpy tails and never climb trees. The 250 types of squirrel are all rodent mammals, cousins of beavers, rats and mice.

▼ At home with the prairie dogs

Named after their doglike 'yips', prairie dogs are ground squirrels of North American grasslands. They dig complicated burrows with many entrances and chambers as a home for one male, several females and their young. The burrow entrance has soil piled around it to keep out water during floods. Many similar burrows over a wide area are called a township.

Word box

hibernate
to sleep very deeply for weeks, usually to survive a long winter

prairie
grasslands or the wide-open plains of North America

▲ Grey squirrel

The grey squirrel originally from North America easily leaps wide distances among the branches of trees, using its tail to balance and steer.

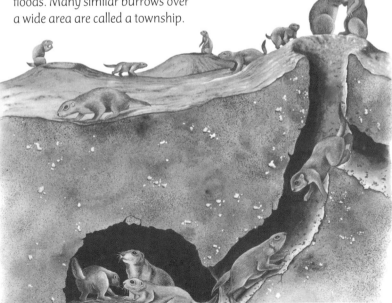

▲ Arctic ground squirrel

This ground squirrel is also called a marmot. It lives in a burrow and eats a wide variety of grasses, seeds, buds and shoots. Like many squirrels in places that have cold winters, it hibernates in its burrow for several months.

Starfish and urchins

Find out more:
Poisonous animals • Sea animals

Starfish are round or circular. They are part of the group of animals called echinoderms. This group includes the ball-shaped spiny sea urchins, sausage-shaped crawling sea cucumbers, flower-like sea lilies and feather stars, which are attached by stalks to the ocean bottom. All 6,000 kinds of echinoderms live in the sea.

▶ Spiny ball

Like starfish, sea urchins have long, wavy, tube-shaped 'feet'. These poke out between their long spines, which can tilt at their bases. A starfish 'walks' on its feet and spines and uses its five-part mouth to scrape tiny animals and plants from rocks.

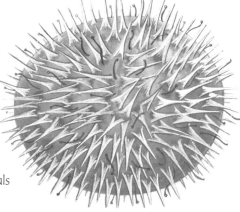

▲ Common starfish

The starfish is a predator. When it finds a shellfish to eat, the starfish slowly pulls the shell open – then turns its own stomach inside out, through its mouth on the underside, to eat the victim's soft insides.

Wow!

If a sea cucumber is in danger from an enemy, it throws its guts out of its mouth!

◀ Pencil urchin

All echinoderms have a circular body shape, like a wheel with spokes. This is usually based on the number five. This means that most starfish have 5, 10 or 15 arms, and so on. Most urchins have a five-part body too, like an orange with five segments. Pencil urchins have spines that look like thick crayons. A few types of urchins have poison in their spines too.

Stars

Have you ever seen stars twinkling?

These stars are part of the Milky Way galaxy, the family of stars in which our Sun lives. Light from faraway stars takes years to reach Earth. Light from our nearest star, the Sun, takes eight minutes to reach us.

Milky Way

▼ Star patterns

Patterns formed by stars are called constellations. Many are named after animals and people from Greek myths. The constellation of Orion is named after Orion the Hunter. A row of three stars across the middle makes up the hunter's belt.

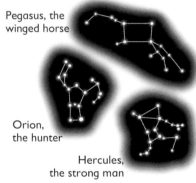

Pegasus, the winged horse

Orion, the hunter

Hercules, the strong man

▶ Star-watching

People who study stars and planets are called astronomers. Modern astronomers use very powerful telescopes. Some telescopes have been placed in space. They send pictures back to Earth. The most famous of these is the Hubble Space Telescope.

Hubble Space Telescope

▼ Life and death

New stars are born all the time – and old ones die. New stars are born inside clouds of dust and gas. Stars swell before they die. Very large stars can explode.

exploding star

▼ Different stars

Stars give off heat and light. A blue-white star is very hot, but a red coloured star is cooler. Our Sun is a main sequence star, which means that it is medium-hot.

supergiant

main sequence star

Word box

constellation
a well-known pattern of stars

galaxy
a huge family of stars

supergiant
a huge red star that is beginning to cool down

Stone Age

Before people learned how to make things from metal, they made tools and weapons from stone, shell, wood, horn or bone. This period is called the Stone Age. People were working with copper in some parts of Asia and Europe by 6000BC, but it took thousands of years for these metal-working skills to spread.

▶ Survival

The Stone Age lasted tens of thousands of years. Although people had less information than we do today, they could be just as clever. They made some progress improving their methods of hunting, fishing and gathering food. In the end, they learned how to farm.

▲ Ring of stone

Towards the end of the Stone Age ancient Britons created a ring of massive stones at Stonehenge. The stones were lined up to follow the path of the Sun across the sky. Historians think that important religious ceremonies were held here between about 3200BC and 1100BC.

▼ Homes for the dead

Between about 5,700 and 4,000 years ago, important people in northwestern Europe were buried in stone tombs, covered with mounds of earth. Some of these tombs, called barrows, can still be visited today.

▲ Cutting edge

Stone Age tools included scrapers, knives, axe-heads, spear-heads, arrows and fish-hooks. Many were made from a hard stone called flint, which could be chipped into the right shape.

burial chamber reached by underground passage

hump of earth

Sun

The Sun is a huge ball of hot, glowing gas. It provides the heat and light that living things on Earth need to stay alive. It is our nearest star, which is why it looks bigger than other stars. The Sun is about 150,000,000 kilometres from the Earth.

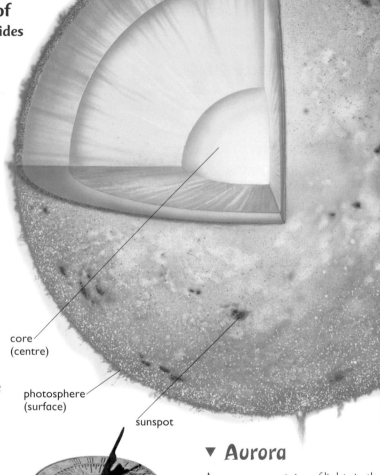

core (centre)

photosphere (surface)

sunspot

▶ Very hot

The Sun is very, very hot. The temperature on its surface is about 6,000 degrees Celsius — that's 60 times hotter than boiling water. The centre of the Sun is almost 3,000 times hotter than its surface.

▼ Spots and flares

Dark spots sometimes appear on the Sun's surface. These are called sunspots. The Sun can give off huge bursts of bright light called flares. They shoot out from its surface.

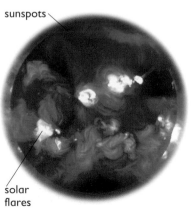

sunspots

solar flares

▲ Telling the time

You can use the Sun to tell the time. A sundial is a kind of clock that shows how a shadow changes as the Sun moves across the sky. You tell the time by looking to see where the shadow falls on the dial.

▼ Aurora

Aurorae are curtains of lights in the sky caused by particles from the Sun. The lights may be blue, red or yellow. They occur in the far north or south of the world.

Swamp animals

Find out more:
Cats • Crocodiles and alligators

Frogs and dragonflies are well suited to swamps, bogs and marshes. A swamp can almost dry out, then flood. So animals must be very adaptable, like lungfish who breathe air, deer who hide in thick reeds, snakes who dive for food and turtles who stay underwater for hours.

▼ Swamp snake

The anaconda of South America is a type of boa-constrictor. It usually squeezes, or squashes, its prey to death.

◄ Swamp croc

Caimans are types of crocodiles found in the Americas. They grow to 6 metres long and eat fish, lizards, snakes, turtles and sometimes mammals.

▼ Swamp bird

The small night heron has a white plume behind each 'ear', which it raises to attract a mate. It stalks or wades quietly at night, hunting a range of smaller creatures.

Wow!

The anaconda is the world's bulkiest snake, weighing up to 250 kilograms — as much as four adult people.

▼ Swamp cat

Of the big cats, the jaguar of Central and South America is most at home in water. It wades, swims and dives in the Amazon river to catch fish and turtles. It also eats snakes and tapirs.

Technology

Technology is how we use science to help us. It began many thousands of years ago, when someone discovered that stones could be broken to make a sharp blade. It has come a long way since then! Today, without technology, we could not travel long distances, surf the Internet or make phone calls to our friends.

▲ Lazy technology

This is a vacuum cleaner that does all the work by itself! It will wander about the room, cleaning away until it is switched off again. This machine contains sensors that stop it bumping into things or getting stuck in corners.

◄ Pocket PC

Powerful computers can now be packed into pocket-sized devices called Personal Digital Assistants (PDAs). They do not have a normal keyboard, and information is loaded from a large computer, or is keyed in by touching the screen with a small pen called a stylus.

Wow!

Scientists are planning to make tiny machines that can be injected into our bodies! They will be used to repair damaged body tissues. This is called nanotechnology.

► Tiny technology

A tiny chip made from silicon contains the whole 'brain' of a computer, even though it is smaller than a fingernail. It may be only 0.5 millimetres thick. The chips do not use much power and can be built into almost any machine. You will not even know they are there!

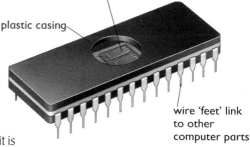

silicon 'wafer'

plastic casing

wire 'feet' link to other computer parts

► Working robots

Computer-controlled robots are used for many jobs, such as making cars and spacecraft. This robotic lifting device, called the Canadarm, was built by the Canadians for use on American space shuttles. It has been useful in assembling the new International Space Station.

Technology for fun

Technology costs millions of euros to develop, but sometimes we can use it just for fun! Whole computers can be packed into toys, and some video games use lots of computing power. Once new technology is developed, people work out all sorts of other uses for it, whether you are at home, at school or on the move.

▶ Cyber dog

This robot dog is powered by a battery, and contains a simple computer that controls its movements. It can also understand and act on basic commands.

▲ On the move

Mini discs are tiny versions of the CD. Mini disc players are small and light, so will fit in your pocket. They have a 'skip-free' device, so that the music will not jump when you are moving around. Most allow you to record from CDs.

◀ Computer power

When you play a computer game, you are actually using a very powerful computer. The computer has to make millions of calculations just to make a single object move across the screen.

▲ Movie star

You can make and star in your own movies! Small digital video cameras like this include the software to let you edit your own movie and create special effects. The camera records information on a memory chip. The end result can then be viewed on a computer screen or sent as emails.

Word box

edit
put together material for a film, TV programme, book or newspaper

software
the programs used by a computer

Theatre

Find out more:
Books

People go to the theatre to watch a play, a musical, avariety performance, an opera or a ballet. The performance usually takes place on a stage at the front of the theatre. The audience sits in rows facing the stage. In ancient Greece, audiences would sit outside to watch plays performed in open-air theatres.

Wow!

In the 1500s, if an audience disliked the play they shouted out rude remarks and threw rotten vegetables at the actors.

▶ In ancient Rome

Roman theatres were huge, well-built structures. One of the best-preserved is at Orange, in France. It has seats for almost 10,000 people. It was so cleverly designed that the audience could hear the actors, even from the back row.

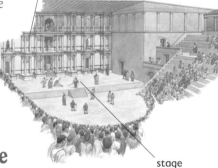

scenery could be complicated, so it was moved around by machinery

stage

▼ Modern theatre

Many new theatres are modern-looking buildings, like the National Theatre in Ghana, Africa.

▼ Famous writer

William Shakespeare (1564–1616) was a successful English playwright (a person who writes plays). Many of his plays were performed at the court of Queen Elizabeth I. Today, Shakespeare is still one of the world's best-known writers.

▶ The Globe

The plays of William Shakespeare were performed in London's Globe Theatre in the 1600s. An exact copy of the original theatre was completed in 1996, close to the original site.

Time

Time can be measured in various ways. You can tell the time roughly by looking at the length of shadows. But the need for accurate time became important, in general, when railways spread around the world in the mid-1800s and train timetables were developed. Now time can be measured even more precisely with atomic clocks, using the vibration of atoms.

▲ First calendars

Calendars help to keep track of days, weeks, months and years. The Mayan people of central America made calendars on the ground, in the shape of the Sun. Signs for the days were carved around the outside. Time was tracked by the Sun's movement.

▼ Night and day

People on opposite sides of the world have day and night at different times. As the Earth spins round, half the world is in daylight and the other half, facing away from the sun, has night. When it is 11 o'clock in the morning in London, UK, the time in Sydney, Australia is 9 o'clock at night.

▼ Giant calculator

Stonehenge, in England, is a huge circle of stones, thousands of years old. Some astronomers (people who study the stars and planets) believe it was built to tell the time of the seasons by the shadows that the stones cast.

▲ Sands of time

An hourglass contains sand in a glass container. The sand runs through a small hole. It was a popular type of clock in the Middle Ages (between the years 470 and 1450), when it was used to measure short periods of time.

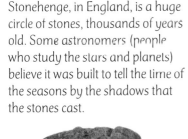

Through the day, time is measured from 12 o'clock midnight. But as the Earth turns, our midnight might be midday on the other side of the world. So we have divided the world into different time zones.

Earth's orbit around the Sun takes about 365 days

▼ Earth's year

The Earth takes 365 and a quarter days to orbit the Sun, so we have three years with 365 days, and a leap year of 366 days every fourth year. The Earth also spins, taking 24 hours to spin around once – one day and one night.

Sun

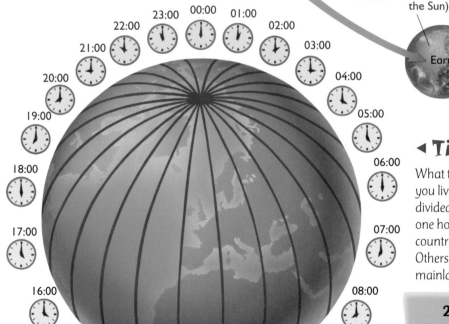

daytime (facing the Sun)

Earth

night-time (away from the Sun)

◀ Time on Earth

What time it is depends on where you live in the world. The world is divided into 24 time zones. There is one hour between each zone. Some countries are within one time zone. Others span more than one – mainland United States has five.

24-hour clock

To avoid confusion between the morning and the evening, we sometimes tell the time using the 24-hour clock. Look at the diagram on the left to find out how we do this. The 24-hour clock time is written next to each clock face.

Towns and cities

Buildings • Homes around the world

Towns and cities are noisy, bustling places where lots of people live. Their streets are usually filled with buses and cars, and their pavements are packed with people. Cities can be centres for government, finance and culture. Many people work in towns and cities – in offices, shops, workshops and factories. Cities are bigger than towns, and have more inhabitants.

Word box

inhabitant
someone who lives in a place

spire
a tall, pointed tower on top of a building

▼ Rush hours

Every morning, city streets are filled with people going to work. They crowd into cities from surrounding areas and nearby towns and villages. They travel by car, bus and train. Each evening they go home again. We call these busy times rush hours.

▼ Ancient spires

The historic city of Oxford has many beautiful, old buildings and graceful spires. It is the home of England's oldest university. The first college was founded in 1249.

▲ Modern and old

The city of Tel Aviv in Israel stretches as far as the eye can see. It is Israel's second largest city, and has some very modern areas. Cafés and fashionable shops exist alongside parts of the city that date back to Biblical times.

▼ Meeting place

The central meeting place in many towns is the town square, like this one in the Greek town of Rhodes. Busy markets are held each week in the town square.

Match the names

Can you match each of these capital cities with its correct country?

1. BEIJING
2. PARIS
3. NEW DELHI
4. WASHINGTON
5. CAIRO

a. INDIA
b. USA
c. EGYPT
d. FRANCE
e. CHINA

answers
1e 2d 3a 4b 5c

▲ New capital city

Canberra is the capital city of Australia. Unlike other capital cities around the world, Canberra is not an old or large city. It was specially built as a capital in the early 1900s.

Towns and cities: animals

Find out more:
Mice and rats

We crowd together in cities. We cause noise and stress, and produce huge amounts of waste. Various animals share this habitat with us, too. They eat our left-over foods, nest in our buildings and enjoy our central-heating. Mammals such as rats, mice and foxes, birds like sparrows, starlings and pigeons, and insects such as flies, silverfish and cockroaches share towns and cities with people worldwide.

Word box

edible
something that an animal can eat

waste
rubbish that nobody wants

▼ Town birds

Starlings live in flocks, which fly out of town by day to feed. They return at dusk (early evening) to roost on roofs. As with pigeons, their droppings cause damage to buildings. Starlings and pigeons can also spread disease.

▼ City-dweller

The red fox is about at night, when there is less traffic and human activity. It learns routines quickly and visits rubbish tips, litter bins and garden heaps to sniff for any kind of food. It lives in a burrow called an earth, in a bank or under an outbuilding.

fox

▼ Sorting the rubbish

In North America the common raccoon is a regular visitor to rubbish bins and bags. It climbs well over fences and rooftops, and sorts out edible bits using its front paws.

raccoon

▶ Rats

Huge numbers of rats are found all over the world in towns and cities. They will eat almost anything and breed very quickly. Rats can cause diseases that are harmful to people.

rat

Toys

Children in the Stone Age probably played with pebbles, seeds, shells, feathers, toy spears and clay figures. Dolls, toys and other games have survived from ancient Egypt and we know that toys were sold at fairs in the Middle Ages. In the 1800s, cheap toys made of tin or wood were made in factories.

◀ Egyptian toys

Children in ancient Egypt played with colourful balls made from linen and rags, spinning tops, dolls and toy lions whose jaws snapped when they pulled a string.

▼ Dice and marbles

The ancient Romans loved playing dice and had many board games with their own pieces or counters.

▼ Rocking horses

In the days when everyone rode about on horseback, little children played with hobbyhorses and wheeled wooden horses. Rocking horses were first made in the 1600s. This one dates from the 1800s.

▼ Yo-yo!

Some toys go through crazes at different times in history. The yo-yo, which was popular in the 1930s, 1950s and 1990s, was also a toy in ancient Greece.

▶ Teddy

Teddy bears were first made 100 years ago. They probably take their name from an American president called 'Teddy' Roosevelt, who is said to have spared the life of a little bear when he was out hunting.

Wow!

The oldest board game surviving today was played by Sumerians at the royal court of Ur, over 4,500 years ago.

Trains carry passengers and heavy loads along thick, metal tracks called rails. Passenger trains carry people on long journeys across a country or on short journeys to and from work. Some passenger trains in countries such as France and Japan travel at very fast speeds. France's *TGV* can travel over 500 kilometres an hour. Goods trains carry heavy loads such as coal, timber and chemicals.

▼ Underwater

The Channel Tunnel, which links England and France, was opened in 1994. The rail tunnels are 50 kilometres long and were built at a depth of 46 metres under the sea. The train journey through the tunnels takes just 35 minutes.

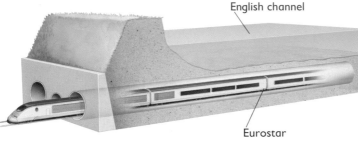

English channel

Eurostar

▼ High speed

Japan's high-speed passenger train is known as the 'bullet train'. It can travel at speeds of up to 260 kilometres an hour.

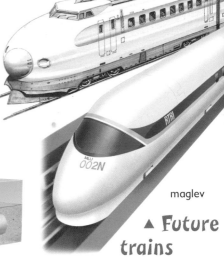

bullet

maglev

▲ Future trains

The maglev train is suspended by powerful magnets above a track. They can reach speeds of up to 500 kilometres an hour!

▶ Underground

In some big cities, underground trains travel along rails in tunnels built beneath city streets. The world's first underground system was opened in London in the 1860s. The first section, between Paddington and Farringdon, was opened in 1863.

Wow!

The city of New York, USA has 468 underground railway stations – that's more than any other city in the world.

Trains in history

In the early 1800s, steam-powered locomotives were invented. The first steam locomotive pulled a train of five wagons. As engines became more powerful, longer and heavier trains were built. Locomotives were able to pull dozens of carriages containing passengers and goods.

▶ Early steam

In 1804, the very first steam locomotive pulled wagons along a railway track in Wales. It was built by an engineer Richard Trevithick. It began the development of the steam locomotive.

Word box

locomotive
a railway engine powered by steam, electricity or diesel fuel, used to push or pull trains

▲ By steam

Once, all trains were steam-powered. The steam was produced by burning coal to heat water in big boilers. Some countries still have steam trains. Most modern trains run on electricity or diesel fuel.

▼ Stephenson's Rocket

In 1825, George and Robert Stephenson opened the world's first steam passenger railway, the Stockton and Darlington in England. They also built the first modern type of steam engine, the *Rocket* in 1829. It reached a top speed of 56 kilometres an hour.

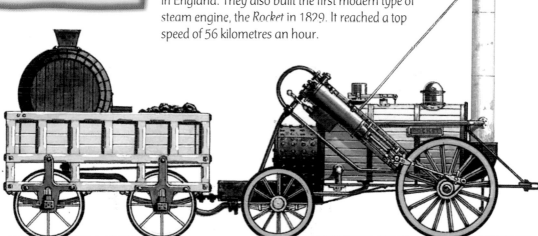

Find out more:
Cars • Engines • Machines • Trains

Transport takes people where they want to go, and takes goods from place to place. Land transport is the most common kind of transport. Cars, trains, buses, motocycles and trucks are the main engine-powered means of transport. All of these vehicles ride on wheels.

▲ Power bikes

Motorcycles were developed from the bicycle. They are powered by a petrol engine, and have a much heavier, stronger frame than a bicycle. This is a 1997 Triumph T595 Daytona motorcycle.

▶ Electric cars

Petrol and diesel cars burn up huge amounts of fuel and pollute the atmosphere. Electric cars, like this one, are powered by chemical batteries rather than petrol or diesel oil, and are a cleaner alternative.

▶ Heavy loads

Most goods are carried by road in trucks. They help transport nearly everything we need in our everyday lives, from food and clothes to the letters we get in the post. Most trucks have more powerful engines than cars, and run mostly on diesel fuel.

◀ Top speed

Some trains now match aeroplanes for speed. France's *TGV* (*Train à Grande Vitesse*, or high-speed train) is on of the world's fastest trains. Normally, it cruises at 300 kilometres per hour, bu it has been known to travel over 500 kilometres per hou

The first water transport was developed by prehistoric (early) people, thousands of years ago. They built rafts made of logs or reeds. The development of boats took many centuries. It was not until the 1400s that ships capable of making long ocean voyages were built. Today, high-speed motor boats take us places in no time at all.

▲ Speedy boats

Hydroplanes are motor boats that skim across the surface of the water. They are a cross between a boat and a plane. They have special 'wings' which raise the hull (frame) above the water.

▲ Getting bigger

During the 1400s, ship-builders began to make ships four times as large as any built before. These ships had a rudder (a piece of wood beneath the back of the ship used for steering) rather than steering oars. Most had three masts and at least three sails.

▲ The steam age

The invention of the steam engine during the 1700s opened the way for transport. By the late 1800s, ships powered by steam engines were quickly taking the place of sailing ships.

◄ Wind power

A catamaran is a raft-like boat powered by the wind. It is made of lightweight materials, with two hulls. These allow the boat to slip through the water easily. Some have outriggers (extra floats). These are developed from traditional Polynesian outriggers.

Trees

Find out more:
Forests • Plant life • Rainforests

Trees are the largest plants of all. The biggest tree alive today, a giant sequoia in California, USA, is over 80 metres tall. Trees provide us with wood for building and to make furniture and paper. They give us fruits such as oranges and apples, and important materials such as rubber and cork. Trees take in carbon dioxide from the air, and give off oxygen, the gas needed by all living things.

▼ Trees in blossom

Blossom is the name for the sweet-smelling flowers of some trees. The flowers then turn into fruit that we pick to eat. Inside are seeds from which new trees can be grown.

apple blossom on an apple tree

◄ Falling leaves

These are leaves from the North American maple tree. It is a deciduous tree, which means it loses its leaves each year and is bare in winter. Its leaves are green in spring and summer and turn gold, red and brown in autumn as they fall to the ground.

▼ Evergreen trees

Non-deciduous trees are called evergreens – they keep their leaves all year round. Some evergreens, such as pines, have needle-like leaves and woody cones. The seeds from which new trees will grow develop inside these cones.

▼ Inside the trunk

A rough, woody layer called bark protects the living parts of the tree beneath. Each year the sapwood beneath the bark grows, leaving a ring. This is how the age of fallen or damaged trees can be determined. Each ring is equivalent to one year.

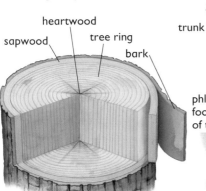

heartwood
sapwood
tree ring
bark

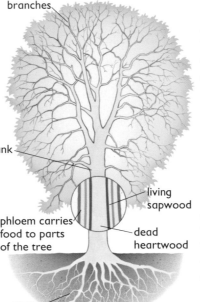

branches

trunk

living sapwood

phloem carries food to parts of the tree

dead heartwood

roots

◄ Parts of a tree

A tree has three main parts: the trunk and branches, the leaves and the roots. The branches and leaves together are called the 'crown'. The trunk supports the crown. The roots are underground and they absorb water from the soil.

Tudors and Stuarts

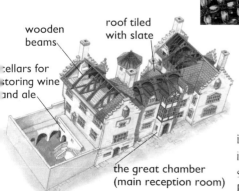

In the 1500s and 1600s, England, Wales and Scotland were ruled by two powerful families, the Tudors and the Stuarts (or Stewarts). This was a time of bitter quarrels between Christians. The Roman Catholics supported the Pope in Rome, but the Protestants wanted to break away from the Roman Church.

▲ Henry VIII

The Tudors reigned over England and Wales from 1485 to 1603. Henry VIII (Henry the Eighth) was desperate for a son to succeed him. When the Pope refused to give him a divorce from his first wife, Henry made himself head of a new Church of England.

▼ Two queens

During troubled times in Scotland, Mary Stuart, Queen of Scots, fled to England. After being tried for plotting against Elizabeth I (below), Mary had her head chopped off in 1587.

▲ Country at war

King Charles I was unpopular. A war broke out between his supporters and the English Parliament. They cut his head off in 1649 and in 1653 handed over power to a soldier called Oliver Cromwell, who ruled the country for the next five years.

▼ King of Scotland

The Stuarts (or Stewarts) ruled Scotland between 1371 and 1714. This is James IV (James the Fourth), one of the greatest Scottish kings. He was killed fighting the English in 1513. In 1603, the Stuarts came to rule England too.

wooden beams

roof tiled with slate

cellars for storing wine and ale

◀ A Tudor town house

This fine house was built by a wealthy businessman in the town of Conwy, Wales, in 1577. It was built in the shape of an 'E', after Elizabeth I.

the great chamber (main reception room)

Istanbul

BLACK SEA

TURKEY

The Turks, led by Osman I, founded an empire in North East Anatolia in 1299. His successors founded a new empire which soon spread across Turkey, Greece and southeastern Europe, Arabia, Egypt and North Africa. The Ottoman Empire came to an end in 1922 and Turkey became a republic.

▲▶ New Turkey

The Ottoman Empire was defeated in 1918, at the close of World War One. The country was built up again by a man called Kemal Atatürk, who was president from 1923 to 1938.

▶ Topkapi

During the 1460s and 1470s, the grand new palace of Topkapi Sarayi was built in Istanbul, looking out over the sea. At times, as many as 5,000 people lived in the palace buildings.

◀ Istanbul

The Turks renamed Constantinople 'Istanbul', and made it the capital of their Ottoman Empire. The graceful Blue Mosque was built for Sultan Ahmet I. It was finally finished in 1619.

Word box

republic
a state that is governed by a ruler chosen by its people

sultan
the king of a Muslim country

▶ Magnificent!

The Ottoman Empire reached the height of its power under a ruler or 'sultan' called Süleyman I, the Magnificent, who died in 1566. His armies marched westwards as far as Austria.

Few animals are slower or safer than turtles, terrapins and tortoises. They form a group of reptiles called chelonians, with almost 300 types. Turtles and terrapins swim in water and have broad, flipper-shaped legs, while tortoises dwell mainly on land. All have a double-layered shell of bony plates covered with horny plates.

Wow!

The largest turtle is the leatherback of the ocean, which has a head and body almost 2 metres long. It measures nearly 3 metres across its front flippers.

Make a turtle shell

1. Put some papier mâché over a balloon, leaving holes for the turtle's head, tail and four legs.

2. When dry, paint the shell and then pop the balloon. Stick on four cardboard legs.

3. Put your arm through the tail hole and out through the head hole, making your fist into the turtle's head – draw eyes and a mouth on your fist!

▲ Diet

Turtles and tortoises survive on a diet of plants, leaves, grass and even prickly cacti. Some turtles such as the Indian softshell turtle are capable of swimming very fast and so can feed on fish. Tortoises and turtles have no teeth, just jaws with sharp edges.

▼ Slow and steady

The alligator snapping turtle of North America lies still in muddy water, with weeds growing on its shell. In its mouth it has a piece of wormlike flesh that it uses for bait. Fish come to look at the 'worm', and *snap*, the prey is caught!

alligator snapping turtle

◄ Race to the sea

Baby sea turtles hatch from eggs laid on a beach. They race to the sea, risking being snapped up on the way by gulls or crabs. Sadly, few young turtles reach adult life.

UFOs and aliens

Find out more:
Astronomy • Internet • Spacecraft • Universe

For a long time, many people have thought that life might exist on other planets. Some believe that 'alien' beings have visited us, and that UFOs (Unidentified Flying Objects) are their spaceships. Certain people who believe this have produced blurry pictures to back up what they say. However, there is still no really solid proof.

▶ Alien craft

For years, humans have imagined what alien craft might look like. No one really knows, as we can't imagine what type of power would let these beings, or aliens, travel freely across space.

▶ Radio signals

Some scientists study the radio waves that reach us from space, trying to find a signal from other intelligent life. They also send signals into space to try and contact alien life but as the stars are so far away it could take thousands of years before their messages reach anyone.

▼ Flying saucers

Starting in the 1940s, many people have reported seeing saucer-shaped flying objects. They are said to be able to fly at impossibly fast speeds. These flying saucers are supposed to be controlled by aliens, but there is no real evidence for this.

United States of America

Find out more:
Atlas: North America

In the 1800s, the new country of the USA grew **very quickly.** It gained lands in the South, the Southwest, California and Alaska. New settlers arrived from Ireland, Italy, Germany, Poland and Russia. Despite a civil war and battles with the Native Americans, farming and factories flourished. By the 1950s, the USA had become the richest and most powerful nation in the world.

▲ North v. South

In 1861, 11 southern states withdrew from the Union that made up the USA. They disagreed with how the country should be governed and wanted to keep slavery. Many people died in this civil war, which lasted until 1865, when the Northerners won.

▶ Statue of Liberty

Many Europeans came to America between 1850 and 1910 in search of a better, fairer life. The Statue of Liberty was a gift from the French people to the United States in 1884. It was a symbol of this fairness and freedom.

◀ 'I have a dream...'

One hundred years after the end of slavery, African Americans were still being treated as second-class citizens in the USA. Martin Luther King Junior led a campaign for justice. In a famous speech, he told people that he had a dream of a land in which all people were free and equal. He was killed in 1968.

▼ Abraham Lincoln

Abraham Lincoln was president of the USA from 1861 to 1865, when he was murdered. He was a great leader who helped to bring slavery to an end.

Martin Luther King Junior

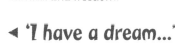

The Universe contains everything that exists.
This includes the Earth, other planets, and billions of
stars. The Universe is about 15,000 million years old –
and still growing. Scientists believe it was probably born
after a very large explosion which they call the Big Bang.

Word box

elliptical
egg-shaped

▼ Galaxy clusters

Out in space there are glowing clouds
made up of masses of floating dust
and gas. These are called nebulae,
and they often look like smudges of
light. Nebulae also contain millions of
stars. Nebulae and stars form huge
clusters called galaxies. Our own
galaxy is called the Milky Way.

▲ Cosmic rays

Stars produce huge amounts of energy. This reaches
the Earth as light and cosmic rays, made of tiny
particles (objects). These particles travel so
fast that when they hit other particles in
our atmosphere they smash them,
forming cosmic ray showers.

▼ Spins and streamers

Galaxies come in different shapes. Many of
them are spinning. The stars they contain
trail out to form long streamers.

| spiral galaxy | irregular galaxy | elliptical galaxy | spiral galaxy with bar across |

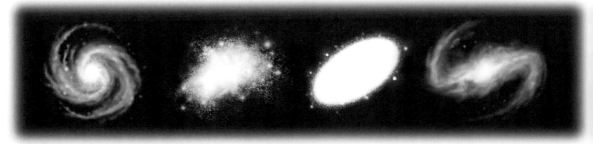

Victorian Britain

From 1837 to 1901, Britain was ruled by Queen Victoria. Her reign is called the Victorian Age. She ruled over large areas of the world, which made up the biggest empire in history. At this time Britain led the world in trade and in building new factories.

▶ Ladies of fashion

During the 1850s–1860s Victorian ladies wore dresses that were stretched over a hooped petticoat called a crinoline. These 1870s models are showing off the bustle, a pad which pushed out the back of the skirt.

▼ A long reign

Queen Victoria was only 18 when she came to the throne, and she ruled for 63 years. She married a German prince called Albert. After he died in 1861 Victoria retired from public life for 13 years. She wore black for the rest of her life.

▲ Crystal Palace

In 1851, a huge glass building called the Crystal Palace was put up in Hyde Park, London. Inside it was the Great Exhibition, organized by Prince Albert. It showed off produce, crafts and new machines from all over the world.

▼ The poor

Some people in Victorian Britain were extremely poor. Their lives were described in stories by the great writer Charles Dickens, who lived from 1812 to 1870.

Be a Victorian fashion designer

1. Draw a Victorian lady in a dress and bonnet, like the ones shown in the picture above.
2. Colour in her costume and add patterns, lace and bows.

Vikings

The word 'Viking' means sea raider.
About 1,200 years ago, Vikings caused terror along the coasts of northern Europe. They sailed from Norway, Sweden and Denmark to attack, plunder and settle new lands. They traded as far away as Russia and the Middle East. They even sailed to Iceland, Greenland and North America.

▲ Meeting up

All free Viking men gathered regularly at a special meeting called the Thing. There they passed new laws and settled any arguments between them.

▶ Life at home

The Vikings built farming settlements, ports and towns. They were great craft workers, traders and storytellers. Family life took place around the fire.

▲ Northern fury

Viking chiefs lead a band of raiders ashore from their longboat, armed with spears, swords and axes. Viking warriors attacked towns and Christian monasteries, seizing gold, silver, cattle and weapons. Sometimes they captured people to sell as slaves.

▶ Thor's hammer

The Vikings believed in many gods and goddesses. Thor, god of thunder, had a magic hammer that he used to fight giants. His chariot was pulled by goats.

Make a Viking treasure hoard

1. Make some coins by cutting out circles of card. Viking coins might be stamped with designs of ships or swords. Cover your coins with silver foil then use a blunt pencil to make a design on them.

2. Cut out a cross and a brooch from card. Again, cover with foil and press a design on them.

Volcanoes

A volcano is an opening on the surface of the Earth. Most volcanoes are cone-shaped mountains. An erupting volcano is spectacular. Hot liquid rock pours out of the volcano and down its sides, clouds of gases and ash rise into the air and lumps of rock are blasted out.

Wow!
The biggest volcano disaster in recent times was an eruption of Mount Tambora in Indonesia in 1815 – it killed around 71,000 people.

▲ Clouds of smoke

Thick clouds of smoke, hot gases and ash stream out of this volcano. Some volcanic clouds are so thick that they block out the Sun's light. When the ash reaches the ground it covers everything around the volcano in a grey blanket of dust.

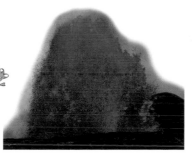

▲ Red hot lava

The fiery red liquid that pours out of an erupting volcano is called lava. It comes from deep inside the Earth. When this hot liquid cools down, it hardens and turns into dark-coloured rock.

▶ Inside a volcano

The red-hot lava travels up through a pipe in the middle of the volcano. It pours out through the vent, the opening at the top of the volcano. Some of the hot lava leaks out through other openings in the volcano's sides.

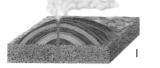

1

2

3

▲ Different kinds

Some volcanoes have runny lava that runs from the vent and makes a domed shape (1). Others have thick lava that explodes, making a cone-shaped volcano (2). A crater volcano (3) occurs when the top of a cone-shaped volcano explodes and sinks into the magma chamber.

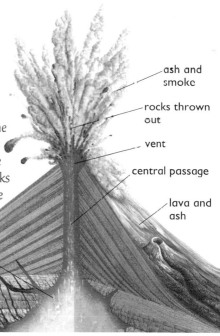

ash and smoke

rocks thrown out

vent

central passage

lava and ash

chamber

rocks

Water

Water fills the Earth's oceans and seas and its rivers and lakes. Water is also found in the sheets of ice around the North and South Poles. It would be impossible to live on the Earth without water – all animals and plants need it to survive.

Wow!

You use about 10 litres of water every time you flush a toilet.

▶ Round and round

Water moves around our world in a continuous circle called the water cycle. During this cycle, water falls to the ground as rain and snow, returns to the air from the sea and the land and then falls back to the ground as rain and snow again.

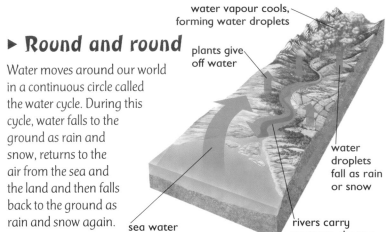

water vapour cools, forming water droplets

plants give off water

water droplets fall as rain or snow

rivers carry water to the sea

sea water evaporates

▼ Water at home

We use water in our homes for washing, cooking and cleaning. Water comes into our homes through pipes underground. Drains take away the dirty water.

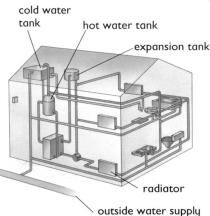

cold water tank

hot water tank

expansion tank

radiator

outside water supply

▲ Lack of rain

Some parts of the world receive little or no rain each year. A long period without rain is called a drought. The ground becomes hard and cracks, and crops shrivel and die. Often there are food shortages during a drought.

▶ Collecting water

In poorer countries, many people have no running water in their homes. Instead they collect water from a well or stream in their village. Some people have to walk a long way to collect their water. They carry it back home in pots and other containers.

▼ Flash floods

If very heavy rain falls in a short period of time, a river cannot always carry the water away quickly enough. When this happens, a mass of fast-moving water called a flash flood spills onto the land.

Water and life

All life depends on water. The microscopic cells in our bodies are made mostly from water. We carry lots of water in our blood. Like most animals, our bodies are usually able to stop us from losing too much water. But as we cannot store water, we still need to drink very regularly. Making sure that people have germ-free drinking water is vital for good health.

◀ Pot plants

Plants in pots can't get water from the ground, so they need regular watering. Too little water means they die. Too much can also kill them, by rotting their roots.

▶ Water holes

Oases are the few places in deserts that have water. Rainwater sinks into the sand, then collects in rock. The water moves through the rock to form a pool where the land dips down. Plants and animals can survive there.

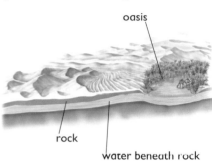

oasis

rock

water beneath rock

▼ Life in a rock pool

Rock pools contain lots of different plants and animals. All of them are adapted to withstand pounding waves and hot sun in the shallow water. Rock pools give you an idea of the huge variety of life in the sea.

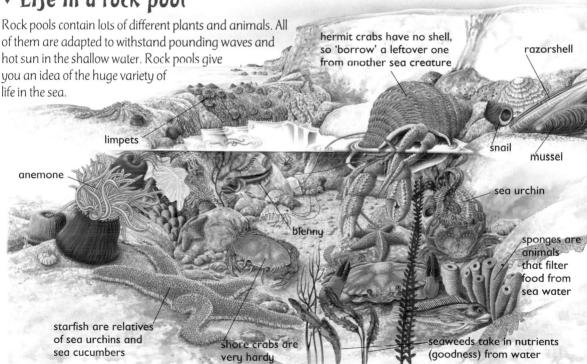

hermit crabs have no shell, so 'borrow' a leftover one from another sea creature

razorshell

limpets

snail

mussel

anemone

sea urchin

blenny

sponges are animals that filter food from sea water

starfish are relatives of sea urchins and sea cucumbers

shore crabs are very hardy

seaweeds take in nutrients (goodness) from water

Sunshine and clouds, winds and storms, rain and snow, frost and ice – these are all different kinds of weather. When the weather is fine, the sun shines and the sky is clear. In stormy weather, dark clouds fill the sky, strong winds blow and rain falls. The weather affects the daily work of many people, from farmers and sailors to aircraft pilots and mountaineers.

▼ Frozen drips

Icicles form when snow or ice melts and then re-freezes. The snow starts to melt during the day. Then the dripping water freezes again in the colder night temperatures.

▲ Strong winds

A tornado is a windstorm that creates a huge funnel of whirling air. The tip of the funnel sucks up everything in its track. In the United States, tornadoes are called twisters. They can reach speeds of up to 50 kilometres an hour.

▼ Farming

Farmers need to know what the weather ahead will be like. Their crops need the right amount of sunshine and rain to grow properly. Farmers like to harvest their crops in dry, sunny weather.

▼ Heavy snow

Snow is frozen crystals of water. Heavy snowfalls can cause a lot of damage and disruption. Snow may pull down electricity wires, delay trains and planes, damage plants and stop people travelling.

► Weather maps

Weather maps help us to predict what the weather for a particular area will be like. They are usually printed in newspapers and shown on television screens. Symbols on the map represent sunshine, rain, clouds, wind and other types of weather.

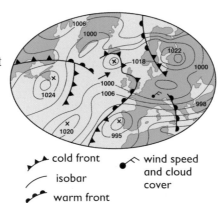

➤◢ cold front
◢ isobar
◢ warm front

● wind speed and cloud cover

Word box

crystals
a tiny multi-sided, regular-shaped object

isobar
line that connects places where air pressure is the same

predict
to say what will happen in the future

Whales

The blue whale is the largest mammal.
There are about 40 different types of whales. They
spend hours underwater, coming up only to
breathe. They spout out stale air and
spray from blowholes
on top of their heads.

▼ Whale with a sword

The narwhal has an amazing tusk – a very long upper left tooth. Usually only males grow the tusk. They 'fence' with rivals at breeding time, as if sword-fighting.

▲ Noisy whales

Belugas are probably the noisiest whales. They chirp, chatter, wail and moan to each other as they swim along the coasts of the Arctic Ocean. Many other whales also send out squeaks and clicks and listen to the bounced-back echoes, to detect objects around them.

▼ Sperm whale

Sperm whales are the world's biggest predators. They can dive more than 1,000 metres into water and stay beneath for more than an hour.

▼ Blue whale

The blue whale opens its mouth wide to gulp in water. It then squeezes the water out through rows of bristly, strap-shaped plates called baleen. Small animals called krill are trapped by the baleen and get eaten.

krill

baleen

In the 1840s, the Europeans who had settled in the eastern United States began to move westwards. They settled on the prairies (grasslands) and seized land from the Native Americans. They planted crops and kept cattle, working as cowboys. Some went all the way across to the Pacific coast, in search of land or gold.

Word scramble

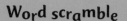

Can you unscramble these names? They all belong to famous people from the Wild West:

a. MALACITY ENJA
b. TAWTY PERA
c. ENNIA KEOLAY

answers
a. Calamity Jane b. Wyatt Earp
c. Annie Oakley

▲ The Oregon Trail

Covered wagons took whole families westwards from Missouri, often as far as Oregon. It was a rough ride and many travellers died from accidents or lack of water.

▲ Buffalo Bill

William Cody was an army scout and buffalo hunter. In 1883, he set up a spectacular 'Wild West Show', which went on tour. In the 1900s, film-makers took up the same story of outlaws, cowboys and 'Indians' (as Native Americans were known).

◄ Lawless times

Gunfights and robbery were all too common. William Bonney was a cattle thief who killed 21 men before he was shot, in 1881. He was better known as 'Billy the Kid'.

◄ The 'Forty-Niners'

In 1849, gold was discovered in California. Prospectors (gold hunters) rushed to 'stake a claim', marking out their own area. They then set up camp and started searching for traces of gold in the rivers.

Women's rights

In the late 1800s, many women across the world were frustrated. They did not have the same rights as men and could not vote in elections. They were paid less than men in factories and mills who did the same work. They were not allowed to go to university or to be doctors or judges. They demanded better lives.

Nancy Astor

◄ Into parliament

The first nation to allow women to vote was New Zealand, in 1893. Nancy Astor became Britain's first female Member of Parliament, in 1919.

▼ 'Votes for women!'

Women that campaigned for the vote in the 1900s were called suffragettes. Suffragettes protested by breaking windows and chaining themselves to railings. Many were sent to prison.

▲ Wars and work

Many men had to go away to fight in wars from 1914 to 1918 and 1939 to 1945. Women were taken on to do work that only men had done before. They worked on farms or in factories. They proved that they were just as good as men, but they were still not paid as much.

◄ Bloomers

Amelia Bloomer was an American who campaigned for a better deal for women in the 1850s. She wanted them to wear more practical clothes, so she invented a new kind of trousers. These became known as 'bloomers'.

Our world is planet Earth, and 6.4 billion people live here. The world's land areas are divided into 191 separate countries, and other areas that belong to certain countries. Each country has its own government and laws, and its own national flag.

▼ Big and small

The world's biggest country is Russia. It is millions of times bigger than Vatican City, the smallest country in the world. The Vatican City lies in the Italian city of Rome.

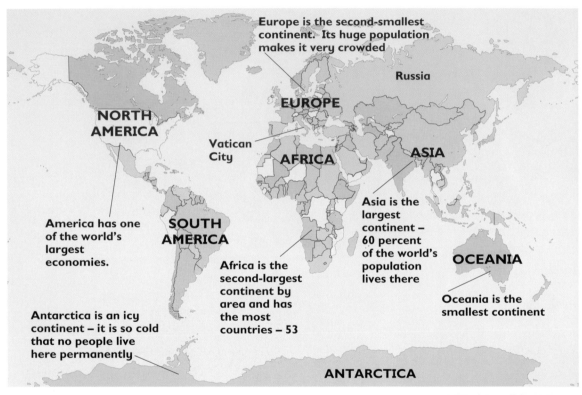

Europe is the second-smallest continent. Its huge population makes it very crowded

Russia

EUROPE

NORTH AMERICA

Vatican City

AFRICA

ASIA

America has one of the world's largest economies.

SOUTH AMERICA

Africa is the second-largest continent by area and has the most countries – 53

Asia is the largest continent – 60 percent of the world's population lives there

OCEANIA

Oceania is the smallest continent

Antarctica is an icy continent – it is so cold that no people live here permanently

ANTARCTICA

Wow!
Around the world people speak more than 3,000 different languages. The six most common ones are: Chinese, English, Spanish, Hindi, Arabic and Russian.

▶ United Nations

The United Nations is an organization that encourages peace between countries. Soldiers from member countries help to keep peace in troubled areas. The UN symbol shows a map of the world surrounded by olive branches, which traditionally stand for peace.

World War One

Find out more:
Flying machines • World War Two

A terrible war broke out in 1914. It was fought in many different parts of the world, so it later became known as a World War. The Central Powers, which included Germany, Austria and Turkey, fought against the Allies, which included the British Empire, France, Russia, Italy, Japan and the USA. Peace was not achieved until 1918.

Word box

barbed wire
tangled wire fitted with sharp spikes

poisonous gas
gas that poisoned anyone who breathed it in

tanks
armoured vehicles with moving tracks instead of wheels

trench
a deep ditch, dug to shelter soldiers from gunfire

▲ In the trenches

The opposing armies faced each other along a line which stretched from Belgium to Switzerland. Soldiers sheltered in long trenches dug into the ground, defended by barbed wire.

◄ War in the air

Planes were used to fly over the enemy, spying out the land, or dropping bombs. This German plane had three wings.

◄ So many dead

Ambulances carried wounded soldiers from the scene of battle. By 1918, ten million soldiers had been killed and many more injured.

▲ New weapons

Terrible new weapons were invented during World War One. The Allies used armoured tanks, like these. The Central Powers attacked their enemies with poisonous gas.

A second World War broke out in 1939 and lasted until 1945. After years of fighting, armies from the British Empire, the Soviet Union (Russia) and the USA defeated those of Germany, Italy and Japan. This was the worst war in human history, leaving 55 million soldiers and civilians dead around the world.

◄ Pearl Harbor

In 1941, Japanese planes attacked an American naval base at Pearl Harbor, in Hawaii. The USA entered the war, fighting in the Pacific islands and across Europe.

▲ Fast warfare

Germany invaded most of Europe, while Japanese troops advanced quickly through East and Southeast Asia. World War Two weapons included high-speed tanks, dive-bombers and deadly submarines.

▼ The Nazis

During World War Two, Germany was ruled by the Nazi Party. Their leader was Adolf Hitler. Anyone who disagreed with the Nazis was put in prison or killed. The Nazis hated Jewish people and set up death camps. Six million Jews died there.

Word box

civilian
someone who is not serving as
a soldier, sailor or airman

► Cities bombed

Many cities all over Britain and Germany were devastated by bombs. Here, thick smoke hangs over the city of London in 1940. St Paul's Cathedral is surrounded by blazing buildings.

Worms are vital for the natural world. As earthworms tunnel through soil, eating bits of old plants, they let in air and moisture, so that new plants can grow. Worms in the sea eat the remains of dying animals, helping to recycle nutrients (goodness). A world without worms would quickly fill up with dead, rotting bodies!

▼ Inside a worm

An earthworm is a segmented worm or annelid. It has a head at one end, a tail at the other, and many segments in-between. Each segment contains much the same set of organs.

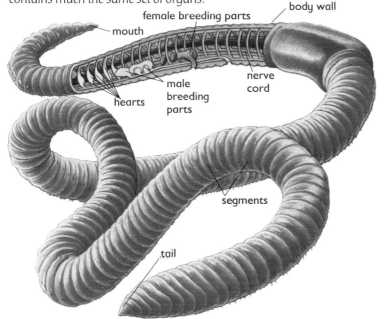

- body wall
- female breeding parts
- mouth
- male breeding parts
- nerve cord
- hearts
- segments
- tail

Make a wormery

1. Ask an adult to help you. In a see-through container, put a 5-centimetre layer of sand, then a 5-centimetre layer of soil, and then alternate the sand and soil until your container is almost full.
2. Add leaves to the very top.
3. Take a few worms from your garden, add these to the container, and keep it in a cool, dark place.
4. Every few days, see how the worms mix up the layers.

▲ Roundworm

Roundworms are mostly tiny and simple. They live almost everywhere including soil, ponds, rivers, seas and inside plants and creatures. Some, such as hookworms and pinworms, cause diseases.

Wow!

The giant earthworms of southern Africa and southern Australia are thicker than your thumb and over 3 metres long!

▶ Fanworm

The head end of the fanworm has beautiful feathery tentacles that catch tiny pieces of food floating in the water. If danger appears, the worm whisks its 'fan' down into its burrow in the mud.

Writing and printing

Find out more:
Schools

Writing began about 5,500 years ago, in the Middle East. It allowed people to keep records and to write down their stories for the people who came after them. All sorts of scripts came into use around the world, from China to Central America. They included patterns, pictures, symbols and alphabets. These signs stood for objects, ideas or sounds.

▶ A B C D...

Alphabets are made up of letters that stand for different sounds, objects or ideas. The alphabet used in this book grew from those used in southwest Asia and southern Europe. Here are the first letters of nine different alphabets and scripts.

Phoenician

Classical Greek

Roman

ABCDEF

Cyrillic

АБВГДЕ

Hebrew

Arabic

Ancient Egyptian

Chinese
人 月 子 水 雨 木

Japanese
星 面 海 水 下

▲ Picture writing

Between about 3200BC and AD400, Egyptian priests wrote using picture symbols called hieroglyphs. These can still be seen on the walls of old tombs or written out on some examples of papyrus.

Word box

papyrus
a kind of paper made from reeds

printing press
a machine in which metal shapes covered in ink are pressed against a page to print words or pictures

script
signs that are used in writing

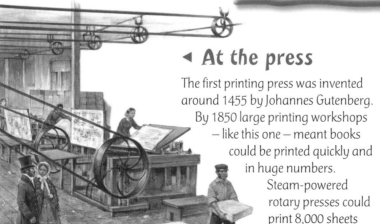

◀ At the press

The first printing press was invented around 1455 by Johannes Gutenberg. By 1850 large printing workshops – like this one – meant books could be printed quickly and in huge numbers. Steam-powered rotary presses could print 8,000 sheets an hour.

▼ Newspapers

Newspapers today are printed on machines called web presses. Paper is fed from huge rolls through the press at a rate of up to 1,000 metres a minute.

The invention of the X-ray machine meant doctors could see what was going on inside a living body. There are now many other types of body-scanner. They 'see' inside the body by using sound waves and other forms of energy that are able to pass through living tissue.

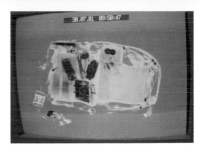

▲ Airport security

To make sure that people do not carry anything dangerous on board an aircraft, their baggage is X-rayed. An X-ray can travel through substances but not the denser ones like metals. This means that even the smallest metal objects can be seen inside a case.

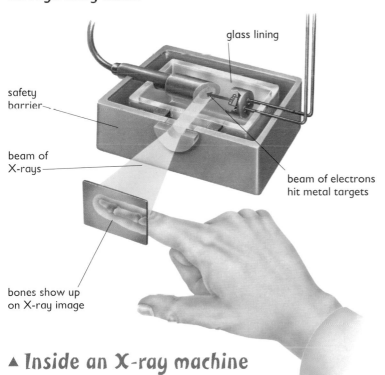

glass lining

safety barrier

beam of X-rays

beam of electrons hit metal targets

bones show up on X-ray image

Word box

discharge tube
vacuum-filled (without air) glass tube through which electricity is passed

electron
a tiny particle

▲ Inside an X-ray machine

X-rays are produced in a glass discharge tube. They pass through the body and make an image on a screen or on photographic film. As bone is denser than flesh, it leaves a shadow that can be seen very clearly.

▶ Dental X-rays

Your dentist may X-ray your teeth to find out what is happening inside a tooth. Any infection and cavities (holes) show up on the X-ray pictures, so the dentist knows what treatment to give you.

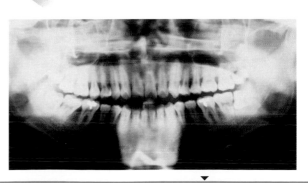

Young animals

Find out more:
Eggs • Mammals and their babies • Nests

Many kinds of young animals survive without help from their parents.
Most insects, fish and amphibians, hatch from eggs and survive on their own. But some reptile parents, and almost all birds and mammals, care for their young.

▲ Mother duck

After hatching, ducklings will follow the first moving thing they see – nearly always their mother. This behaviour is called imprinting. Ducklings use sounds when in trouble, cheeping loudly if they are lost.

▼ Helpless baby

Like all baby mammals, the young baboon feeds on its mother's milk. It clings to its mother for warmth. As with most other large mammals, baboons usually have just one baby.

▲ Big baby

A young elephant is a 'baby' longer than almost any other animal. It feeds on its mother's milk for two years, and stays near her for another three. Many females in the herd help to protect the baby.

Baby quiz

What animal will each of these babies grow up to be?

1. foal **2.** cub
3. leveret **4.** calf **5.** kid

Choose from:
a. tiger **b.** goat
c. whale **d.** horse **e.** hare

1d 2a 3e 4c 5b
answers

▼ Help with hatching

The female of nearly all crocodiles and alligators makes a caring mother. She guards her eggs and young fiercely. The young squeak loudly in their eggs. The mother helps them to hatch, carries them gently to a quiet pool, and guards them for several weeks.

American alligator

Zoos

Animals from many different parts of the world are kept in zoos. The word 'zoo' is short for zoological gardens. Thousands of visitors come to a zoo to watch and study its animals.

◄ Nature reserves

To help protect endangered animals there are more than 10,000 national parks and wildlife reserves all over the world. These are safe areas where people cannot tamper with the natural habitat and the animals are protected from poachers. In some areas there are even several 'animal orphanages' where young animals whose parents have died are cared for until they can survive in the wild.

▲ Water works

Zoos that have only fish and other aquatic animals are called aquariums. Dolphins are intelligent and require a stimulating environment. In many zoos, dolphins are taught tricks, often using balls and hoops, to perform for visitors.

► Entertainment

People of all ages enjoy viewing animals that they wouldn't see in their daily lives. Animals in zoos are often grouped by type, for example different kinds of monkeys and apes, (such as this orang-utan), might be kept in the same building. To combat boredom, many exhibits contain toys and climbing structures to encourage active behaviour. Meals are often hidden in trees or shrubs so animals have to forage as they would in the wild.

◄ In the wild

Many zoos have helped to breed animals that are disappearing in the wild. When enough animals have been bred, some can be returned to the wild. Without this work, animals such as the Arabian oryx (left) and the European bison would have disappeared.

How to use the maps

Maps can look very puzzling. What are all those squiggly lines and strange colours and shapes? How can you fit a whole town or country onto one page?

You can read a map – just like you are reading this book now! Instead of letters and words, the map uses symbols and colour codes to give you information. Therefore to read a map you need to understand the symbols.

A feature on a map is much smaller than it is in real life. Maps show places at different sizes. So one centimetre on a map might represent one kilometre (that's 100,000 centimetres) on the ground.

Reading a book may open up whole new worlds – and so does reading a map. Just looking at the page of an atlas will help you to imagine jungles or mountains or deserts. You can work out journeys and measure how far it is from one place to another. Maps can even help you to discover why people's lives are so different.

▼ Physical map pages

Here you will find information about what the land in each continent looks like. Does it have mountains and rivers, deserts or rainforests? Can you tell if it is hot or cold? You will also discover amazing animals and wonderful natural places to visit.

| 1 | 2 | 3 | 4 | 5 |

Europe

Europe is the second smallest continent in the world – less than a quarter the size of Asia. Yet it is also the most crowded, with its population contained in 47 different countries.

Europe is able to support such a large number of people because it is lucky enough to have good farmland covering half of the continent. But there is less space for wildlife. The European brown bear is one of the few big animals to live in Europe.

There is a wide variety of birdlife, as well as smaller animals such as badgers, foxes, deer, hedgehogs, squirrels and wild boar.

Copper butterflies can live almost anywhere. They are tiny, growing to only 36 millimetres across their wings.

This fallow deer is guard The white spots on their coa camouflage them amongst they live. The fawn may sta mother for more than a yea

A red fox's natural habitat is woodland, but many have living in towns. They mainly hunt for food at night. They v anything, from rabbits and earthworms to fish and apples

Best of Europe

HOTTEST PLACE Seville in Spain recorded a high of 50 degrees Celsius in August 1881.

LARGEST SEA The Mediterranean Sea covers about 2,503,000 square kilometres.

350

Two types of maps

In your atlas you will find two different kinds of map. They are called physical and political maps. Physical maps show natural features, such as mountains and rivers, seas, lakes and islands. They would be there even if there were no people around. Political maps show countries and states, which would not exist without people.

This physical map of Europe shows the rivers, mountains and seas.

This political map of Europe shows the countries in different colours.

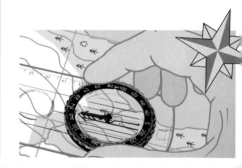

▼ Political map pages

Here you will find information about the places in each continent and facts about each country. You will also learn about the people who live there and what their lives are like.

▼ Grid lines

Can you see the numbers that run across the top of each page and the letters that run down the right of the border? These are called grid lines. You can use them to locate places on the map. For example, look for Belarus on the political map – its grid reference is D11. Trace a line with your finger across from D and down from 11 and you will find Belarus. See if you can find the grid references for Finland.

◀ Using a compass

A compass has a small needle in it that always points to the north (N). This helps you to find out where you are when studying a map. For example, it can help you to find which way you need to walk to get to a particular place.

Reading symbols on a map

Find out how to read the maps in this atlas by looking at the land colours and symbols used for the different features.

Desert	Grassland or forest	Mountains

POLAND / **UKRAINE**
National borders

HIMALAYAS
Mountain range

■ Warsaw
Capital city

Murray River
River

SAHARA DESERT
Desert

Lake Superior
Lake

Earth in space

Imagine you are far out in space.
You turn and look back at the planet we call Earth. What does it look like? It is round like a ball, and coloured, mostly blue and green with smudges of white.

It is also small – much smaller than most of the other planets that are near us. Some of these are huge, and could swallow up the Earth many times over. But, even bigger, is the Sun, a giant mass of fire and flame that is the brightest thing in our small corner of space. The Earth gets all its heat, light and energy from the Sun.

If you watched for long enough, you would see that the Earth does not stay in one place. It moves in a big circle around the Sun. This circle is called Earth's orbit. One whole journey around the Sun takes a year, or just over 365 days.

▲ The Moon

The Earth has a rocky ball, the Moon, that circles around it as it moves through space. It is one-quarter the size of the Earth. The Moon's surface is full of great holes called craters.

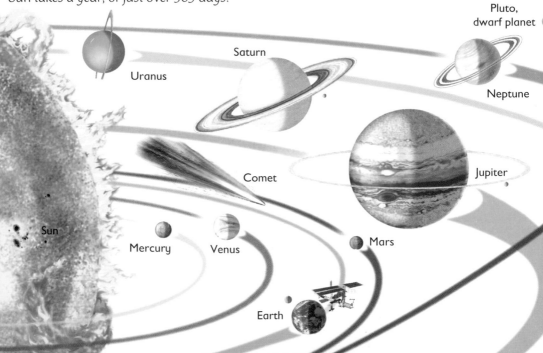

Pluto, dwarf planet

Uranus

Saturn

Neptune

Comet

Jupiter

Sun

Mercury

Venus

Mars

Earth

▲ Spinning in space

Earth does not just move through space, it also spins round, like a top. Imagine a line drawn through the middle of the Earth from top to bottom. The Earth spins around that line, making a complete turn every 24 hours – a day and a night.

▼ Parts of the Earth

The Earth is split up into lots of layers, almost like an onion. If you could cut open the Earth you would be able to see all the different layers inside. The outside layer is called the crust. This is up to 50 kilometres deep in some places, but compared to the whole Earth it is very small. If the Earth was an apple, the crust would be as thick as its skin! The next layer is called the mantle. This is a layer of soft, hot rock that is nearly 2,900 kilometres thick. After this is the outer core which is made up mostly of molten metals, iron and nickel. In the middle is the inner core, where temperatures reach as high as 7,000 degrees Celsius.

inner core

outer core

mantle

crust

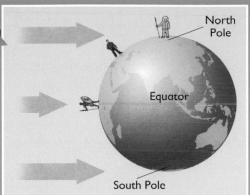

North Pole

Equator

South Pole

▲ Poles and the Equator

At the very top of the world is the North Pole. At the bottom is the South Pole. And halfway between is an imaginary line called the Equator. The Equator is the part of the world nearest to the Sun, so it is always hot. The poles are furthest from the Sun, so they are cold.

Day and night

The Earth is constantly spinning like a top. At any time, the Sun only shines on one half of the Earth's surface. As the Earth spins around, the sunshine moves onto a different part of the surface. On the side of the Earth where the Sun is shining, it is light and day. On the side of the Earth that is facing away from the Sun, it is dark and night.

► The seasons

The Earth tilts over slightly as it spins around. This means that for half of the year the top half of the Earth is tilted towards the Sun. This gives us the warmer seasons of spring and summer. When the Earth is tilted away from the Sun, we have the colder seasons of autumn and winter.

Spring in Northern Hemisphere

Winter in Northern Hemisphere

Sun

Summer in Northern Hemisphere

Autumn in Northern Hemisphere

Looking at the Earth

How can we know what the Earth looks like? If you were an astronaut you could see it very well from your spacecraft. But the rest of us have to stay on the Earth's surface. We can't see the shape of a whole coastline or mountain or river. We can't tell how far it is across an ocean or between two cities.

Instead, we look at a map of the Earth. A map is a diagram, which shows where things are on the Earth's surface. Each kind of feature has its own sign or symbol. Symbols come in many different lines, colours and shapes to show rivers, mountains, towns, and so on.

There are many kinds of map. Some show the main features, using different colours for rainforest, desert or highland areas. Others use boundary lines and colours to show how the world is divided up into countries and states. Maps can be big or small. A map can show the whole world — or just your street!

▲ Continent map
This is the continent of Oceania. You can see Australia, New Zealand, and the small islands in the Pacific Ocean.

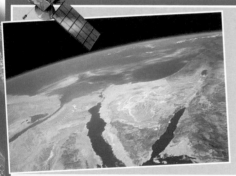

◄ Eye in the sky
Modern mapmakers use photographs taken from the sky by satellites or aircraft. Special machines transfer the shapes from the photos onto paper. Mapmakers can measure distances from these photographs. The information, stored in a computer, can be used to control a drawing machine called a plotter.

► Country map
Maps like this one of Australia show you where different towns and cities are. They will also tell you where to find other land features, such as mountains, rivers, lakes and deserts.

► Round into flat
An exact map of the world would be a globe or sphere. But how do you draw this onto flat paper? One early method was to peel the Earth like an orange, then spread the peel out in sections (see right). A better way was invented by Mercator in 1538. He wrapped a sheet of paper in a tube shape around a globe map, then copied the lines of the map onto it. When he unwrapped the tube, he had a flat map.

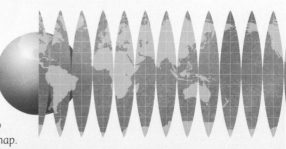

▼ Zooming in on Earth

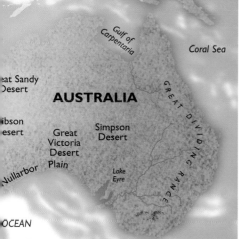

Different maps are used to study the Earth. A globe shows the whole of the Earth. The detail on Earth can be shown at different sizes. As you zoom in you see more detail. A state or county map will show you a small part of the Earth, while a street map will help you find your way around a city or town.

▼ Making maps

As soon as people started exploring the world, they began drawing maps. Travellers brought back rough plans from around the world. The first person to put these together into a large map was the Greek, Ptolemy, about 1,900 years ago. But it had gaps – because large parts of the Earth were still unknown. Slowly, these gaps were filled in. The first complete world map did not appear until the last century.

▲ World from afar

We cannot see all the countries on a globe because some are hidden. Here you can see Oceania, and some of Antarctica and Asia.

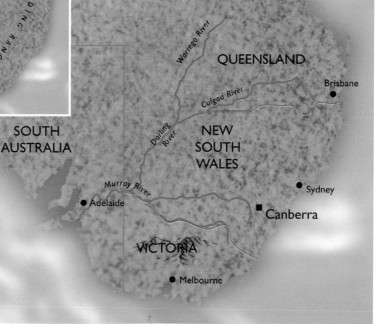

▶ State map

Zooming in a bit more, you can see state or county details. You can also find the names and places of major cities and towns. You might use a map like this if you wanted to find out about the states of Australia. For example, from this map, can you tell in which state you would find the city of Brisbane?

337

The world

Here is a map of the whole world – on two pages!

It shows you all the main land areas of the world, and the oceans and seas. Can you see how much of the map is coloured blue? This is because there is so much water. Oceans, lakes, rivers and other water cover over two-thirds of the Earth's surface.

ARCTIC
OCEAN

NORTH
AMERICA

NOF
ATLAN
OCE

PACIFIC
OCEAN

SOUTH
AMERICA

SOU
ATLAN
OCE

North America

Population	515 million
Climate	All types
Land features	All types
Area	24 million square kilometres

South America

Population	373 million
Climate	Hot and wet, hot and dry
Land features	Rainforest, desert, grassland
Area	18 million square kilometres

Antarctica

Population	No permanent population
Climate	Always very cold
Land features	Ice and snow
Area	14 million square kilometres

Europe

Population	727 million
Climate	Mild
Land features	Plains, uplands, mountains
Area	10 million square kilometres

ARCTIC
OCEAN

ASIA

EUROPE

AFRICA

PACIFIC
OCEAN

Asia

Population	3,875 million
Climate	All types
Land features	All types
Area	45 million square kilometres

INDIAN
OCEAN

OCEANIA

Oceania

Population	32 million
Climate	Hot and dry, hot and wet, mild
Land features	Rainforest, desert, grassland
Area	18 million square kilometres

NTARCTICA

Africa

Population	885 million
Climate	Hot and wet, hot and dry
Land features	Desert, rainforest, grassland
Area	30 million square kilometres

The continents

The land on the Earth's surface is split up into seven large areas that are called continents. Their names are North America, South America, Europe, Asia, Africa, Oceania and Antarctica. Some of these, such as Europe, are very crowded, while nobody at all lives permanently in Antarctica. Some are big blocks of land, while others, such as Oceania, are made up of thousands of islands – some enormous and some tiny.

If you look closely, you will see that some of the continents are joined together. North and South America are linked by a narrow strip of land, called an isthmus. Asia and Europe are really part of the same huge land mass, and only a narrow canal separates Africa from Asia.

NORTH AMERICA

SOUTH AMERICA

AFF

Comparing countries in each continent

Do you know how many independent countries there are in each of the continents? Africa is not the largest continent, but it has the most countries – 53 in total. The continent with the fewest is South America – it has only 12.

53	48	44	23	14	12
AFRICA	EUROPE	ASIA	NORTH AMERICA	OCEANIA	SOUTH AMERICA

Highest and lowest temperatures

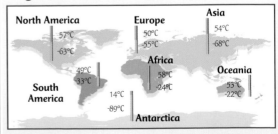

North America
57°C
-63°C

Europe
50°C
-55°C

Asia
54°C
-68°C

49°C
-33°C

South America

Africa
58°C
-24°C

Oceania
53°C
-22°C

14°C
-89°C

Antarctica

JROPE

ASIA

QUIZ

1. Which is the largest continent?
2. Which is the smallest continent?
3. Which continent has the most people?
4. Which is the coldest continent?
5. Which continent has the most countries?

Answers on page 384.

Oceania 0.5%

Asia 63%

Africa 12.5%

Europe 10.4% Antarctica 0% South America 6.7% North America 6.9%

People and places

In the diagram above, the Earth is shown as a circle divided into the seven continents. It shows you how much bigger the area of Asia (purple) is than Oceania (orange). You can also see how many people live in each continent – the population. Sixty-three percent of the world's population lives in Asia while nobody lives in Antarctica.

OCEANIA

Time difference

The world spins around as it orbits, or circles, the Sun. This means that while it is daytime in one part of the world, it is the middle of the night in another! This is called time difference.

It is 7 a.m. in New York, USA, and people are getting up.

It is 12 midday in London, England – playtime!

In Tokyo, Japan, it is 9 p.m. – and time for bed.

RCTICA

North America

North America contains three huge countries!
These are Canada, the United States of America and
Mexico. It also includes smaller countries in Central
America and the islands in the Caribbean. This
third biggest continent in the world stretches
from the North Pole down to the Caribbean
Sea. Here, a spindly strip of land containing
the countries of Central America
eventually joins South America.

In North America you can see
cold white ice-caps, mountains,
rainforests, deserts and forests
– almost all the different kinds
of land that can be seen
anywhere in the world!

▼ An area of swampy land in the USA is
home to the very rare Everglade jaguar –
and lots of alligators too!

◀ Kings Canyon is the deepest
canyon in North America. Gradually
worn away by the Kings River that
flows through it, the canyon is
2,499 metres at its deepest point.

*PACIFIC
OCEAN*

Best of North America

LARGEST GULF
The Gulf of
Mexico covers
1,543,000 square
kilometres.

LONGEST GORGE
The Grand Canyon,
a valley with
rocky sides, is 446
kilometres long.

LARGEST CRATER
Clearwater Lakes
Crater is 60 kilometr
across.

A

B

C

D

E

F

G

Great Bear Lake

Mackenzie River

Great Slave Lake

Hudson Bay

Lake Winnipeg

ATLANTIC OCEAN

ROCKY MOUNTAINS

Missouri River

Lake Superior

Lake Huron

St Lawrence River

Lake Michigan

Lake Ontario

Great Salt Lake

Missouri River

Lake Erie

Mississippi River

Rio Grande

Gulf of Mexico

Caribbean Sea

▲ Many animals live in the cold forests of Canada, including moose and bears. The moose is the largest deer in the world. Its antlers can grow up to two metres across.

HOTTEST PLACE
In Death Valley temperatures can rise as high as 57 degrees Celsius.

TALLEST LIVING THING
This giant redwood tree grows in America. It is 112 metres high.

LARGEST FRESHWATER LAKE
Lake Superior covers 82,350 square kilometres.

343

North America
People and places

Some of the richest and poorest people live here. North America contains some of the world's largest cities, but also vast areas of remote land. The USA is the richest country in the world, and big cities such as Washington D.C. are centres of wealthy living. But many people in countries like Nicaragua and El Salvador in Central America are very poor.

The USA has become wealthy because it produces most of the world's silver, nickel and copper, as well as large amounts of coal, oil and gas.

By contrast, the people of Central America are not so lucky. The country does not have many natural resources, and the wealth they create is not evenly shared amongst everybody. Most people now live in cities, while the rest are small farmers growing just enough wheat, beans and rice to survive.

The Native American Indians lived in North America for a long time before anyone else arrived. Then people from Europe came to live there, and now there is a huge number of people who have come from many different places.

▲ Racing monster trucks like this one is a popular sport in Canada and the USA. The huge wheels and powerful engines mean that they can easily crush ordinary cars that get in their way!

QUIZ

Can you find out which cities are in the following squares by using the grid around the map?

D10, G9, E11, F11

Answers on page 384.

◀ The Empire State Building is one of the most famous places in the USA. Its 102 storeys rise to a height of 381 metres.

North America Facts

Biggest country Canada – 9,970,610 square kilometres
Biggest city population Mexico City – 19,232,000 people
Most TV sets USA – 81 out of 100 people own televisions
Fewest doctors Haiti – one doctor for every 7,140 people
Fewest TV sets Haiti – 5 out of 100 people own televisions

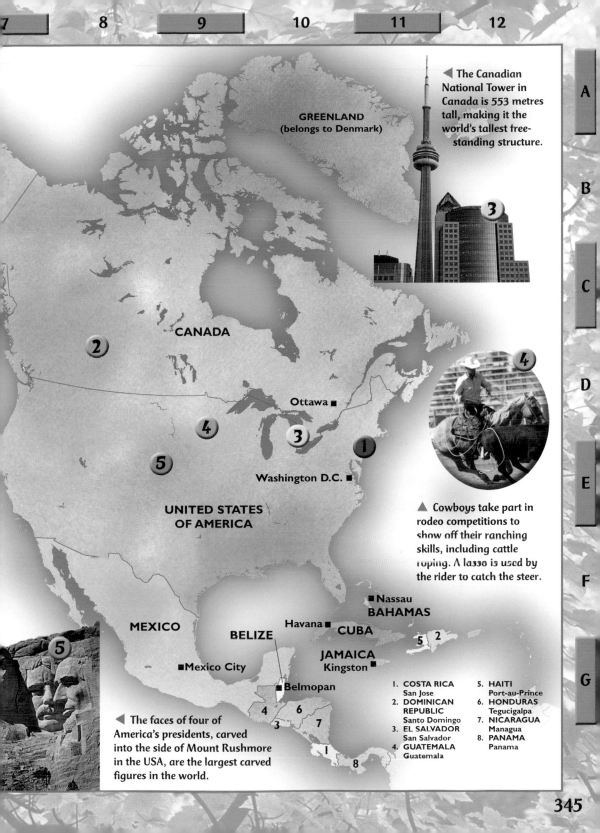

A

B

C

D

E

F

G

◀ The Canadian National Tower in Canada is 553 metres tall, making it the world's tallest free-standing structure.

3

GREENLAND
(belongs to Denmark)

CANADA

2

Ottawa ■

4

3

1

5

Washington D.C. ■

4

▲ Cowboys take part in rodeo competitions to show off their ranching skills, including cattle roping. A lasso is used by the rider to catch the steer.

UNITED STATES
OF AMERICA

■ Nassau
BAHAMAS

MEXICO

BELIZE

Havana ■   CUBA

5 2

■Mexico City

JAMAICA
Kingston ■

5

■Belmopan

4   6

3   7

I

8

◀ The faces of four of America's presidents, carved into the side of Mount Rushmore in the USA, are the largest carved figures in the world.

1. **COSTA RICA**
   San Jose
2. **DOMINICAN REPUBLIC**
   Santo Domingo
3. **EL SALVADOR**
   San Salvador
4. **GUATEMALA**
   Guatemala
5. **HAITI**
   Port-au-Prince
6. **HONDURAS**
   Tegucigalpa
7. **NICARAGUA**
   Managua
8. **PANAMA**
   Panama

South America

South America means – jungle! The biggest tropical rainforest in the world covers an area ten times bigger than France. Through this forest winds the giant Amazon. It may be only the world's second longest river, but it carries two-thirds of the Earth's river water.

The continent contains many other marvels too. There are beautiful waterfalls, snowy mountaintops, and smoking volcanoes. It is a paradise for wildlife. A quarter of all known mammals live here, including the giant anteater and the vampire bat.

The rainforests are alive with beautiful birds, insects and animals. They also contain a staggering variety of plants, some of which give us vital medicines.

▲ The capybara is the largest rodent in the world. Rodents are animals like mice and rats, but the capybara can reach up to 1.4 metres in length!

▼ The anaconda, found in swampy river valleys in South America, is the widest snake in the world. It can measure 110 centimetres around its stomach!

Best of South America

LONGEST RIVER
The Amazon river runs for a total length of 6,448 kilometres.

HIGHEST WATERFALL
The water at Angel Falls plunges down a cliff 979 metres high.

DRIEST PLACE
The Atacama Desert has had no rain for over 400 years!

▶ The sloth is the slowest mammal on Earth. It normally moves at only 0.27 kilometres an hour – that's 15 seconds to move one metre!

Negro River

Amazon River

Purus River

Tapajos River

São Francisco

Lake Titicaca

Lake Poopo

PACIFIC OCEAN

Andes

Atacama Desert

Parana River

Uruguay River

Parana River

ATLANTIC OCEAN

◀ Jaguars are the largest cats in South America. They can reach up to 2.2 metres in length, and eigh up to 90 kilograms.

▶ At the junction of two rivers, 275 individual cascades form the spectacular Iguazú Falls.

ANDES

LONGEST RANGE
The Andes mountain chain runs for 7,200 kilometres. It is the longest in the world.

MOST PLANTS
The tropical rainforest contains more varieties of plant than anywhere else in the world.

347

South America
People and places

South America is the fourth largest continent but it has one of the smallest populations. This is because much of the land is difficult to live on, and the cutting down of the rainforests has forced native people to leave their homes.

Some of South America's farms are the biggest in the world and cover areas larger than some countries. However, most are small and farmers own or rent little plots of land, struggling to grow enough food to survive.

Three-quarters of the people in South America now live in towns and cities. Many of these people are very poor and cannot afford houses. They crowd into flimsy shelters on the outskirts of towns. Meanwhile a few South Americans are very wealthy. These are mainly the landowners, factory bosses and political leaders.

Until the Spanish and Portuguese invaded in about 1,500 only native tribes lived in South America. Now most people are a mix of Native American and European.

QUIZ

1. Which countries does Chile share a border with?
2. Can you find the capital city of the largest country in South America?

Answers on page 384.

▶ **This Bolivian woman is dressed in traditional clothes – blankets and a bowler hat. Life in rural Bolivia has not changed for many years.**

South America Facts

Smallest country Suriname – 163,270 square kilometres
Countries where most people live in cities Uruguay – 91 out of 100 people live in cities; Argentina – 90 out of 100 live in cities
Country that produces most silver Peru – 14 percent of world total
Most TV sets Argentina – 22 out of 100 people own televisions
Fewest doctors Guyana – one doctor for every 6,220 people

◀ This beautiful statue of a bird with a snake is carved out of stone. It was made in Colombia about 2,000 years ago.

▶ Pipes like these are used by musicians who live in the Andes mountains.

3

A

B

C

D

E

F

G

■ Caracas

VENEZUELA

GUYANA

Georgetown

■ Paramaribo
FRENCH GUIANA
(belongs to France)

■ Bogota

COLOMBIA

2

■ Quito

ECUADOR

SURINAME

PERU

BRAZIL

3

■ Lima

1

■ La Paz

■ Brasilia

■ Sucre

BOLIVIA

PARAGUAY

4

CHILE

■ Asunción

▼ Artists live in these brightly coloured flats in Buenos Aires, capital of Argentina. They have painted their houses in wonderful colours.

ARGENTINA

Santiago
■

URUGUAY

Buenos Aires ■ Montevideo

5

▼ Deforestation means cutting down forests. This is happening at an alarming rate. A total of 370,000 square kilometres was cleared between 1990 and 2000.

4

Europe

Europe is the second smallest continent in the world – less than a quarter the size of Asia. Yet it is also the most crowded, with its population contained in 47 different countries.

Europe is able to support such a large number of people because it is lucky enough to have good farmland covering half of the continent. But there is less space for wildlife. The European brown bear is one of the few big animals to live in Europe.

There is a wide variety of birdlife, as well as smaller animals such as badgers, foxes, deer, hedgehogs, squirrels and wild boar.

▲ **Copper butterflies** can live almost anywhere. They are tiny, growing to only 36 millimetres across their wings.

▲ **This fallow deer is guarding her fawn.** The white spots on their coats help camouflage them amongst leaves where they live. The fawn may stay with its mother for more than a year.

▲ **A red fox's natural habitat is woodland,** but many have adapted to living in towns. They mainly hunt for food at night. They will eat almost anything, from rabbits and earthworms to fish and apples.

Best of Europe

HOTTEST PLACE
Seville in Spain recorded a high of 50 degrees Celsius in August 1881.

LARGEST SEA
The Mediterranean Sea covers about 2,503,000 square kilometres.

LARGEST ISLAND
Britain is the larges island in Europe, covering 218,041 square kilometres

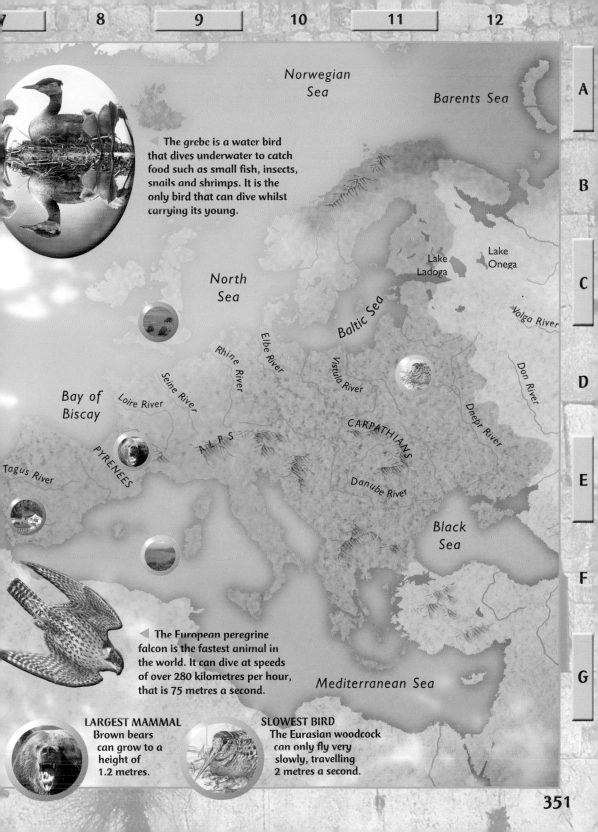

Norwegian Sea

Barents Sea

The grebe is a water bird that dives underwater to catch food such as small fish, insects, snails and shrimps. It is the only bird that can dive whilst carrying its young.

Lake Ladoga

Lake Onega

North Sea

Baltic Sea

Volga River

Rhine River

Elbe River

Vistula River

Don River

Seine River

Bay of Biscay

Loire River

Dnepr River

CARPATHIANS

A L P S

PYRENEES

Danube River

Tagus River

Black Sea

The European peregrine falcon is the fastest animal in the world. It can dive at speeds of over 280 kilometres per hour, that is 75 metres a second.

Mediterranean Sea

LARGEST MAMMAL
Brown bears can grow to a height of 1.2 metres.

SLOWEST BIRD
The Eurasian woodcock can only fly very slowly, travelling 2 metres a second.

351

Europe
People and places

Europeans have changed the world.

Despite its small size, Europe has produced writers, artists, scientists and explorers whose lives have influenced the rest of the world since the time of the ancient Greeks.

Most Europeans are descended from the tribes that roamed the area long ago. More than 70 different languages are spoken by the people living in Europe today. Over the last fifty years, many new settlers have come to Europe from Asia, Africa and the Caribbean.

Europe is a wealthy continent, with many modern kinds of industry. Today, Europe produces more manufactured goods than any other of the world's continents. Several countries, though, especially those in the east, remain poor.

Europe Facts

Biggest country
Russia – 2,800,000 square kilometres
(in Europe, the rest of Russia is in Asia)
Biggest city population
Moscow, Russia – 12,500,000 people
Country where most people live in cities
Monaco – everybody lives in a city
Longest average length of life
Andorra – 84 years

Reykjavik ■
ICEL

▲ The London Eye is the world's highest observation wheel, standing at 136.1 metres. Views all over London can be seen from the top.

Ireland

▲ Venice in Italy is a city built on water. Boats, such as these gondolas, are used to get around. They are moved with long poles that touch the bottom of the canals and drive the gondolas forward.

SPAIN
PORTUGAL
Madrid ■
■ Lisbon

◀ Neuschwanstein castle in Germany was the model for the Magic Kingdom castle in Walt Disney's theme park in the USA.

◀ Greece is very popular with tourists. They visit the islands to enjoy the hot sunshine and visit the beautiful old buildings.

QUIZ

Find the European countries, hidden in these jumbled up names.

OLD SCANT	ANGRY ME
MARK END	RAIN BIT
SIR USA	CAR FEN

Answers on page 384.

A

B

C

SWEDEN

FINLAND

NORWAY

Helsinki ■

Oslo ■   Stockholm ■

■ Tallinn   RUSSIAN
ESTONIA   FEDERATION

Moscow ■

cotland

■ Riga

■ Edinburgh

ED KINGDOM   DENMARK

LATVIA

LITHUANIA

Vilnius ■

5

■ Minsk

England

Copenhagen ■

ales

ardiff

London

BELARUS

■ Berlin

Warsaw ■

3

Brussels

GERMANY

POLAND

Kiev ■

BELGIUM

UKRAINE

5

7

4

■ Paris

SLOVAKIA

14

Vienna ■ ■ Bratislava

MOLDOVA

1

■ Budapest

■ Chisinau

FRANCE

AUSTRIA

HUNGARY

6

ROMANIA

13   3

2

ITALY

2

■ Belgrade   ■ Bucharest

10

SERBIA

BULGARIA

12

MONTENEGRO

Podgorica ■

■ Sofia

1

8

Rome

Tirana ■

15

ALBANIA

4

GREECE

■ Athens

9

CYPRUS   Nicosia

▲ France is the most visited country in the world. The Eiffel Tower is one of its main attractions.

1. **ANDORRA**
   Andorra La Vella
2. **BOSNIA-HERZEGOVINA**
   Sarajevo
3. **CROATIA**
   Zagreb
4. **CZECH REPUBLIC**
   Prague
5. **Kaliningrad**
   (part of Russian Federation)
6. **LIECHTENSTEIN**
   Vaduz
7. **LUXEMBOURG**
   Luxembourg
8. **MACEDONIA**
   Skopje
9. **MALTA**
   Valletta
10. **MONACO**
    Monaco
11. **NETHERLANDS**
    Amsterdam, The Hague
12. **SAN MARINO**
    San Marino
13. **SLOVENIA**
    Ljubljana
14. **SWITZERLAND**
    Bern
15. **VATICAN CITY**
    Vatican City

D

E

F

G

Asia

Asia is big in many ways. It is the biggest continent, covering a third of the world's land area. It also has the biggest population by far — nearly two-thirds of all the people in the world live in Asia.

Asia also has the biggest range of scenery. It contains the highest place on Earth (Mount Everest) and the lowest (the Dead Sea), as well as deserts, jungles and frozen plains. There are vast stretches of empty land which is no good for farming, but there are also river valleys which have some of the best farmland anywhere in the world.

◀ The giant panda spends up to 16 hours a day eating bamboo – this means that they eat between 10 and 20 kilograms of bamboo every day!

Mediterranean Sea

Black Sea

Euphrates

Red Sea

Arabian Peninsula

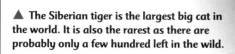

▲ The Siberian tiger is the largest big cat in the world. It is also the rarest as there are probably only a few hundred left in the wild.

Best of Asia

FRESHWATER SEALS
The Lake Baikal seals are the world's only freshwater seals.

HIGHEST MOUNTAIN
Mount Everest, on China and Nepal's borders, is 8,863 metres high.

LOWEST PLACE
The Dead Sea is situated 408 metres below sea level.

A B C D E F G

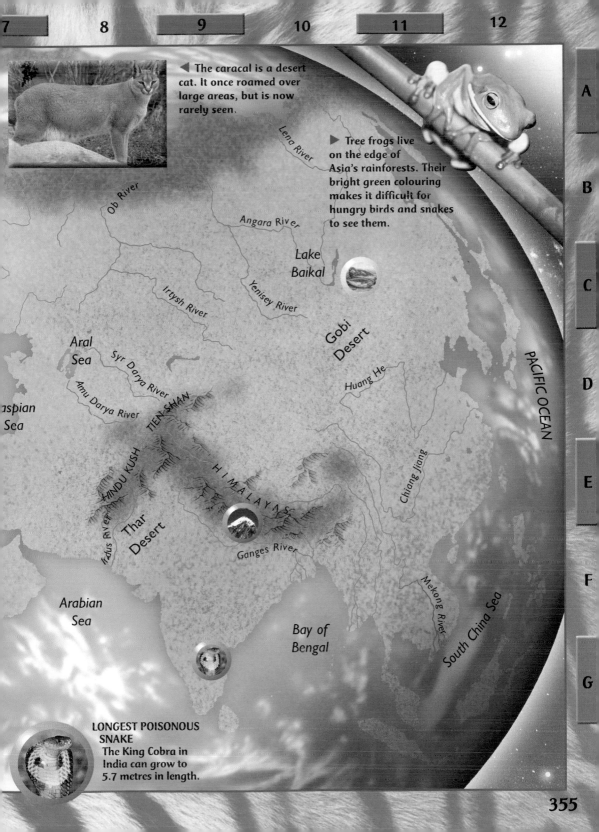

◄ The caracal is a desert cat. It once roamed over large areas, but is now rarely seen.

Lena River

► Tree frogs live on the edge of Asia's rainforests. Their bright green colouring makes it difficult for hungry birds and snakes to see them.

Ob River

Angara River

Lake Baikal

Irtysh River

Yenisey River

Gobi Desert

Aral Sea

Syr Darya River

Amu Darya River

TIEN SHAN

Huang He

Caspian Sea

HINDU KUSH

HIMALAYAS

Chiang Jiang

Indus River

Thar Desert

Ganges River

PACIFIC OCEAN

Arabian Sea

Bay of Bengal

Mekong River

South China Sea

LONGEST POISONOUS SNAKE
The King Cobra in India can grow to 5.7 metres in length.

Asia
People and places

Asia contains a huge number of different races.

Each speaks a different language and follows a different way of life. There are Mongolian herdsmen living on the vast grasslands, and city-dwellers living in modern Japan. Oil brings wealth to many Arab people, while most people in India work on small farms. Big cities such as Tokyo are among the most crowded in the world. The world's major religions – Christianity, Islam and Hinduism – all began in Asia.

▲ A few Mongolian people live on the grassland steppes of central Asia, where they raise herds of goats, cattle and yaks. They live in felt-covered tents called yurts.

TURKE
Ankara ■

13
19
9 10
8

Riyadh ■
SAUD
ARABI

Sana ■
YEMEN

Asia Facts

Biggest country Russia – 14,300,000 square kilometres (in Asia, the rest of Russia is in Europe)

Biggest country population
China – 1,284,960,000 people

Biggest city population
Tokyo, Japan – 36,760,000 people

Most children in a family
Yemen – an average of 6

Longest railway line Trans-Siberia line – 9,297 kilometres (part of which is in Europe)

▲ In India and other Asian countries, bicycles are used as taxis. These taxis are called rickshaws – they are also used for moving heavy goods about.

◀ Muslims believe that the Dome of the Rock in Jerusalem is the holiest place on Earth. It was built over the rock from which, according to Muslim belief, the Prophet Muhammad rose to heaven.

▶ China holds a New Year's Day parade. A group of people dress up and dance in a large dragon costume. They believe that the dragon helps prevent evil spirits from spoiling the New Year.

QUIZ

1. Which one country would you have to travel through to get from Iran to India?
2. Mongolia shares a border with two other countries, what are they?

Answers on page 384.

1.	AFGHANISTAN Kabul
2.	ARMENIA Yerevan
3.	AZERBAIJAN Baku
4.	BAHRAIN Manama
5.	BANGLADESH Dhaka
6.	BHUTAN Thimphu
7.	GEORGIA Tbilisi
8.	IRAQ Baghdad
9.	ISRAEL Jerusalem
10.	JORDAN Amman
11.	KUWAIT Kuwait
12.	KYRGYZSTAN Bishkek
13.	LEBANON Beirut
14.	MALDIVES Male
15.	NORTH KOREA P'yŏngyang
16.	QATAR Doha
17.	SINGAPORE Singapore
18.	SOUTH KOREA Seoul
19.	SYRIA Damascus
20.	TAJIKISTAN Dushanbe
21.	TURKMENISTAN Ashgabat
22.	UNITED ARAB EMIRATES Abu Dhabi
23.	UZBEKISTAN Tashkent

◀ This army of terracotta warriors is in the world's largest tomb in China. Qin Shi huangdi's, Emperor of China, was buried here 2,210 years ago.

A
B
C
D
E
F
G

357

Africa

Africa is the second biggest continent in the world. You could fit Europe into it nearly three times over! But fewer people live in the whole of Africa than in Europe.

There are many wonderful natural sights in Africa, such as Mount Kilimanjaro and the wildlife of the jungles and grasslands.

The longest river, the Nile, flows through the northeast of the continent. It provides water for the farmland along its banks. But much of Africa is an extremely hot and dry place to live because it lies across the Equator. The largest desert in the world, the Sahara Desert, takes up most of the north of the continent, but there are tropical rainforests further south.

Even though there are plenty of minerals, such as gold, diamonds, and even oil, two-thirds of the world's poorest countries are on the African continent.

◀ The lion is the largest big cat in Africa. It can grow to 3 metres in length.

ATLANTIC OCEAN

▶ The African elephant is the largest land animal in the world. It can grow up to 7.5 metres tall and can weigh as much as 90 adult humans!

Best of Africa

TALLEST MAMMAL The giraffe can grow to a height of 6 metres. Its legs are 1.8 metres long.

HIGHEST MOUNTAIN Kilimanjaro soars to 5,894 metres.

A

B

C

D

E

F

G

ATLAS MOUNTAINS

Mediterranean Sea

SAHARA DESERT

Nile River

NUBIAN DESERT

Blue Nile River

GREAT RIFT VALLEY

Niger River

Lake Chad

Volta River

Benue River

Ubangi River

White Nile River

Lake Turkana

Congo River

Congo River

Lake Victoria

GREAT RIFT VA-LLEY

Lake Tanganyika

INDIAN OCEAN

Lake Nyasa

Zambezi River

NAMIB DESERT

KALAHARI DESERT

Orange River

▲ The meerkat is a type of mongoose. It lives in large groups of up to 30 animals in connecting underground burrows.

LARGEST BIRD
The ostrich grows to 2.75 metres tall and weighs up to 156 kilograms.

BIGGEST DESERT
The hot Sahara Desert covers 9,269,000 square kilometres.

359

Africa
People and places

Africa is a very large continent, but it has few people living there.

Nigeria has the biggest population with 108 million people, but a lot of other countries have much smaller populations – less than five million.

African people come from many racial groups. In the north, most are Arabs. South of the Sahara Desert, most people are black. They are divided up into over 800 different groups, each with its own language, religion and way of life.

Very few people live in the deserts or the dry grasslands. The most crowded areas are the Nile Valley, the Algerian coast and the South African coast.

Over 60 percent of Africans live in villages. They grow crops and raise cattle and other animals to feed themselves. This is a hard way of life, because the soil is poor and the climate is harsh.

▼ Camels are still a very important method of transport in Egypt. They are known as 'ships of the desert', and can travel for days without drinking or eating.

▲ The Bolga people of Ghana paint their houses in bright colours. Most are farmers whose main crop is cacao beans. They sell these beans to other countries who use them to make chocolate!

▲ These children from the Masai tribe live in Kenya. The traditional clothing of the Masai people is a single piece of cloth wrapped around them. These children are wearing traditional decorative beads.

Africa Facts

Biggest country Sudan – 2,505,815 square kilometres

Smallest country Seychelles – 455 square kilometres

Biggest city population Cairo, Egypt – 12,200,000 people

Shortest people Pygmies – about 140 centimetres

Largest producer of gold
South Africa – 33 percent of world total

Most children in a family
Niger – an average of 7

Shortest average length of life
Swaziland – 32 years

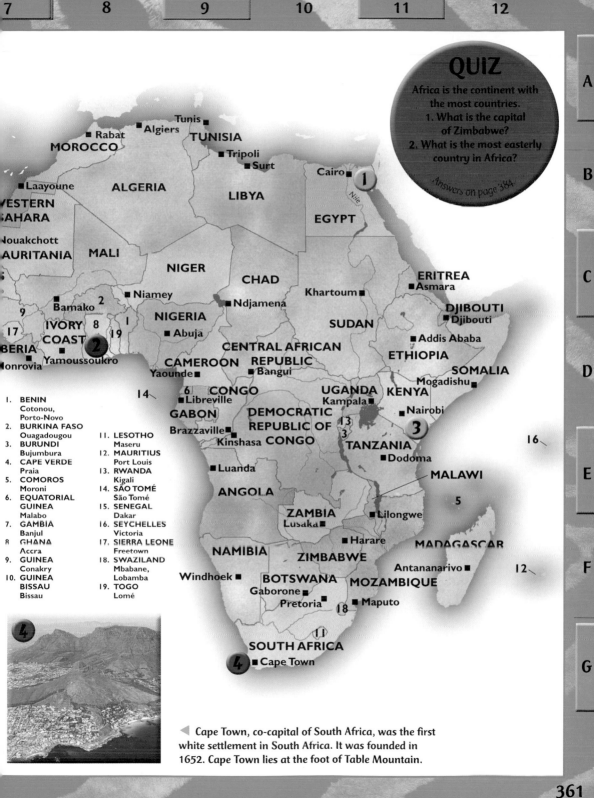

QUIZ

Africa is the continent with the most countries.

1. What is the capital of Zimbabwe?
2. What is the most easterly country in Africa?

Answers on page 384.

Tunis
Algiers
TUNISIA
Rabat
MOROCCO
Tripoli
Surt
Cairo ① 1

Laayoune
ALGERIA
LIBYA
WESTERN SAHARA
EGYPT
Nouakchott
MAURITANIA   **MALI**
NIGER
CHAD
ERITREA
Asmara
Niamey
Ndjamena
Khartoum
DJIBOUTI
Djibouti
Bamako
NIGERIA
SUDAN
Addis Ababa
IVORY COAST
Abuja
ETHIOPIA
LIBERIA
Yamoussoukro
CENTRAL AFRICAN REPUBLIC
SOMALIA
Monrovia
CAMEROON
Bangui
Yaounde
Mogadishu
CONGO
UGANDA **KENYA**
Libreville
Kampala
Nairobi
GABON
DEMOCRATIC REPUBLIC OF CONGO
Brazzaville
Kinshasa
Nairobi
TANZANIA
Dodoma
Luanda
MALAWI
ANGOLA
Lilongwe
ZAMBIA
Lusaka
Harare
MADAGASCAR
NAMIBIA
ZIMBABWE
Antananarivo
Windhoek
BOTSWANA   **MOZAMBIQUE**
Gaborone
Pretoria   Maputo
SOUTH AFRICA
Cape Town

1. **BENIN**
   Cotonou,
   Porto-Novo
2. **BURKINA FASO**
   Ouagadougou
3. **BURUNDI**
   Bujumbura
4. **CAPE VERDE**
   Praia
5. **COMOROS**
   Moroni
6. **EQUATORIAL GUINEA**
   Malabo
7. **GAMBIA**
   Banjul
8. **GHANA**
   Accra
9. **GUINEA**
   Conakry
10. **GUINEA BISSAU**
    Bissau

11. **LESOTHO**
    Maseru
12. **MAURITIUS**
    Port Louis
13. **RWANDA**
    Kigali
14. **SÃO TOMÉ**
    São Tomé
15. **SENEGAL**
    Dakar
16. **SEYCHELLES**
    Victoria
17. **SIERRA LEONE**
    Freetown
18. **SWAZILAND**
    Mbabane,
    Lobamba
19. **TOGO**
    Lomé

◀ Cape Town, co-capital of South Africa, was the first white settlement in South Africa. It was founded in 1652. Cape Town lies at the foot of Table Mountain.

Oceania

Oceania is really more than one continent. It is the name we give to a group of islands covering an enormous area in the Pacific Ocean. The biggest of these islands is Australia, and there are 14 other countries. Oceania is the smallest of the continents.

The next biggest parts of Oceania are New Zealand (which is made up of two islands) and Papua New Guinea. The rest of this strange continent is made up of at least 30,000 small islands.

Much of this area has been isolated from the rest of the world for millions of years, so many unique animals are found here. Animals like the duck-billed platypus, the kangaroo and the koala are found nowhere else in the world.

▲ Koalas are only found in Australia. They are covered with soft, thick brown and grey fur. They eat the leaves and young shoots of eucalyptus trees.

INDIAN OCEAN

▼ Ayers Rock, now called Uluru, in Australia is the largest free-standing rock in the world. It is 300 metres high and over 600 million years old.

▲ The duck-billed platypus is one of the strangest mammals in the world. It has fur like a mammal, but it has webbed feet like a duck. It also has a bill like a bird, and it lays eggs!

Best of Oceania

LARGEST BUTTERFLY
Queen Alexandra's birdwing has a wingspan of 280 millimetres.

LONGEST CORAL REEF
The Great Barrier Reef in Australia is 2,025 kilometres long.

OLDEST ROCKS
Zircon crystals from Australia are 4,276 billion years old.

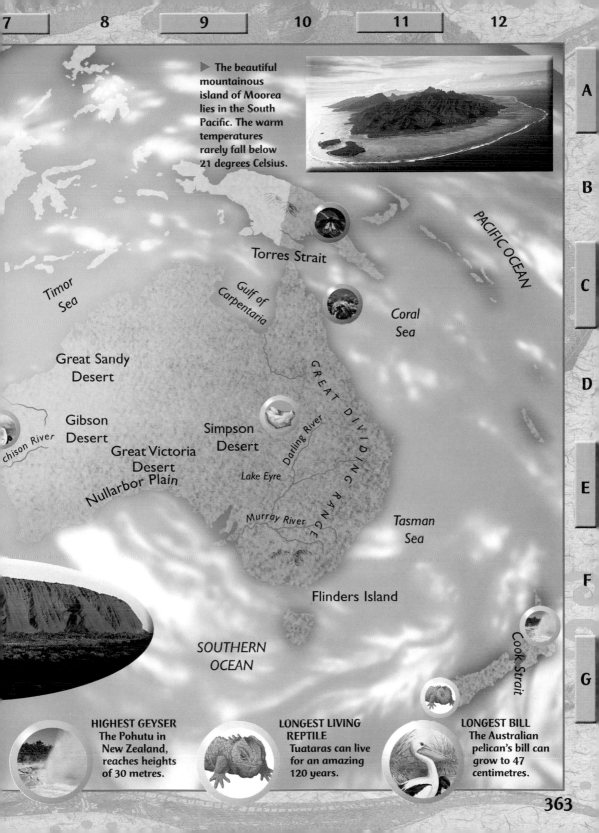

▶ The beautiful mountainous island of Moorea lies in the South Pacific. The warm temperatures rarely fall below 21 degrees Celsius.

A

B

PACIFIC OCEAN

Torres Strait

Timor Sea

Gulf of Carpentaria

Coral Sea

C

Great Sandy Desert

GREAT DIVIDING RANGE

D

Gibson Desert

chison River

Simpson Desert

Darling River

Great Victoria Desert

Lake Eyre

Nullarbor Plain

Murray River

Tasman Sea

E

Flinders Island

F

SOUTHERN OCEAN

Cook Strait

G

HIGHEST GEYSER
The Pohutu in New Zealand, reaches heights of 30 metres.

LONGEST LIVING REPTILE
Tuataras can live for an amazing 120 years.

LONGEST BILL
The Australian pelican's bill can grow to 47 centimetres.

363

Oceania
People and places

QUIZ

Many places in Oceania take their name from early explorers who came from Europe. Can you find on the map on page 363 places named after: James Cook, Abel Tasman, Matthew Flinders, Luis de Torres, Edward Eyre?

Answers on page 384.

About 80 percent of Australians live in the south-east corner. Nearly all the major cities are here, including the capital, Canberra. The land is good for farming and the climate is mild and wet. Almost nobody lives in the centre of the country, known as the outback. It consists of vast deserts and grasslands.

Most Australians come from families that moved here from Europe during the 20th century. Aboriginals, the first people to live in Australia, now make up less than one percent of the total population. However, it was not always like this. Aboriginals, like the other first people of Oceania, travelled from Southeast Asia 40,000 to 70,000 years ago. They sailed from island to island for thousands of years, setting up homes in many places. When the British came to Australia 200 years ago they destroyed the Aboriginals' way of life.

Farming and mining make Australia and New Zealand wealthy countries, and Papua New Guinea produces timber and copper. The smaller countries have little to sell and are much poorer. However, the tourist industry is growing fast in the Pacific and this is helping to create jobs and bring money to the islands.

Oceania Facts

Biggest country
Australia – 7,682,300 square kilometres
Smallest country Nauru – 21 square kilometres
Biggest city population
Sydney, Australia – 4,119,000 people
Longest average length of life Australia – 81 years
Country that produces most diamonds
Australia – 34 percent of the world total

▶ The Sydney Opera House looks over the harbour in Australia. The building was finished in 1973.

▶ The people of Papua New Guinea speak more languages than anywhere else in the world – about 869! Each language is only spoken by an average of 4,000 people.

A

B

PAPUA NEW GUINEA

Port Moresby ■

SOLOMON ISLANDS ■ Honiara

C

VANUATU

Port Vila ■

NEW CALEDONIA
(belongs to France)

D

AUSTRALIA

E

▲ This sheep is being sheared – shaving the sheep's coat for its wool. New Zealand has about 58 million sheep and 8 million cattle – that's about 25 farm animals to every person!

F

■ Canberra

NEW ZEALAND

■ Wellington

Tasmania

G

365

Antarctica

Antarctica is the most difficult place to live in the world. It is the coldest continent, and 98 percent of the land area is covered with ice and snow. Some of the ice is nearly five kilometres deep – more than ten times the height of the world's tallest building! The ice reaches out into the sea forming huge ice shelves that break off to form vast floating icebergs.

Almost nothing grows here, so it is not surprising that Antarctica has no permanent population. However, a few explorers and tourists visit, and there are several camps where scientists work studying animals and the ice.

Even animals find it difficult to live here. The few that do, live mainly in the air or in the sea. Penguins, seals and whales survive because of their thick layer of blubber, or fat, which keeps them warm. They feed off fish and tiny animals called krill that live in the sea.

▲ The first person to reach the South Pole was Norwegian Roald Amundsen in 1911. He beat a British explorer, Captain Scott, who also reached the South Pole, but only after Amundsen.

▲ The albatross has the largest wingspan of any living bird. Its wings measure 3.6 metres across!

Best of Antarctica

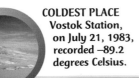

COLDEST PLACE
Vostok Station, on July 21, 1983, recorded –89.2 degrees Celsius.

DEEPEST ICE
Ice has been found to a depth of 4,776 metres.

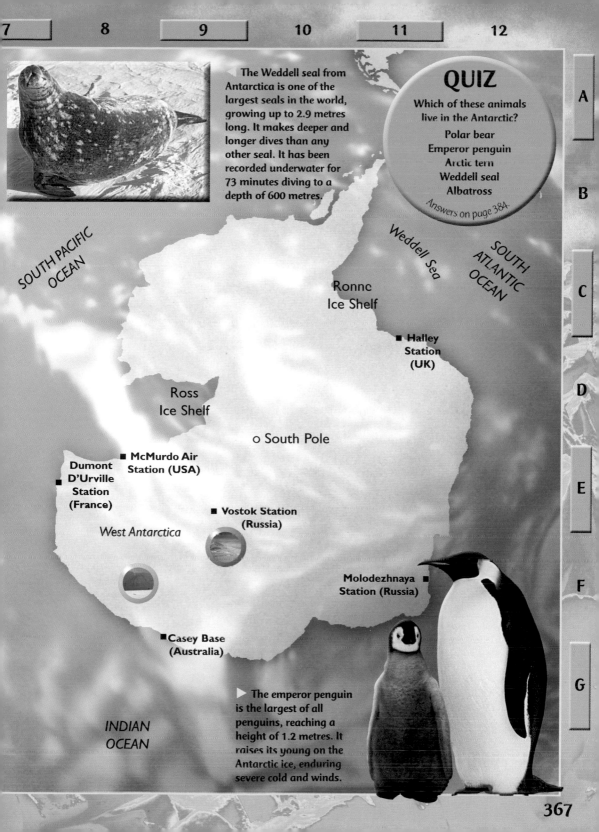

The Weddell seal from Antarctica is one of the largest seals in the world, growing up to 2.9 metres long. It makes deeper and longer dives than any other seal. It has been recorded underwater for 73 minutes diving to a depth of 600 metres.

QUIZ

Which of these animals live in the Antarctic?

Polar bear
Emperor penguin
Arctic tern
Weddell seal
Albatross

Answers on page 384.

A

B

C

D

E

F

G

SOUTH PACIFIC OCEAN

Weddell Sea

SOUTH ATLANTIC OCEAN

Ronne Ice Shelf

■ Halley Station (UK)

Ross Ice Shelf

o South Pole

■ McMurdo Air Station (USA)

■ Dumont D'Urville Station (France)

■ Vostok Station (Russia)

West Antarctica

Molodezhnaya ■ Station (Russia)

■ Casey Base (Australia)

▶ The emperor penguin is the largest of all penguins, reaching a height of 1.2 metres. It raises its young on the Antarctic ice, enduring severe cold and winds.

INDIAN OCEAN

Index

Entries in **bold** refer to main subject entries; entries in *italics* refer to illustrations.

A

Acknowledgements

The publishers would like to thank the following sources for the use of their photographs:

59(b/r) Pavel Losevsky/Fotolia;
198 Salter Housewares;
193 Garmin International 2008;
197 Forgiss/Fotolia
208 Maria Brzostowska/Fotolia;
209 Hervé Collart/Sygma/Corbis;
260 Bettmann/Corbis;
272 Princess Cruises;
284 ESA/CNES/CSG;
296 Cassio;
364 Glenn Morales/Corbis;
365 Mats Tooming/Fotolia

All other photographs are from:
Corel, digitalSTOCK, digitalvision, iStockphoto.com, John Foxx, PhotoAlto, PhotoDisc, PhotoEssentials, PhotoPro, Stockbyte

All artworks from the Miles Kelly Artwork Bank

Every effort has been made to acknowledge the source and copyright holder of each picture. Miles Kelly Publishing apologises for any unintentional errors or omissions.

Atlas Quiz Answers

Page 341
1. Asia
2. Oceania
3. Asia
4. Antarctica
5. Africa

Page 344
D10 Ottawa
G9 Mexico City
E11 Washington D.C.
F11 Nassau

Page 348
1. Argentina, Bolivia and Peru.
2. Brasilia (capital of Brazil)

Page 353
Scotland (OLD SCANT)
Denmark (MARK END)
Russia (SIR USA)
Germany (ANGRY ME)
Britain (RAIN BIT)
France (CAR FEN)

Page 357
1. Pakistan
2. Russia and China

Page 361
1. Harare
2. Somalia

Page 364
Cook Straight G12
Tasman Sea E11
Flinders Island F10
Torres Strait C10
Lake Eyre E9

Page 367
Emperor penguin
Weddell seal
Albatross